Famous
FOR A TIME

Famous FOR A TIME

Forgotten Giants of Canadian Sport

JASON WILSON
RICHARD M. REID

DUNDURN PRESS

Publisher and acquiring editor: Kwame Scott Fraser | Editor: Dominic Farrell
Cover designer: Laura Boyle
Cover image: Ethel Catherwood, 1928: public domain

Library and Archives Canada Cataloguing in Publication

Title: Famous for a time : forgotten giants of Canadian sport / Jason Wilson, Richard M. Reid.
Names: Wilson, Jason, 1970- author. | Reid, Richard M., 1943- author.
Description: Includes bibliographical references and index.
Identifiers: Canadiana (print) 20230203256 | Canadiana (ebook) 20230203280 | ISBN 9781459749955 (softcover) | ISBN 9781459749962 (PDF) | ISBN 9781459749979 (EPUB)
Subjects: LCSH: Sports—Canada—History. | LCSH: Athletes—Canada—History.
Classification: LCC GV585 .W55 2023 | DDC 796.0971—dc23

Canada
Canada Council for the Arts | Conseil des arts du Canada
Ontario
ONTARIO ARTS COUNCIL
CONSEIL DES ARTS DE L'ONTARIO
an Ontario government agency
un organisme du gouvernement de l'Ontario
ONTARIO CREATES

We acknowledge the support of the Canada Council for the Arts and the Ontario Arts Council for our publishing program. We also acknowledge the financial support of the Government of Ontario, through the Ontario Book Publishing Tax Credit and Ontario Creates, and the Government of Canada.

Printed and bound in Canada.

Dundurn Press
1382 Queen Street East
Toronto, Ontario, Canada M4L 1C9
dundurn.com, @dundurnpress

For the "shes" who must be obeyed

Contents

FAMOUS:
AN INTRODUCTION

Men are great in various ways. The topmost crest is for kings to climb,
And do not think to look or strive beyond it.
It is for you, then, in the time remaining,
To stride along those heights; for me,
Poet who speaks with victors,
to be seen pre-eminent every place where they speak Greek.
— from "Olympian Ode I," Pindar (518–446 BCE)

IF THE POET SPEAKS, THE VICTOR WILL BE FOREVER FAMOUS. THESE chosen ones are accorded a place in the sacrosanct places of memory constructed to celebrate sporting excellence. For the heroes and heroines of Canadian sports, this means being inducted into a hall of fame. The last half of the 20th century saw an explosion in the number of sports halls of fame across the country. It was driven by the growing social importance Canadians have placed on sports, as well as by the increased commercialization and media coverage of sports.

In 1936, the National Baseball Hall of Fame and Museum — the first sports hall of fame in North America — was established in Cooperstown, New York, to promote baseball. The Hockey Hall of Fame was established shortly thereafter, with its first inductees of players and builders selected in 1943. In 1955, Canada's Sports Hall of Fame (CSHF) inducted its first athletes. The emergence of the CSHF triggered the creation of a plethora of other sports halls of fame. Soon, every province and most municipalities in Canada had their own sports hall of fame. Universities added their own halls. By the mid-1990s, there were some 300 sports halls of fame in North America, and the number keeps growing.[1] Every province and two of the three territories now has its own not-for-profit sports hall of fame.

As not-for-profit organizations, most halls could not function without significant popular financial support. And yet, most of these halls thrive. This is because Canada's sports fans recognize the importance of remembering. For these lovers of games, forgetting those who were famous on the pitch, the track, and the rink is unthinkable.

Fans are drawn to these institutions for a spectrum of reasons. Some ardent supporters see the halls as shrines, where acolytes can worship their own favourite or chosen sport. Some are nostalgic for what they consider a happier time and seek to recapture it when looking at the mementoes gathered in those halls.

On balance, these memory museums reflect the competitive desire — across sports and regions — to identify, publicize, and venerate those athletes who *should* be regarded as the best of their time. They lend an authoritative stamp of approval to the athletes and their achievements that deserve remembering. Naturally, all halls, even the most "scientific," are biased, full of contradictions, cliquey, and, in the end, exclusive. As a result, some of the undeserving are remembered, and some of the deserving are, lamentably, forgotten.

The answer to the question of who deserves to be immortalized is inevitably contentious and subjective. For any athlete to be deemed forever famous, two critical factors are required: 1) they need to have achieved sporting accomplishments and standards that are exceptional; and 2) they also need to have a large fan base, one that places high value on their accomplishments and is therefore willing to grant them fame. Importantly, both factors are time and value sensitive.

As social values change and evolve, so too do attitudes toward fame: opinions about "who" and "what" deserve memorializing can change over time. Lacrosse, for instance, was popular across Canada before the First World

Lacrosse Match between the Montreal Club and Caughnawaga Indians, 1870.

War. This was a result of how the game fit into the "Men of the North" identity that was emerging — or, more accurately, was being manufactured by the anglophone elites after Confederation. Here, the stoic, hearty pioneer in the cold northern clime of Canada played hearty and muscular games to survive in it. This image, which borrowed heavily from both Indigenous and French-Canadian cultures, could ostensibly be found on the various fields of play across the nascent nation, and would be replicated in Canadian art as well as in the studio of Scottish-Canadian photographer William Notman.

However, when another sport came along that captured the imagined idea of what it was to be "Canadian," lacrosse was soon replaced. Hockey was well matched to the northern climate narrative, was better known internationally, was a game that Canadians could dominate, and was even better suited to the sort of nation-building needs — or, at least, *perceived* needs — of the 20th century. After the First World War, hockey surpassed lacrosse — the purported "national sport" at the turn of the century — in popularity.

The legacy of this early replacement can be seen in the representation of players in sports halls of fame. At the time of writing, only 9 lacrosse players or builders have been inducted to the CSHF, compared with 125 hockey players and builders. Even boxing and curling have sent more inductees to the CSHF: 18 and 15, respectively. Moreover, despite the dominance of Indigenous players within lacrosse, only three have made it to the Hall: Bill Isaacs (2015), Gaylord Powless (2017), and Ross Powless (2020–1). Again, returning to the notion of fame being "time and value sensitive," readers will likely be unsurprised at *when* these three players were inducted. It is only now, during this slow march to Reconciliation, that the efforts, of any kind, by Indigenous people are being recognized.

A feature common to all the halls is the opacity of the selection criteria. The CSHF, as a typical example, relies on sports organizations, regional or sport-specific halls of fame, sports historians, and members of the public to nominate candidates. The candidates are then reviewed by the CSHF's Selection Committee, which, in turn, makes the final choice. Thus, the results of this process can only ever reflect existing social values and attitudes, sometimes of specific groups, at a particular time in Canada. For much of the time that these halls have existed, athletes from minority groups have been marginalized and under-selected while athletes from dominant groups and classes have been well- and over-represented.

Waneek Horn-Miller was the first Haudenosaunee (Iroquois) woman to compete in an Olympic Games. She became the first water polo player inducted into the CSHF — but only in 2019.[2] At that time, only 11 of the 665 inductees were Indigenous athletes. Over time, as social attitudes change and previously ignored groups are seen as deserving, the halls have sought greater diversity.

Sport historians and their histories have also all too often been focused on the most popular. It sells, after all. A close examination of the works written to celebrate particular sports and athletes — which are celebrated; what is written about them — shows that sports can serve as a valuable lens through which to examine the social values of an era. Sports can be a gauge of social values and a measure of a group or individual's acceptance or, indeed, rejection by society. Looking through such a lens brings many questions.

How did a sanitized version of an Indigenous game inform a nascent Canadian identity? Why, at least in Canada, did baseball win and cricket lose? What did the bicycle mean to the people of the nation? Why — with apologies to the nerdiest sports geeks among us — have you *probably* heard of the Matchless Six and Percy Williams, *maybe* heard of Tommy Burns, Sam Langford, and Tip O'Neill, and likely *never* heard of Teddy Ogden, George Godfrey, George Dixon, Louise Armaindo, Karl Creelman, and Walter Knox? Let us then consider *Famous for a Time* as something of a written testament: a micro-museum, a completely incomplete hall of fame for those precious few unbelonging but perhaps deserving Canadian athletes.

I

THE CREATOR'S GAME AND CANADIAN IDENTITY: LACROSSE, 1800s

IN CANADA, AS ELSEWHERE, SOME PARTICIPANTS HAVE USED SPORT as a way of expressing and maintaining their cultural identity. At the same time, involvement in sports has afforded new immigrants the opportunity to signal their assimilation *into* and acceptance *of* the broader Canadian society. Less constructively, though, sport has sometimes served as a powerful mechanism for exclusion and elitism. The struggle for participation and status within sport is often only a reflection of the larger "real-life" struggle for rights, freedom, and recognition that exists within society.

Such was the case with the game the Iroquois called *tewaarathon* ("the little brother of war"), the game that became lacrosse. With the emergence of a codified and "improved" version of the Indigenous game in Canada during the 1860s, sport offered a faithful rendering of Canadian society at that time, where ugly prejudices and injustices were laid bare, sometimes deliberately, in the name of nation building.

This was a time when the "Myth of the Vanishing Indian" was being constructed across North America. The myth played on the belief that the Indigenous populations of both Canada and the United States were

Kahnawà:ke Lacrosse Club, Montreal, QC, 1867.

slowly dying out as a result of disease and that their various cultures would eventually vanish after they had been assimilated into the dominant Euro-Canadian society. The Gradual Civilization Act (1857), predating the Indian Act (1876) by two decades, was a particularly aggressive policy aimed at "civilizing" the Indigenous peoples of Canada. It was, unsurprisingly, met with resistance from Indigenous communities. While politicians and legislators were considering how best to deal with the perceived "Indian Problem," Anglo-Saxon Canadians sought to make a somewhat sanitized version of lacrosse the national sport. All the while, Indigenous people looked on from the touchlines to see their Creator's Game appropriated to satisfy a nascent and manufactured national narrative.[1]

On August 29, 1844, the first recorded lacrosse game involving Indigenous and non-Indigenous players was played in Montreal. A group of

Anglo-Canadians from the Montreal Olympic Athletic Club (MOAC) had for years watched nearby Kahnawake teams play and decided to take up the sport.[2] Having organized a lacrosse team in their club, they challenged the Indigenous players to a match. Despite being allowed two extra players, the MOAC team was badly beaten. However, it was not deterred.[3] By the middle of the century, lacrosse was rapidly growing in popularity across Canada. It was the start of the cultural appropriation of an Indigenous game that would be used by anglophone Canadians to help define a distinct cultural identity for the nation and, with bitter irony, exclude Indigenous participation at the elite levels of the game.

The centrality of lacrosse in the nation's sporting minds was ephemeral. As mentioned earlier, by the end of the First World War, the game, although still popular among specific groups, ceased to be the nation's dominant sport. And by the time Canada was headed into the Great Depression, lacrosse's star had long faded. In 1929, for instance, amateur sports enthusiast and journalist Henry H. Roxborough wrote an article for *Maclean's Magazine* titled, "Can Lacrosse Come Back?" It was, in fact, a requiem for the sport. Roxborough claimed that in 1900, lacrosse was "so deeply enshrined in the heart of sporting Canada that its permanency and supremacy seemed absolutely assured."[4] Just two decades later, however, lacrosse had been left behind, replaced by hockey as the nation's more "permanent" and "supreme" sport. There were simply fewer lacrosse teams and fewer players. Lacrosse registration in Ontario alone had fallen by two-thirds. It was much the same on the West Coast, in cities such as Vancouver.[5] Although the sport would make some gains with the introduction of box lacrosse and the expansion of university field lacrosse, professional teams had collapsed and their players, no longer amateurs, had little choice but to retire.

THE CREATOR'S GAME

The ways in which Indigenous games have been perceived, described, explained, and — in the case of lacrosse — appropriated offer an example of Mary Louise Pratt's concept of the "contact zone." Pratt defines this as the public places where "cultures meet, clash and grapple with each other, often in contexts of highly asymmetrical relations of power, such as colonization, slavery, or their aftermaths as they live out in many parts of the world today."[6]

As the evolution of lacrosse shows, asymmetrical power relationships dominate but do not deny all power to the marginalized group. Within constrained choices and limited options, Indigenous people used lacrosse for what they saw as their own advantage and agency. A century and a half after its appropriation by Montreal sportsmen, lacrosse would become a tool for Indigenous empowerment and nationalism.

Lacrosse provides an excellent example of the role that sport plays in creating, defining, and reshaping cultural, individual, and even national identity. Appropriated from the Haudenosaunee (Iroquois) and given a French-Canadian name, lacrosse became a major factor in creating a national identity for the new Dominion of Canada.[7] Because these identities were shaped and constantly updated by cumulative historical, cultural, and personal factors changing across time, they remain in a state of flux. As such, one hundred years after it was called Canada's national game, the Creator's Game was reduced to a minor sport.

INDIGENOUS SPORT BEFORE COLUMBUS

Before European contact with North America, Indigenous men played a range of different stickball games. These varied in forms and rituals, for there were few fixed rules, but all of them involved the use of a racquet of some sort to pick up a ball and throw, carry, or pass it. Given the players' sticks and balls, and the goals used in play, the ethnomusicologist Thomas Vennum — who also wrote on Indigenous culture writ large — identified three quite different versions played in three regions of eastern North America: the northeast, the Great Lakes, and the southeast.[8]

The stick used in the northeastern game among the Haudenosaunee along the St. Lawrence River became the model for all lacrosse sticks used today: a hickory shaft, one end curved back on itself; a thong fastened from the end of the crook to partway down the hickory shaft; and the resulting triangle filled in with rawhide webbing that could take up half the stick. However, with the divergence in form from place to place, the terms of play, size of the field, number of players, and length of game were all up for negotiation before the start. Perhaps one of the only cardinal rules that governed almost all versions of the game was that the ball was never to be touched by the hand.

The game demanded a lot from its participants, including speed, endurance, dexterity, and a tremendous tolerance for pain. It should be noted that while these stickball contests had strong recreational and athletic components, they were seldom merely games. Indeed, for the Indigenous people who played or watched them, these contests were a communal act, involving a whole range of cultural complexities, including spiritualism, warfare, the demonstration of physical prowess, prestige, gambling, dreaming, mourning, celebration, curing, and shamanism.[9]

Several different names were conferred on the game by the many nations who played it. The Anishinaabe (Algonquin), for example, referred to it as *baggataway*; the Wendat as *kahwendae*; and the Kahnawake (Mohawk) as *tewaarathon*. For their part, the Haudenosaunee referred to it as the "Creator's Game," as it was played for the entertainment of the Creator.

And spirituality was indeed a key feature of the contests. Spiritual leaders, for instance, were the initiators and mediators of most games. Before playing, warriors might fast, purge, and exercise to make their mind, body, and spirit acceptable to the Creator. During the political disruption and social change within Indigenous communities between 1700 and 1800, however, the connection of *tewaarathon* to the Creator waned as some Kahnawake individuals converted to Christianity.[10] Here, for the first time, we see non-Indigenous elements being introduced and, over time, altering the very meaning of the game. Soon, members of Montreal's anglophone elite would repackage and *repurpose* the Indigenous sport.

EARLY IMPRESSIONS: 1630s–1800

Early explorers and missionaries frequently described the Indigenous games they witnessed. While most observers stressed the fortitude, physical prowess, and aggressive and violent nature of the players, few fully understood the contest's spiritual and cultural importance. Jesuit missionaries, who were among the first Europeans to leave partial records of these games, recognized the Indigenous spiritualism embedded in the game. They opposed it. The Jesuits also opposed the high level of gambling that was associated with the contests.

There were other observers, though. The *coureur des bois* Nicolas Perrot witnessed games while trading for furs in the West. Perrot was impressed by the fact that contending sides wanted to ensure fair games and balanced the numbers of players, but he was surprised by the violent nature of the contests. If a player had the ball at his bare feet, Perrot recorded, he had to "fend off blows from his opponents who continually strike his feet, and if in this situation he is injured, it is his own concern."[11] Perrot added that it was "common to see players maimed permanently," but it did not alter how they played, nor did it generate hard feelings.

In 1796 Jonathon Carver, a Connecticut-born militia captain and self-declared explorer, watched and described a game played in Chippewa. Carver echoed Perrot, writing that he was struck not only by the violence of the game but also by the players' reactions to injury: "They play with so much vehemence that they frequently wound each other, and sometimes a bone is broken; but notwithstanding these accidents there never appears to be any spite or exertions of strength to affect them, nor do any disputes ever happen between the parties."[12] Just as violence is still so much a part of hockey today, it seems that it was just as much a part of lacrosse centuries earlier.

In some instances, the violence extended beyond the field of play. Such was the case during one game played at the start of Pontiac's War in 1763. Angered at British policy changes in the West, a group of Anishinaabe used lacrosse as a ruse to successfully capture the Brits' important Great Lakes post, Fort Michilimackinac.

The fort, protected by a wooden palisade and guarded by a small army garrison, was too formidable a target for any frontal attack. So, to capture the fort, the Indigenous warriors gathered there used an unusual and surprising tactic.

The Anishinaabe notified the British Garrison that they would be playing a game of lacrosse against the visiting Sauk near the main gate. About 100 warriors participated, and in due course, senior British officers came out to observe. While the officers watched, Anishinaabe women entered the fort wearing blankets that hid tomahawks and guns with cut-down barrels. After one of the players threw the ball over the gate of the fort, the warriors raced inside. There, the Anishinaabe women armed their men, who then overwhelmed the garrison, killing 15 soldiers. The rest of the garrison and a dozen merchants were made prisoners.[13]

In truth, the capture was not a critical event in the war; the victors soon abandoned the fort and it had been reoccupied by the British by the end of the year. It did, however, become a feature in the mythology surrounding Indigenous warriors. Henceforth, Indigenous people were regarded as duplicitous and prone to violence. Indeed, when newspaper writers introduced lacrosse to their readers more than half a century later, their articles invariably began with an account of the attack on the fort. In the minds of the British, every game played between Indigenous and non-Indigenous teams in the 19th century had the potential to become a symbolic re-enactment of that event.

In the ensuing years, through to the end of the War of 1812, Indigenous people suffered disruption and, for many, devastation. For instance, the American government, at the end of that country's revolution, assumed that it had — automatically and despite Indigenous claims to the contrary — acquired rights to all lands east of the Mississippi River. The failure of the American authorities to arrive at a satisfactory agreement with the various First Nations gathered in 1793 at Sandusky, Ohio, resulted in a renewed outbreak of fighting along the frontier, which ended the following year with the American victory at Fallen Timbers.

In the War of 1812, Indigenous communities were forced to choose between expansionist Americans and the unpredictable and unreliable British. The war marked the last time that northeastern Indigenous warriors, who would suffer serious casualties and the loss of Tecumseh while supporting Britain, were critical participants in a military conflict. The important role they had played as allies, the funds they received, and the political influence they exercised were soon diminished in concert with a massive increase of British migration to Canada. The British government's response was to try to force Indigenous communities onto small, isolated reserves, which, of course, further disrupted traditional Indigenous ways of life.

MONTREAL

Although Europeans and colonists had viewed and described the various stickball games played by Indigenous people across North America for a century, few of these observers had tried to play them. The one exception was in New France, where political, economic, and cultural relationships between the two communities were somewhat more equitable. Certainly, early French survival would not have been possible without Indigenous assistance and the transfer of skills relating to hunting, snowshoeing, canoeing, and so forth. Many French males — *les Canadiens* and the *coureurs des bois* — greatly respected and often emulated Indigenous examples of masculinity, stoicism, and fortitude.[14] One way for young Frenchmen to test and compare their physical prowess and endurance was through lacrosse. Beginning in 1740, games were held in the French colony and the sport's popularity persisted throughout the political paradigm shifts that were occurring in North America at this time.[15]

With Britain's victory over the French in 1763, the francophone population experienced what it was to become both colonizer and colonized. At the same time, the establishment of the American republic and the flood of British immigration after the War of 1812 marked the end of Britain's dependency on her Indigenous allies. Now in control of the Canadas, the British would soon consider how to manage and reimagine the variety of cultures living within the colony. Out of such diversity, government (and later immigration) agents sought to fashion a new, British, and perhaps romantic idea of the stoic frontiersman braving the elements in a new land. Here, one could feel the birth pangs of what people living in the latter part of the 19th century might have referred to as the "Canadian identity." And lacrosse was a complementary accessory to this idea.

The move toward anglicizing Indigenous sport came relatively swiftly. The Haudenosaunee game of *tewaarathon*, for example, which had been played almost entirely by Indigenous men, was stripped of its cultural and religious components, codified, called by its French-Canadian name (lacrosse), and wholly adopted by the anglophones of Montreal. The game quickly expanded to other parts of Canada and became so popular in the newly created Dominion of Canada that supporters soon referred to it as "Canada's Game."

Dr. W. George Beers, St. Georges Snowshoe Club, Montreal, QC, 1881.

Tewaarathon was the natural model for modern lacrosse. First, that Indigenous game was being played in close proximity to Montreal, a city where anglophone sportsmen saw the muscular and often violent game as one that suited their interests in building a uniquely Canadian identity. These men were eager to learn and eventually reimagine the new sport — new to them, at least. Equally important was the large and receptive audience in Montreal with a vested interest in the popularization of the activities linked to an earlier Indigenous and French-Canadian way of life. For this audience, watching lacrosse was a way to take part in the practice of romantic remembering, filled as it was with melancholic notions of the "Vanishing Indian" and the wistful play of the colourful *coureur des bois*. However, with neither "Indian" nor Frenchman invited, the activity was, in fact, unadulterated appropriation.

Part of the success of this peculiar appropriation had to do with location, timing, and social need. The Haudenosaunee community of Kahnawake was situated about 16 kilometres from Montreal, across the St. Lawrence River. During the previous century, the Kahnawake community had been forced to relocate from the Mohawk Valley in upstate New York. Following a series of disruptive moves, by 1716 that community had settled in its present location south of Montreal.[16]

There, the community's resources were limited and the people of Kahnawake survived by farming and working outside the community in the forest or on the river. By the 1840s, they were also increasingly engaged in the commercialization of Indigenous produce and performance. In this way, Montreal's sporting community became familiar with *tewaarathon* and how the game was played in Kahnawake.[17] By 1844, enough members of the MOAC had become familiar with the game and how to play it that they challenged a Kahnawake team to a match. The Kahnawake team allowed their competitors several extra players but still won easily. During the next decade, more exhibition games were played, and interest grew exponentially. By 1856, enough anglophone athletes had taken up the sport that the Montreal Lacrosse Club (MLC) was formed.

Beyond the sheer love of the game, though, the anglophones of Montreal saw the potential for lacrosse to serve as a crucial accessory to the nascent Canadian identity. Ideally, this new identity would provide cohesion for the new nation and justification for the British-Canadian dominance and sensibilities that would come to inform all matters — cultural and otherwise — across the land.

In the early 19th century, many in the growing English population were concerned about their identity. Second-generation anglophones no longer felt simply "British": they had strong roots in North America; they resented being called "colonials" because that smacked of "provincial"; and the term "American" was already taken by an expanding and, for many in the British colonies, threatening United States. Describing themselves as native or "true" Canadians was awkward because the Indigenous and francophone populations had more convincing claims in this regard. The challenge for British immigrants was to portray themselves as having equal claim to being native Canadians while also justifying a dominant status. In *Becoming Native in a Foreign Land,* historian Gillian Poulter, surveying the architects of a new Canadian identity in Montreal, argues that the development of this new identity occurred between 1840 and 1885 and was based on Montreal anglophones' cultural adoptions and appropriations of activities long associated with Indigenous people and French Canadians.

At the same time that there was a growing need to create a new nation out of the separate British colonies in North America, there was considerable difficulty creating an imagined cultural identity that could bind disparate groups together. In conscious and unconscious ways, anglophones in Montreal began creating a new way to imagine an identity that would be calibrated to the needs of the new nation of Canada. Through the public and visible adoption of particular activities and sports (e.g., snowshoeing, tobogganing, winter hunting, and especially lacrosse), Montreal's elite could portray, at home and abroad, a set of gendered characteristics and behaviours that were seen as defining Canadians as "Men of the North."[18]

This invented tradition emphasized "northern*ness*" and gave agency to the cold and unforgiving climate; the landscape then became a central figure in the Canadian story. This idea of geography as an active character in the history of Canadian*ness* was attractive *to* and elaborated *on* by social agents, novelists, historians, artists, and sportsmen alike. Just as the "Old Boys' Clubs" of Quebec and Ontario were codifying the nation's games under the "Men of the North" model, so, too, would the likes of famed author Lucy Maud Montgomery, Group of Seven painter J.E.H. Macdonald, and historian Donald Creighton look to Canada's land and lakes to serve as their guiding muse in the 20th century.[19]

Meanwhile, back in the middle of the 19th century, anglophones hoped that their adoption of Indigenous and French-Canadian sports would help to forge an identity that drew on a mostly imagined way of life in previous times. The chosen sports were ideal for several reasons. First, they were activities that were categorically *not* British and *not* American. The performance of these sports was also, in itself, an Indigenizing experience — it helped the anglophones' claims of being "native." Yet, all these early activities were framed within a British paradigm. In this way, snowshoeing, tobogganing, and lacrosse — reformed and "scientifically" improved as they had been — suited 19th-century British values and sensibilities. At once, we have the robust pioneering Men of the North meeting the refined, white, middle- and upper-class anglophone men of Montreal who privileged the British public-school tenets of discipline, order and — at least as far as sport was concerned — fair play.[20]

The first such activity adopted by Montreal's sporting community was snowshoeing. The Montreal Snow Shoe Club (MSSC) — the first of many organized sports clubs — was formed in 1843. The club held weekly "tramps," social events, and organized races. In order to better envision themselves as the heirs and kin to the voyageurs and fur traders of old, club members also appropriated the voyageurs' style of dress; on all the tramps, members wore white blanket coats tied with a sash, plus leggings and moccasins and a tasseled toque. Clearly, the leggings and moccasins were an adoption of Indigenous dress while the blanket coat with sash and toque came courtesy of the French Canadians.

The weekly tramp represented more than just exercise; rather, it was, as Poulter observes, a "cultural performance in which members envisioned themselves as Nor'wester voyageurs." These clubs grew in popularity among the anglophone communities in Montreal. By the 1880s, when that city's population was approximately 200,000, there were some 25 snowshoe clubs in the city, with the largest, the MSSC, having 1,100 active members. These clubs, perhaps unsurprisingly, were *not* representative of Montreal's overall demographics. The bulk of the members were professional and commercial middle-class males, first- or second-generation British immigrants with strong ties to Empire, and all with a desire to be seen as "true" Canadians.

Also unsurprisingly, Indigenous people were absent from the clubs' memberships, and the number of French Canadians who joined was very limited. This presented a problem for members when Indigenous athletes entered the various clubs' competitions. There were — not for the first time — competing ideas on how to address Indigenous participation in Canadian sport. Some members claimed that snowshoeing could provide a common bond between new and old Canadians, and as such, Indigenous participation should be encouraged. On the other hand, other members remained steadfast in the belief that Indigenous people as a whole were inferior. Observing the subordinate status of Indigenous people was, obviously, at odds with the idea of inviting them to compete.

Club races were, nevertheless, initially open to Indigenous athletes. However, their subsequent success in these events hastened a reduction in the number of "open" or "Indian" races. They were not done away with altogether, though, as such races drew large crowds. At the same time, some Indigenous athletes challenged the extant racist system. For example, in 1873, Peter Thomas, an Indigenous snowshoer, won a Maple Leaf Snow Shoe Club race. The white racers, however, denied his victory. Although the race was advertised as an open one, organizers had really meant open to other clubs — not the general public. Thomas challenged the organizers' implied restrictions, won the race, and overcame his opponents' appeal. In this unfortunately rare case, the officials' sense of fair play trumped racism.

It may not have been coincidental that in the same year, the Montreal Pedestrian Club adopted a strict exclusionary rule banning professionals from the club's races. Under the new rules, anyone who had ever competed for money or had been paid for any activity relating to athletics was banned from competition (a theme we will return to later). Just to ensure that only real "amateur" athletes were allowed to compete, the club also excluded anyone who was "a labourer or Indian." In this way, the British-centric sports clubs of Montreal became the first gatekeepers of organized sport in Canada, liberally excluding on the basis of class, ethnicity, or race when it suited.

EXPANSION

When the Prince of Wales (later King Edward VII) visited Montreal in 1860 on his goodwill Royal Tour, lacrosse games were a major part of the spectacle that organizers held in his honour. There was more than a little irony in the fact that the newly adopted and widely advertised "Indian Games" were played on the city's cricket grounds. The event was designed to play up the city's reputation as a sports centre and to use the Indigenous teams to draw a larger paying audience.

The first game featured an Anishinaabe and a Haudenosaunee team, while the second one saw a Kahnawake team take on members of the MLC. Immediately following the two games, Kahnawake and Kanesatake warriors put on "Indian war dances" in which, as historian Ian Walter Radforth has assured, they "brandished tomahawks and knives, mimicking a bloody battle complete with the scalping of enemy captives."[21] Some spectators saw it as a frightening reality while others, including the players, understood it was theatre.[22]

The spokesman for the MLC believed lacrosse to be a laudable example of Anglo-Canadians borrowing and improving an Indigenous activity. The spokesman argued that lacrosse was "a manly sport peculiar to Canada, one derived from the aboriginal Red Man of the forest, and pre-eminently adapted to test their swiftness of foot, quickness of ear and vision, and powers of endurance."[23] Whatever appropriation processes — nefarious and otherwise — might have been at play here, the exhibition games put on for the Royal Tour in 1860 accelerated the popularity of the game in other parts of the country and did much to codify the governing rules and regulations of the sport.

The growth of the game that followed the exhibition was both immediate and remarkable. In the spring of 1867, there were 10 lacrosse clubs across Canada. Six months later, there were 80, with 2,000 players from Halifax to Hamilton.[24] In the decade that ensued, more and more clubs popped up across the western reaches of the new Dominion, and by the mid-1880s, there were something in the neighbourhood of 20,000 registered lacrosse players.

Perhaps as important as the popularity of the game with players was the fact that matches were highly entertaining and were able to consistently draw large crowds. These crowds, with enthusiasm, offered their stamp of approval to the sport and what it represented. Such enthusiasm was apparent to those outside of Canada. In 1887, for instance, the *Chicago Tribune* claimed that lacrosse "is to the Canadian what base-ball is to the Yankee and cricket to the Englishman."[25] No other sport in Canada, the paper added, had achieved the same support and affection. Lacrosse had secured its centrality in the blossoming cultural identity being crafted by those who sought to forever entwine "Men of the North" with the public-school tenets of the Old Country.

Part of the sport's attraction was that, unlike the quintessentially English game of cricket, lacrosse was seen as a bona fide Canadian sport. It was, after all, the only popular sport in the country that did not have European roots. There were also the healthy quotients of danger and violence in the game, which appealed to player and audience alike. Despite the attempt of some to "tame" the game, lacrosse offered a more physically aggressive notion of masculinity that was in many ways the exact opposite of more conservative games such as cricket.

This expectation of sanctioned violence within the game anticipated that of other organized sports — particularly hockey — and even helped and defined the career trajectories of individual Canadian athletes. The heavyweight boxing champion Tommy Burns, for example, played lacrosse in his youth and credited the sport for making Canadian sportsmen unique: "The only really tough athletes in the world are Canadians, who played lacrosse as roughly and toughly as the Mohawks ever did."[26] Such sentiments seem remote from those who tried to proselytize on the merits of cricket's gentlemanly play and, at the same time, did much to galvanize lacrosse's position within the enduring "Men of the North" mythology.

Indigenous teams outside Quebec also fuelled the growing interest in the sport and were at times able to use it for their own advantage. In September 1867, for instance, a game played in Toronto between a Haudenosaunee team from the Grand River and the Toronto Lacrosse Club drew a paying crowd of more than 3,000 spectators.[27] Similarly, Indigenous teams in other communities were able to capitalize on financial offers from non-Indigenous teams and eager promotors who were keen to set up exhibition games.

Invariably, after such exhibitions, the Indigenous players were called upon to provide a "war dance" to please the desires of the white audience. For their part, the performers knew well what was expected. Historian Johnny Beauvais described similar "desires" in Kahnawake:

> During the first years of Kahnawake participation in the entertainment industry, some attempts were made to maintain traditional Iroquois values, but in light of the audience's preference to see the "real" Wild West, our Indians had to adopt the "Sioux look," to make up new dance and songs and to learn trick horse-riding.

It mattered little, then, that the white audience's desires might have been incongruous with material history. A fictitious or at least generic rendering of Indigenous culture could, it seemed, be provided for a fee.

BEERS AND THE NATIONAL GAME

The Victorian era saw a shift toward a more regulated and controlled society that included what has been described as a sporting revolution in Britain and North America. So-called vernacular sports — largely recreational pastimes informally organized by local communities — had been codified, commercialized, and institutionalized. As it was in Britain, "modern" sport in Canada became yet another way for the elite classes to control the lower classes. Social entrepreneurs, the anglophone elites, and "Social Gospellers" (such as the Methodists) wanted to solve the various issues that came with the newly urbanized society, such as alcoholism, gambling, and general poor health. In response, there was a dramatic increase in the number of sports clubs. Each had its own governing body. These governing bodies outlined a given sport's rules and regulations in the hopes of limiting the violence and chaos of the vernacular sports of an earlier time. Organized sport was — or so thought its key proponents of the time — an effective way to civilize and moderate the rougher and more violent pastimes of the lower class or newly colonized people.[28] Lacrosse would soon undergo such a metamorphosis.

The Royal Tour of 1867 had done much to raise the awareness of the sport, but lacrosse owed perhaps a greater debt to the Montreal team's 19-year-old goaltender, who featured in the loss against Kahnawake. William George Beers began playing lacrosse at the age of six and would be a lifelong advocate of the sport. While growing up in Montreal in the 1850s, Beers attended numerous games played between the Kahnawake and Kanesatake teams. Although he loved the game, he felt the Indigenous players were often too wild and violent. The young netminder was, as it turned out, something of a visionary. In the same year as the Royal Tour, Beers published a brochure outlining his proposal for a standard set of rules and regulations to govern the game. Largely as a result of his efforts, the National Lacrosse Association (NLA), whose slogan was "Our Game and Our Country," was formed in September 1867. Representatives from 29 clubs from across Quebec and Ontario met in Kingston, Ontario, and appointed Beers as the association's secretary. Importantly, the NLA adopted the rules that Beers had proposed back in 1860. Two years later, he published *Lacrosse: The National Game of Canada.*

Beers was exactly the type of Canadian nationalist identified by Poulter: he was a second-generation English Canadian, a fervent patriot, and a believer in Muscular Christianity à la Thomas Hughes's *Tom Brown's School Days.* Beers's love of sports extended beyond lacrosse; besides belonging to the MLA, he was a member of the MSSC, the Olympic Club, a tobogganing club, and was a founder of the Montreal Amateur Athletic Association. Beers was swept away by the romance of the fledgling Canadian nationalism in Montreal. He was keenly aware, though, that in order to arrive at something distinctly Canadian, the architects — and Beers was certainly one of them — would need to consciously move away from those ideas rooted in British imperialism. Instead, Beers and company partook in the conscious creation, or imagining, of a national history rooted in the conditions of the New World. Beers, as professor Michael Robidoux explains, "turned to Indigenous sport as a means of portraying the soul of a nation."[29] The NLA began operations only nine years before the Indian Act came into effect. With all the suffering that sprang from that single piece of legislation, the "soul" of the nation was certainly a troubled one.

Montreal Snowshoe Club on Mount Royal, Montreal, QC, 1884.

Although Beers may have loved the Indigenous sport, his opinion of Indigenous people was disappointingly common and racist. In his capacity as a sportswriter, Beers argued that Indigenous athletes played lacrosse "mainly by instinct" and could never play "as scientifically as the best white players." He claimed that his version of lacrosse "improved and reduced to rule by the whites, employs the greatest combination of physical and mental activity white men can sustain in recreation, and is as much superior to the original as civilization is to barbarism."

The vigorous nature of Indigenous stickball games had, in his opinion, "developed an amount of splendid physical energy sufficient to have made their race masters of this continent forever, had mind not been so entirely subservient to body."[30] Beers believed the Indigenous style of play to be inferior to that of the Anglo-Canadians, who he felt were better at "team play" or, as he put it, "scientific regulations." Many of the adapted rules — such as a shorter field, limited time of play, breaks in the play — seemed to reduce the apparent Indigenous advantages of fitness and endurance. In time, however, many of claims were undermined when Indigenous teams continued to defeat non-Indigenous teams in games played *under* Beers's rules. When that happened, the involvement of Indigenous players in NLA games was greatly limited.

At least as far as Beers was concerned, the extant Indigenous game was too savage and was "midway between a sport and a deadly combat, because of its serious results to limb and life." Reforming the game, however, turned out to be more difficult than first imagined and involved much more than drafting rules and regulations. A game played before an audience becomes governed to a significant degree by the values and expectations of that audience. A match played in August 1879 between the Montreal Shamrocks, and an Indigenous team shocked a reporter: "I have never witnessed such rough play, in fact almost brutal play as was indulged in today, so far from being sport, they might as well put down their sticks and fight at once."[31] It may, however, have been what middle-class anglophones had expected from the two teams.

As its popularity rose during the latter part of the 19th century, lacrosse would indeed become more structured, but not necessarily less violent. In one particularly nasty game in St. Catharines, the home team openly declared they would disable any opposing Orangeville player trying to score. By the end of the game, one Orangeville player had a ruptured kidney, another a fractured kneecap, a third a punctured lung, and a fourth needed seven stitches to his head. Two members of the home team were later jailed for assault causing bodily harm. This was an extreme case, but for many spectators, roughness and violence was an inherent and attractive part of lacrosse. Beers, nevertheless, regulated and restructured lacrosse into something he thought was slightly more palatable for Canadian society.

SELLING CANADA

Beers also took part in several lacrosse tours to Britain to spread the sport's popularity and to associate the game, in the mind of the British public, with a uniquely Canadian national identity. At the same time as the NLA had begun making it more difficult for Indigenous teams to compete at the highest level in Canada, Indigenous teams were being recruited for lacrosse tours that were trying to sell the sport and a Canadian identity in Britain and the United States. The first of the three lacrosse tours of England was organized in 1867, the same year the NLA began its operations and, of course, the year of Canadian Confederation. The tours, out of financial necessity, included a team of Indigenous players to attract British spectators.[32]

The organizers had planned the tours to be both an expression of imperial loyalty and one that displayed the distinctly Canadian themes of a wintry climate and a Northern character. This task proved difficult given that the tours were set during a warm English summer. One of the solutions was to hold snowshoe races on England's green and pleasant land after the lacrosse games.[33] The inclusion of such exotica worked: the exhibitions of the Canadian sport raised sufficient interest among English observers that the English Lacrosse Association was formed in 1868.

A more significant tour of Britain — one played before the royal family, no less — took place in 1876. This particular sojourn included a Kahnawake team. Here, there occurred again the dressing *up* and repackaging *of* Indigenous culture and sport at a time when Indigenous players were actively being excluded from the NLA. Lasting from May until July, the tour was jointly organized by George Beers, the MLC, and the English Thames Hare and Hounds Club. The latter requested that an Indigenous team be included in the tour, to draw spectators. The games were advertised as "Twelve Canadian Gentlemen" meeting "Twelve Iroquois Indians."

All games, with the exception of the private royal event, were played before a paying audience. For their participation, the Indigenous players were promised that their travel costs would be covered, and that each player would receive $20 a month and a new suit. Through this promise, the tour organizers effectively made all of the Indigenous players "professional," which of course contravened the codes as set forth by many of the organized clubs back in Canada.

Certainly, the tour provided the possibilities of profit for player and promoter alike. For many of the individual players, however, a greater motive was the chance to travel internationally and represent their community before British spectators and the royal family. For decades after, Kahnawake

Kahnawà:ke Lacrosse Team with Dr. W. George Beers and Hugh Beckett, about 1867.

residents told and retold stories about the royal family being charmed by the players, especially Big John Canadian (Sawatis Aiontonnis), who proved that it was possible to be both "rustic" and a "gentleman." These rustic gentlemen played across Ireland, Scotland, and England and, even in inclement weather, attracted crowds of upward of 2,000 spectators.[34] In terms of igniting interest and support for the sport in Britain, the 1876 edition was far more successful than the previous endeavours.

The success of the tour also garnered considerable attention in the United States. As a result, James Gordon Bennett, the publisher of the *New York Herald*, contacted the organizers of the tour to arrange a game at the Polo Club in Newport, Rhode Island. The Polo Club picked up all the travelling, hotel, and incidental expenses. Notification of the event triggered enthusiasm across Newport. All the town's carriages and other conveyances were booked long before the match, which forced hundreds of spectators to walk to the polo field. It seemed everyone wanted a chance to see the Montreal club square off against the Indigenous team. The Montreal players were, according to the *New York Herald*, "small, wiry and well knit," and surpassed their opponents in running and jumping, but the Kahnawake, "dark" and "slender," were more skilled at throwing and receiving the ball. The newspaper predicted that lacrosse would soon be a favourite game in the United States.[35] Certainly, it was popular enough in Newport that the teams were persuaded to play another game a few days later. That contest attracted an even larger crowd, of more than 3,000.

Beyond the objective of promoting the game for the game's sake, these international exhibitions served another purpose: in 1883, the final British tour that included an Indigenous team was sponsored by the Canadian Department of Agriculture as part of its efforts to encourage British immigration to the Dominion. In this way, lacrosse — and Indigenous players in particular — were used to "sell Canada" to the British. Promotional literature distributed to the spectators throughout the tour trumpeted the benefits of immigration to Canada. Officials believed that the tour would "do much to disseminate a knowledge of the Dominion and the advantages it offered to emigrants from the rural districts of Great Britain."[36]

George Beers served as the Canadian team captain and was also responsible for the distribution of the pro-immigration material at the various matches. By tour's end, 150,000 leaflets had been distributed to spectators. Although some in the Indigenous community believed that the game and the players were being exploited, there were always more Indigenous players who wanted to go on the tours than there were positions available for them. The Kahnawake, it seemed, believed the personal benefits of being part of such a tour outweighed other considerations. The truth of the matter was, however, that while Big John Canadian and company were shilling on the government's behalf for the great wave of Scots and English who would soon leave Britain for the Dominion, these same Indigenous players were not allowed to compete in Canada's national championship when they got home.

"Big John" and the Kahnawà:ke Lacrosse Team, European Competitors, Scarborough, England, 1883.

PROSCRIPTION

The sporting revolution of the mid- to late-19th century fuelled a growing debate over the nature of amateur and professional athletics. By definition — a definition established in British public schools and universities and imported to Canada — an amateur was someone who received no material reward for their involvement in sports and who displayed fair play and a respect for umpires and opponents. By contrast, a professional was defined as someone who made their living from a sport or, more strictly, received money or prizes from any aspect of participation in sport. In practice, the definitions were often blurred; "amateurs," for example, were in some cases able to receive money or prizes.

Right from its inception, the NLA was concerned with the issue of professionalism. In its very first meeting, the NLA classified white teams as "amateur" while judging the teams from Kahnawake and Akwesasne to be "professional." This judgment had less to do with financial remuneration than with social status, class, and, of course, race. A pervasive belief among spectators at the time was that amateurs played for the love of their sport, and professionals were primarily motivated by profit and the need to win at all costs.

In 1867, men from Kahnawake won the first Dominion lacrosse title. Here, in its inaugural year, the NLA began its campaign to restrict the opportunities available to Indigenous players to compete at the highest levels. Beers, the driving force behind the association, believed that the game should be civilized and regulated to reflect British-Canadian notions of fair play, progress, modernity, and scientific regulations. His philosophy found expression in the governing regulations of the NLA. One of the first rules established by the association was that "no Indian must play in a match for a white club, unless previously agreed upon."[37] This rule effectively banned non-Indigenous teams from adding talented Indigenous athletes for league competition. Indigenous teams could, however, still belong to the NLA and compete for the national championship, and individual Indigenous players could be added for exhibition games. In 1869, Kahnawake players again won the national championship. As a result, the rules were once again altered: individual Indigenous players who were paid to play, such as the Kahnawake players who had taken part in the British tours, could no longer belong to the NLA.

In 1876 yet more rules were introduced by the NLA, the effect of which further limited Indigenous participation. Now, any Indigenous team that competed in the NLA championship was no longer able to play for money. Any Indigenous team that took money for exhibition games was also barred from championship games. Such teams could continue to earn money from exhibition games with non-Indigenous NLA teams, but they were excluded from championship play.

The distinction between amateur and professional further threatened Indigenous participation at the highest levels of the sport. In the 1860s and 1870s, it was assumed that Indigenous teams were made up of working-class athletes and, by implication, were professionals. Indigenous teams usually charged playing fees for exhibition games against non-Indigenous teams out of necessity. The players who had been part of lacrosse tours were subsidized. As a result, many of the very best Indigenous athletes faced the charge of being professional.

There had been a general allowance for Indigenous teams that allowed them to receive some subsidies, but this changed in 1880 when the NLA, responding to a growing concern about professionals among the non-Indigenous teams, became the National Amateur Lacrosse Association (NALA). Henceforth, all questions surrounding the nebulous nature of status and participation were resolved: Indigenous teams were barred from NALA competition.[38] Specifically, the NALA claimed that Indigenous players were professional athletes because they were not gentlemen by social class, that they were involved in manual labour, and that their expenses were sometimes paid by the opposing club.[39] Individuals could be retained as a trainer or as players in exhibition games, but they were barred from league competition. After having sold the exotica of lacrosse and Canada to would-be immigrants, First Nations athletes were now on the outside looking in at their own Creator's Game.

THE WOMEN'S GAME

While the British tours were unable to solidify the game as a major sport in the United Kingdom, men's *and* women's lacrosse would, over time, flourish at elite American universities. The evolution of collegiate lacrosse in America, however, occurred differently for men and women. Contemporary photographs bear witness: women's normal protective equipment, excluding goalies, included only mouthguards and eye protectors, while the men are adorned with helmets replete with face guards, a mouthguard, shoulder pads, lacrosse gloves, and elbow and arm protectors. The difference can be explained by how men's and women's lacrosse was transmitted from Canada across the North Atlantic borderlands.

In North America, lacrosse — and the stickball games from which it grew — had always been a sport played primarily by men.[40] Even after its acculturalization by Beers, lacrosse remained a male-only sport that emphasized aggression, strength, and controlled violence. This was the form of men's lacrosse that organized tours and exhibition games carried into Britain and the United States. Women's lacrosse, though, emerged after 1890 and evolved in its own unique way, with different class and gender expectations. This evolution was such that men's and women's lacrosse can today be seen as fundamentally different games.

Certainly, the women's game offered an interesting foil to one feature of the men's game: its level of violence. Recall that Beers and other supporters of lacrosse wanted to create a game that was less violent than *tewaarathon*. Despite these efforts, however, violence remained a thrilling and expected part of men's lacrosse, one that spectators would gladly pay to watch. The violent nature of lacrosse was perhaps less the result of the legacy of its origins or a failure of new rules governing play than it was about gendered expectations: boys and men were *supposed* to be violent. This was particularly so during Canada's perceived "crisis in masculinity."

The so-called crisis began in 1871 after the British Garrison quit Canada, leaving Canadians to defend themselves. At the time, there was a move to militarism around the globe. It seemed that every country was preparing for war. Certainly, in the years between Confederation and the First World War, there seemed a very real chance of conflict between Canada and the United States. Despite its increasingly vulnerable situation, Canada remained ill prepared to defend itself.

The public unease with what was perceived as the government's and military's failure to keep Canada strong was compounded by anxiety over the fact that young boys were now left to be brought up by their mothers as many men moved to factory and office work. Some feared for what might become of the Canadian male.

For many, sport was seen as a solution to the problem and offered the added benefit of preparing young athletic men for future military service. Lacrosse, in particular, served as a corrective to the deleterious effects of urbanization and industrialization; it was a space where violence was permitted and tacitly enjoyed.[41]

These same violent tenets were not, however, transferable to the women's version. Although it was also rooted in the Indigenous game, women's lacrosse evolved much differently. When lacrosse was introduced as a women's sport in Scotland, it was stripped of its physicality.

In 1884, Louisa Lumsden, headmistress at St. Leonards School in Scotland, visited parts of eastern Canada on her way to give a paper on women's education in Britain at a conference at Sarasota Springs in New York. While visiting Montreal, she watched a match between the MLC and a Kahnawake team organized by White Eagle. From the start, Lumsden was smitten with both the game and its players: "these Indians live not far from Montreal, above the Lachine Rapids, and are, of course, civilized, and many are very wealthy.... Their chief was called White Eagle. But the whites were a stronger team and won the game."[42]

The experience of watching a single lacrosse game had a powerful impact on her. "It is a wonderful game," she later wrote; "beautiful and graceful." So charmed with the game was she that Lumsden introduced it to St. Leonards.

One can make a direct link between Lumsden and two other important champions of the women's game: Frances Dove and Rosabelle Sinclair. Dove, Lumsden's successor at St. Leonards, took over the crusade for lacrosse in the United Kingdom when Lumsden moved on from the school. When Dove left St. Leonards to found Wycombe Abbey School in England, she established the women's game immediately. On the strength of Dove's proselytizing for lacrosse, by the turn of the century, several colleges and universities in Britain featured the game in their curriculum.

A graduate of Dove's Wycombe Abbey School, Rosabelle Sinclair would carry the version of lacrosse created by Lumsden back across the Atlantic. Sinclair, who had specialized in physical education, became the athletic director at Bryn Mawr in Pennsylvania, where she introduced women's lacrosse. Sinclair was such a force in popularizing the game in elite U.S. colleges that she became known as the "Grand Dame of Lacrosse."

The women's game, as imagined by Louisa Lumsden those many years before, had come back to Canada. By 1898, students at Wellesley College, an elite women's school, were playing lacrosse. Because real lacrosse involved "violent running," a *Globe* reporter assumed that it "had to be different from any game seen in Canada." To be fair, the paper was partly correct. By the time women's lacrosse began flourishing in American schools, it was most certainly a different game from that played by men in Canada. The rules that Lumsden had introduced prohibited physical contact, especially stick and body checking.

Perhaps more importantly, at the turn of the century sport was governed by certain social expectations regarding the appropriate forms of exercise for young women. Educators believed that women had to balance the need to be physically active while also conforming to white, middle-class, heterosexual norms of femininity. Sinclair claimed, "Lacrosse, as girls play it, is an orderly pastime that has little in common with the men's tribal warfare version … whereas men resort to brute strength the women depend solely on skill." Many others agreed with Sinclair about the differences.[43]

Yet, removed as their game might have been from the men's, the women partaking in team sports were, in fact, challenging some prevailing societal expectations. At a time when many physicians recommended moderate physical activity for women only because of the reproductive health benefits they believed it conferred, games with sticks must surely have crossed the line.

THE 1904 OLYMPICS

By the start of the 20th century, any Indigenous presence in senior levels of lacrosse had been essentially purged — excepting, of course, when it was used to generate public interest. The 1904 Olympics offered perhaps the last example of this type of exploitive inclusion. Advocates of lacrosse had managed to get the game included as a medal sport at the 1904 Olympic Games, held in conjunction with the St. Louis World Fair. An Indigenous team from the Six Nations Reserve was included in the Games to encourage public interest. Little is known of this team except for the record of their names and the fact that they won the bronze medal.[44] On the strength of its popularity at the 1904 edition of the Games, lacrosse was once again included in the 1908 London Olympics.

The Canadian team selected in 1908 to the first "modern" Games starkly revealed the position of Indigenous athletes in Canadian lacrosse. Participants in the London Olympics would compete under a national flag.

In preparation for the 1908 competition, Canadian Olympic officials selected lacrosse players from across Canada to make up the team. Despite the large pool of Indigenous players, including those who had played in the 1904 Olympics, no Indigenous player was selected for the 1908 team.

By this time, lacrosse had become associated with white Canadian culture and nationalism. Indeed, the game was used to assimilate Indigenous children in residential schools. The government believed that this "education," as provided by churches, would also decrease Indigenous people's dependence on public funds. For their part, Christian organizations saw the development of residential schools, with government funding, as a means of converting, "civilizing," and assimilating Indigenous people into a Christian Euro-Canadian society. The residential school system that emerged, administered by various Christian churches, was an ad hoc structure with enormous variation. At its best, the system was underfunded, had too few administrators, and countenanced little empathy for the students or their Indigenous culture.[45] But at its worst, the residential school system was tantamount to a cultural and, for thousands of young students, actual genocide.[46]

The overall experience of Indigenous students was negative. When they arrived, their hair was cut, they were given uniforms, and they were to speak only English or French. The under-funding of the "schools" meant that many students were malnourished and forced to live in overcrowded conditions. The results left students vulnerable to a range of diseases and abuses. The staff was generally underpaid and often unqualified, and some were sexual predators. Students were in class only half the day and worked for the school the rest. The schools, then, seem to have doubled as child-labour camps.

By the 1890s, residential school directors encouraged time for sports, owing to the belief that a healthy life required some physical exercise, the students enjoyed it, and that an exhausted child was a docile child. Another reason for offering sport in the school schedule was, as Allan Downey, an Indigenous scholar and author, observes, "the desire to introduce Indigenous youth to Western Muscular Christian ideas about progress, civility, morality, gender, language and, of course, nationalism."[47] For the administrators, sports such as cricket, soccer, basketball, and boxing seemed ideal ways to transmit an introduction to Euro-Canadian behaviour and "whiteness." Lacrosse, now seen as a symbol of Canadian identity, was increasingly played at residential schools, too. Here was a cruel irony: an Indigenous game, with strong cultural and spiritual significance, had been appropriated, redefined, and reintroduced as a symbol of Euro-Canadianism that could be used to assimilate Indigenous children.

Of course, if lacrosse offered a means of assimilating Indigenous youth, it also offered the possibility of reaffirming Indigenous agency and revitalizing core Indigenous values and identity. After all, if an English colonist, adorned in his blanket coat and snowshoe costume and standing in the snow overlooking Montreal, could envision himself as a hardy "Man of the North" with cultural ties to the earlier voyageurs, so, too, could an Indigenous boy in a residential school playground, with a lacrosse stick in his hands, imagine himself, at least for a moment, as an independent Indigenous warrior and a servant of the Creator. Unwittingly, the architects of these schools had sown the seeds for an Indigenous renaissance.

RENAISSANCE

Although by the early 20th century, Indigenous athletes had been banned from the highest levels of amateur lacrosse, the game remained a powerful Haudenosaunee expression of Indigenous culture.[48] In the depths of the Great Depression, new opportunities opened for Indigenous players who had been previously barred from amateur lacrosse. The Depression, with its massive job losses and social hardships, changed attitudes toward professional sports and professional athletes. The amateur code became a luxury that many could not afford. In August 1931, sports journalist Ted Reeve announced the formation of a new game: box lacrosse. As Reeve explained, "the old, old game of lacrosse [was] taken indoors and speeded up to hockey pace."[49] The catalysts were Joseph Cattarinich and Léo Dandurand, owners of the Montreal Canadiens, who had built professional hockey into a major sport and wanted to create a new professional league.

There was little question that the emergence of box lacrosse was concerned with profit and entertainment. In short, the motive was to fill hockey rinks, empty in the summer, with paying customers. This required talent. Once excluded as professionals, Indigenous players were now welcome to join the new old game. Players from Kahnawake, Akwesasne, and Six Nations were on the first rosters.

Perhaps surprisingly to some, this profit-oriented incarnation of lacrosse would play a significant role in the articulation of Indigenous and, in particular, Haudenosaunee nationhood. A new generation of Indigenous players, drawn from different regions and often playing on all-Indigenous teams, gravitated toward box lacrosse. A sport largely forgotten underwent a rebirth. As all-Indigenous lacrosse associations formed, so too did the demand for the recognition of Indigenous nationhood rise. The sport would soon be linking arms with First Nations activism.

Although the first professional league lasted only two years, other professional leagues soon followed. With rules and team size similar to those of hockey, box lacrosse quickly surpassed the field version in popularity, especially among Indigenous groups. Shut out at the highest levels of the 10-on-10 field game, Indigenous players flocked to the faster, more physical indoor version with 5-on-5 plus goalies. In 1932, the Mann Cup, the most prestigious lacrosse trophy, was played under box lacrosse rules.

Indigenous players now had renewed visibility in non-Indigenous organizations. By the 1970s, the next generation of Indigenous lacrosse players had become increasingly politicized by the newly formed American Indian Movement (AIM). Events such as the occupation of Alcatraz Island, the AIM's seizure of Wounded Knee, and Pierre Trudeau's white paper of June 1969 recommending the dismantling of the Indian Act drew attention to the special legal relationship between Indigenous people and the Canadian government. Many Indigenous athletes became activists. Indigenous players such as Oren Lyons, Rick Hill, and Wes Patterson, drawn from both box and university lacrosse teams, began to envision a Haudenosaunee cultural revitalization that could unite "traditionalists" and "modernists" while also reappropriating lacrosse at the international level. The end result was a drive to create a Haudenosaunee team that would represent a sovereign nation.

In 1982, Roy Simmons, coach of the Syracuse University lacrosse team, suggested to Oren Lyons that he organize an Indigenous team to play an exhibition field lacrosse match at the 1983 NCAA Championships in Baltimore. Even though most Indigenous athletes were playing little field lacrosse, Oren and others saw the invitation as an opportunity to show how lacrosse could promote cultural revitalization. In 1983, the Grand Council of the Haudenosaunee Confederacy agreed to establish and sanction the Iroquois Nationals as the national team of the Confederacy. A mixed group of high-school and college players was cobbled together.

Although the Nationals were badly beaten in their two games in Baltimore, their loss only provided greater motivation. The team subsequently contacted the Los Angeles Olympic Committee and obtained permission to play an exhibition game against Canada before the opening of the Games in 1984. The Australian team, then touring Canada, heard about the Iroquois Nationals and the exhibition game and wanted to join. They were quickly followed by representatives of the English and U.S. teams. The six-team tournament became the centre part of the Jim Thorpe Memorial Games and Pow-Wow.

In an effort to involve other Indigenous people, the Iroquois Nationals organized the "Great Jim Thorpe Longest Run," with a series of Indigenous communities participating in a relay run to carry a commemorative staff across the country to Los Angeles.[50] During the tournament, the Nationals achieved their first victory over a national team, beating England. The Nationals were then invited to tour England the following year. The tour saw them win all but one game. More importantly, the Iroquois Nationals completed the tour while travelling on their Haudenosaunee passports.[51] They had established two precedents: the Iroquois Nationals were recognized as a "national" team and their Haudenosaunee passports had been accepted as legitimate travel documents by a foreign country. While the Nationals were, at first, denied membership in the International Lacrosse Federation (ILF), the team was accepted as a full member nation in 1988. The recognition of the Nationals as a sovereign nation had implications for all other Indigenous people.

However, the terrorist attacks in 2001 on the World Trade Center in New York resulted in nations imposing stricter security measures. In its effort to tighten its borders, the European Union refused to recognize the legitimacy of the Haudenosaunee passports. When the Nationals attempted to travel to England for the 2010 World Lacrosse Championships using these passports, they were denied admission. As a matter of principle, the players refused to use Canadian or U.S. passports and therefore missed the championships. When the championships were held in Israel in 2018, the Canadian government indicated that returning players could not re-enter Canada using Haudenosaunee passports. Only with the mediation of the ILF and local organizers did the Israeli and Canadian officials ultimately waive the travel restrictions. The Nationals finished third in the tournament.

The Iroquois's National Olympic Committee has applied to compete at the 2028 Olympic Summer Games. A decision will be made in 2024. Whatever the result, this development has been something of a victory for Indigenous athletes and has completed the full circle in a curious trajectory for lacrosse: by the 21st century, a sport appropriated by British colonists, touted as Canada's national game, and later used to assimilate residential school students has become a powerful tool to foster the resurgence of Indigenous culture.

II

TIP AND TEDDY: BASEBALL v. CRICKET, 1887

ON A CLEMENT AUGUST 2, 1887, A GROUP OF CANADIANS TOOK TO the field in London, England, for a second day of cricket against their English hosts. This was no ordinary occasion. The opponent was, after all, the Marylebone Cricket Club (MCC), a legendary institution responsible for drafting the laws that today govern the sport. The deeply impressed tourists found themselves at Lord's — the world's most famous cricket pitch — to face, as best they could, a side that was the personification of Englishness and the natural custodian of the summer sport they played. Adding to the intimidating reputation of the Canadian's opponents was the fact that the MCC was celebrating its centenary in this, the same year Queen Victoria was celebrating her 50th jubilee. The visiting colonials were, it would seem, fortunate to have even featured in this grand English sporting narrative. Most every noteworthy Canadian in London was in attendance, to be seen and to witness the auspicious moment at hand.[1]

Few expected much in the way of cricket. If the Canadians had been soundly thrashed, no one would have blamed the players for taking consolation in having had the privilege simply to play at Lord's. As it happened, there was no thrashing. In MCC's second inning on this lovely August day, Dr. Edward Russell Ogden — a.k.a. "Teddy" — of Oakville, Ontario, managed to give up only 83 runs, while taking a remarkable and record-establishing nine wickets for the Gentleman of Canada. The resultant draw ran contrary to the anticipated script the English surely had in mind. More, on the strength of this sensational performance, Teddy Ogden would soon be recognized as one of North America's greatest cricketers of the 19th century.

On the very day Teddy Ogden was making Canadian cricket history at Lord's in London, another story was unfolding 5,700 kilometres across the Atlantic, in Philadelphia. As a member of baseball's St. Louis Browns, Woodstock, Ontario's James Edward O'Neill — a.k.a. "Tip" — was emerging from a mid-season slump during a three-game series against the Philadelphia Athletics. The Browns would take two of the three games played against the Athletics, and much of the credit was owing to Tip's stunning return to form as he scored or drove in 10 of the Browns's 21 runs over the course of the series. On August 2, O'Neill went three for five in a convincing 14–6 Browns victory.[2] From there, Tip maintained a dizzying pace through to the end of the season, resulting in the highest recorded single-season batting average in the history of major league baseball. While O'Neill's .492 average from the summer of 1887 remains somewhat controversial (base on balls, or "walks," counted as a hit for that year), it was still a staggering accomplishment.

At the same time that these two men summited their respective games, a struggle for fan support between baseball and cricket was occurring every summer in the small towns and cities across a Canadian nation in its infancy. In terms of class consciousness, cricket played "top down" to baseball's "bottom up," reflecting as it did a very particular Englishness that outlined a very particular social order. The elite classes of both pre- and post-Confederation Canada were trying to re-create such an order and were loath to share the game with those who weren't a part of the fledgling country's exclusive preserve. Baseball was not circumscribed by any such imperial agenda.

The divide between the sports was manifest in the careers of these two men, born only two years apart: Tip O'Neill, the son of a hotelier, and Teddy Ogden, the son of a doctor. The former attended a Catholic preparatory school in Toronto; the latter, the bastion of old, Orange, Protestant

Ontario, Upper Canada College (UCC), which was also in Toronto. In 1887 both men were considered the best in North America in their chosen sports. In true Canadian fashion, both men had achieved their successes *outside* the country of their birth. By 1890, both men would be plying their sporting trade in Chicago.

At the same time, there were other, non-playing movers and shakers who took part in this yearly battle for the hearts of Canadian sports fans. The Guelph brewer George Sleeman, for example, was proselytizing for baseball, while the Oxford-educated postmaster of Toronto, Thomas Charles Patteson, sought to establish the civilizing pastime of cricket as Canada's game. When Tip and Teddy died — both in their early 50s and, eerily, only two years apart, in 1915 and 1913, respectively — baseball could claim victory over cricket.

EARLY CANADIAN CRICKET

Canada was very much a satellite of Britain during the 19th century. All things in vogue in the mother country were enthusiastically adopted by the tastemakers in the new nation. Sport was no exception. And cricket occupied the most prominent place among all English sports in this regard. At the behest of numerous social agents — including those within influential governmental and viceregal circles — Canada welcomed several visiting English cricket sides at different times throughout the 19th century. These tours were not so much about cricket as they were about enacting a certain sort of Englishness.

The English cricketer and MCC secretary R.A. Fitzgerald spoke to this shared cultural sensibility between tourist and host in a travelogue detailing one English club's tour of Canada in 1872. In it, Fitzgerald recognized an apparent commonality between his teammates travelling across the country and the English-speaking people of the young nation: "We were *made* sensible that our reception was mainly owing to the fact that we were Englishmen. The people were glad to see us, because they feel themselves to be no less Englishmen than ourselves."[3] And British institutions were well represented wherever cricket was played in Canada. In Toronto, Fitzgerald

Master William McF. Notman and Master Chipman posed for a photograph holding symbols — a cricket bat and ball — of their social status, 1863.

confirmed that "luncheon was set out in the log-hut; a great attendance on the first day was well sustained throughout the week. Royalty, in the person of the Lieut.-Governor and his Lady, honoured the performances each day."

As the game dovetailed nicely with the prevailing political and cultural attitudes of the day, Canada's elite stumped for cricket with zeal. Various governors general offered their own stamp of approval. As the *Patriot* observed in 1836, Sir Francis Bond Head, the lieutenant governor of Upper Canada, was

> too accurate an observer of human nature not to know that the amusements of youth tinge the character of the man, and that British feelings cannot flow into the breasts of our Canadian boys through a more delightful or untainted channel than that of British sports. A cricketer, as a matter of course, *detests democracy, and is staunch in allegiance to his king.*[4]

Outside of the viceregal realm, cricket found champions within other "thoroughly English" institutions. The York (later Toronto) Cricket Club (TCC) was founded in 1827 by the English-born educator George Anthony Barber, whom many consider to be the "Father of Canadian Cricket." With the TCC, Barber was endeavouring to reimagine the fabled MCC in London. Upper Canada College, which was founded in 1829 and where, perhaps unsurprisingly, Barber taught, followed the blueprint of English public schools such as Eton and Harrow in privileging cricket above all other sports. For many years, UCC cricketers would find their way into the TCC side.

This development of the game would be replicated in various centres across the country in the decades to come. With the incipient development of the railroad during the 1830s, cricket clubs were formed in Halifax, Kingston, Montreal, Hamilton, Darlington, Guelph, and Woodstock.[5] Here, members of Canada's elite and their children played cricket — first and foremost — as a celebration of their connection to Britain. Playing cricket in the last quarter of the 19th century was also to take a stand in favour of the "amateur ideal." In this way, cricket acted as a bulwark against the general rise of professional sport, and American baseball in particular.

The popularity of the sport, though, changed over time. The situation in Guelph, Ontario, serves as a good example of this evolution. In the 19th century, more than 90 percent of the town's population was British in origin, and those demographics were reflected in its sporting culture. Not surprisingly, the town's first sports club was the Guelph Cricket Club. An elite social club as much as a sports club, it reflected the efforts of J.C.W. Daly, the agent of the Canada Company (a British land development company established, in part, to aid in the colonization of Upper

Canada). Daly requested funds from the company's commissioners to lay out a pitch, along with money for bats and balls, to make the settlement attractive to the "right sort" of immigrant.[6] Until structured leagues were established in the 1880s, the club played only sporadic cricket matches, most frequently against "socially appropriate" opponents, such as the students at the Ontario Agricultural College and UCC.[7] In 1881, the Guelph team competed in a playoff with teams from Galt, Brantford, and Mount Forest in a "Cricket Championship."

Having the time to play protracted games in expensive formal attire on a playing surface maintained by a grounds crew was a test of social status and wealth. Those agents promoting the game regarded their sport as the bedrock of an organized and conservative society. Those who were not the "right sort of immigrant," however, saw cricket as an expression of British cultural elitism and social dominance. As a result, by the mid-1870s baseball was a far more popular sport in Guelph. The same was true elsewhere.

Nevertheless, many influential members of the social elite did their level best to establish cricket, *their* game, as the dominant sport of Canada. One such cricket crusader was the English-born Thomas Charles Patteson. Educated at Eton and later Oxford, Patteson was the managing editor of the Conservative newspaper the *Mail* and was also instrumental in the founding of the Ontario Jockey Club. In 1879, Prime Minister John A. Macdonald appointed Patteson the postmaster of Toronto. Importantly — at least in terms of our story — Patteson represented Canada in various cricket matches and captained the Canadian Cricket XI in 1859 and 1860.

Patteson was committed to turning back the impinging Americana that was having great influence on the Canadian nation. The postmaster was foremost among those agents who sought to bring touring English clubs to Canada. This was the case when he served as the official organizer of the tour that brought Fitzgerald's MCC side over in 1872. This particular incarnation of the club from Marylebone just happened to include the world's most famous cricketer, W.G. Grace, who would bat with impunity in various Canadian cities.

The 1872 tour was, as earlier tours of this kind had been, more a celebration of the ties that bound Canada to Britain than it was about the actual games themselves. In a heartfelt letter at that tour's conclusion, Fitzgerald thanked Patteson for the hosts' hospitality:

> We can certainly report that, if our eyes and ears do not misjudge us, one common interest unites Canada and England, that a Canadian is American only by the intervention of a vast ocean, and that Englishmen have only to see the country and its people to learn its value and their attachment to British institutions.[8]

While the sentiments of kindness and kinship in Fitzgerald's letter may have been received with thanks, Patteson could hardly have been pleased with the Canadians' actual cricket against the English visitors. It was as it had always been: abysmal. In fact, four years earlier, an All-England touring club had easily crushed Canada's XXII in Montreal by the humbling margin of 310 to 28.

In most instances, the Canadians were afforded the luxury of a 2:1 ratio of batting. That is to say, the Canadians fielded 22 players to England's 11. This was the case when they faced the most famous cricket club and cricketer in the world in September 1872, where Patteson's Canadians were still soundly thrashed. In the first match against Montreal, the MCC's XI scored 255 in one inning against the Canadian XXII's 115 over two innings. It wasn't much better in Ottawa, where MCC managed 201 in one inning against the Canadians' meagre 92 over two innings. Toronto was an improvement: MCC made 319 on the strength of W.G.'s 142, but the Canadians surprised with 214. London, too, was a bit better for the hosts — it took two innings for MCC to hit the 250 mark. Yet, the Canadians could only reply with a thin 120. In the final match, in Hamilton, Ontario, the Canadian XXII mustered only a miserable 115 over two innings to MCC's commanding 181 in one inning. The cricket played by the 22 Canadians was, as far as the otherwise charitable Fitzgerald was concerned, "feeble."[9]

Canada's showing wasn't just poor against the English; the United States claimed twice as many victories as Canada in matches between them during the 19th century. Indeed, a drought of Canadian wins in what was usually

Gentlemen of England Cricket Group, Montreal, QC, composite, 1872.

an annual affair against the United States began in 1857 and was interrupted only by the Teddy Ogden–led teams of the mid-1880s, which restored some dignity to the Canadian side.[10] This dismal performance in international cricket was chief among the many reasons that baseball would, in time, claim summer supremacy in the hearts of Canadians.

EARLY CANADIAN BASEBALL

Organized, competitive Canadian baseball first emerged in those small towns and cities in southwestern Ontario, close to New York and Michigan. As a result, the early evolution of the sport in Canada occurred in a "baseball borderland," where the game was widely perceived as an American cultural activity. As the better Canadian baseball teams sought to prove their competitiveness against good American teams, they were drawn into the commercialization, professionalization, and Americanization of the sport.

The bat-and-ball games played in much of Canada and parts of the United States before the 1850s was more in the "folk" tradition of sport and play: limited regulations, flexible rules, and played mostly on holidays. All such games owed a big debt to the British games of rounders (a bat-and-ball game, sometimes called base ball, which also directly informed the evolution of American baseball) and cricket.

The pastime of baseball was attractive to many different people for a variety of reasons. First off, the game had different levels of intensity and competition with which it could be played. The game was also class-cutting and could be enjoyed by a multi-generational group of non-athletes at a family picnic and could be played purely for fun and with little concern for the score and, perhaps, the rules. It could likewise satisfy the need of physically fit and competitive young men to show off their skills and abilities. Most of these early games left no records. When they were mentioned, little was explained. Such was the 1819 notification during Hamilton's celebration of King George IV's birthday that, along with drinking and marches, a game of "the old style of base ball" was played.[11] How or between whom it was played was not described.

Because there were no leagues in existence in this early period, there was little need for uniformity or widely accepted rules of play. As a result, there was considerable variation in how games were organized across the province. As in rounders, batters tried to circle four bases after hitting the ball. At least some of the games, however, were played with five bases, the extra base being the batter's position between home plate and first base. Often, round bats instead of flattened cricket bats were used. In some games, there was no foul territory, and any ball hit by the batter was in play. Many contests followed the cricket practice of having all players on one team bat before the other side had a chance to hit. It seems clear that the bat-and-bases games played in the first half of the 19th century were strongly local versions of whatever games had been handed down to the players by the previous generation.

Certainly, baseball shared much of cricket's DNA. As late as 1856, a game between the London Tecumsehs and a neighbouring Ontario team demonstrated the prevailing influence of cricket. The final score was 34 to 33, and as the *New York Clipper* reported, "London was declared winner on the second inning without losing a man."[12] The report also reveals the growing interest in inter-town competition, which would change the very purpose of the sport for many.

Although the new game retained much of the scaffolding of cricket, it was nevertheless influenced by American innovations. In 1858, for example, baseball clubs in the New York area, including the New York Knickerbockers, came together to form the National Association of Base Ball Players (NABBP). It was the first organization to govern the sport and to establish a championship. They determined the distance between bases at 90', limited teams to nine players, and set the length of game at nine innings.

Baseball played by Northern soldiers during the Civil War introduced the new rules to players from different regions and helped to nationalize these new rules. Club membership in the NABBP grew rapidly after the war and reached 400 by 1867. By then, the New York City brand of baseball had achieved national dominance, in part because players and spectators preferred its rules. As the rules had been established in the business, transportation, and media capital of the United States, the NABBP's version of the game enjoyed wide appeal, including to those on the northern side of baseball's borderland.

The provenance of the new sport, however, has been contested on both sides of said borderland. In fact, it has been a critical issue for many American nationalists for decades.[13] In 1903, Henry Chadwick, a sportswriter originally from England who had written about and popularized baseball for decades, speculated in an article that baseball was derived from the British game of rounders that he had played in his youth.

It was not a new argument on his part, but many Americans baseball fans were outraged by the idea that baseball was not an "American" game. Few cared to countenance America's sporting debt to Britain. Indeed, Albert Spalding, a former player and a sporting goods magnate, established a commission of sports executives in 1905 that ultimately (and incorrectly) ruled that Abner Doubleday had invented America's national pastime. The evidence that the commission had found most compelling was a claim received in April 1905. An aging Colorado mining engineer, Abner Graves, said he had been present some 65 years earlier when Abner Doubleday, a student at Cooperstown, had transformed and modernized the old game of town-ball and renamed it baseball. The commission and Spalding were eager to believe that baseball had been invented in 1839 in the United States by an American.

Graves was not, coincidentally, the only elderly Denver resident to write a letter identifying what they believed to be the origin of baseball. In 1886, Dr. Adam Ford wrote a letter to *Sporting Life* in which he recounted having watched a game of baseball played 48 years earlier in the small Ontario town of Beachville on Militia Muster Day, June 4, 1838.[14] Given the fact that he was only seven at the time, it is remarkable that Ford was able to provide a remarkably precise account of the details of the game and its players.

In 1988, Canada issued a postal stamp commemorating the 150th anniversary of baseball in Canada, even though the early bat-and-ball game played at Beachville did not closely resemble modern baseball. The game Ford described had five bases, with the first base only six yards from where the batter stood. The number of players, he had observed, had to be equal, although the team size could range from 7 to 12 players. The exact rules and length of time for any game were often negotiated just before play began.

The accounts of both men have since delighted some sports fans in their respective countries.[15] The interesting aspect of the letters is less their historical accuracy than it is the question of "ownership." For Canadians, the question of the ownership of baseball was less critical. Still part of the British Empire, Canadians tacitly accepted that many, if not most, of their sporting traditions were inherited from Britain.[16] For Americans, however, the idea that "theirs" was a British game was distasteful. At the same time, American insistence that baseball was their sport made some 19th-century Canadians, fearful of encroaching Americana, less likely to support the game.

Nevertheless, by the early 1860s, southwestern Ontario had become the centre of baseball activity in Canada, with organized teams in Hamilton, Burlington, Flamborough, London, St. Thomas, Guelph, Ingersoll, and Woodstock. The increased competition between the Ontario teams had been facilitated, as with cricket, by the railway boom. By 1854, the Great Western Railway had finished laying tracks from Niagara Falls to Windsor via Hamilton. The line ran through the area of both baseball's and cricket's greatest Canadian hub.

Yet, unlike cricket, which had an exclusive membership, intercity baseball rivalries developed an ad hoc space, shared by a relatively large and diverse — at least, compared with cricket — group of people. Sports historian William Humber argues that emerging rivalries, often among towns just decades old, "were the glue that created a regional and in some cases a national sense of unity." By the 1860s, further railway developments increased baseball's reach. From Niagara Falls and Windsor, Canadian baseball enthusiasts could now access the baseball-loving centres of Buffalo and Detroit. Across this culturally porous borderland, numerous American baseball clubs were ready to play.

Exhibition games between teams in Ontario and America were ubiquitous. As a result, baseball culture in Canada was entirely analogous to baseball culture in the United States. This was objectionable to those attempting to preserve the Englishness of Ontario's and Canada's sporting culture. To be sure, this was, of course, exactly what the organizers of Canadian cricket were trying to do.

The participants competing in the two sports were usually quite different from one another. If cricket counted doctors, lawyers, and members of the gentry (such as it was in 19th-century Canada) among its ranks, baseball was played by middle-class sportsmen, respectable artisans, clerks, and shopkeepers and, later, general labourers and members across the working classes.

At first, this fraternal club of men played after work for the pure enjoyment of the game and to enact the manliness that some felt had been compromised with urbanization. In time, however, a variety of influences changed the very nature of baseball in Canada. A sense of community pride, for instance, demanded that one town beat another. There was also the rise of the American practice of professionalism; acquiring the best players — regardless of where they were born — cost money. All these factors contributed to the unremitting desire for communities and owners to win at all costs. Indeed, by the 1880s, organized baseball had ceased being about personal pleasure and the enacting of manliness and had become a full-blown entertainment industry run by owners and managers who understood that success was measured by gate receipts.

With an emphasis on the gate, the game attracted an entirely different clientele from the one that attended cricket matches. Baseball appealed to men who favoured drinking, gambling, and robust male fellowship in those few hours away from the drudgery of 19th-century labour they were afforded each week. From its very beginnings, then, beer and baseball were inextricably linked. Canadian taverns welcomed the "big game," as it was very good for business. So, too, did the bookies — there was unrepentant gambling in most sports at this time in Canada and baseball was not immune. The working-class male (and it was mostly male) showed little interest in the slower-moving game of cricket, and less still in its haughty celebration of queen and empire. Instead, with a very modest disposable income and precious little time to enjoy it, these men chose to support baseball as a refuge from the constraints of the new industrial society.

By the 1870s, the local papers carried increasingly detailed accounts of baseball games. Many of these reports reflected local rivalries between competing factories or trades. In Ingersoll, workers at Noxon's Agricultural Works challenged players from Brown's Carriage Works, Hault's and Ellis's furniture companies, and other local factory baseball teams. In Woodstock, players from Scharff's Carriage Shops, Richards Soap Factory, Thompson's Mills, and other businesses played baseball on Saturday afternoons.[17] In the 1870s, the Guelph finishers were playing the moulders at the Cossit's Agricultural Works.[18] At Bell's Organ Factory, it was the tuners challenging the finishers, while numerous matches took place between the city's printers and railwaymen. The growth of play among the industrial workers in these developing urban centres strengthened support for baseball culture at the intercity level.

While cricket had its viceregal patronage and Oxford-educated champions, baseball got support from other men of other means. George Sleeman, for instance, was a prominent entrepreneur from Guelph. An ardent sportsman and an incessant booster (and eventual mayor for four terms) of his hometown, Guelph, Sleeman had worked with his father at the Silver Creek

Brewery, of which he eventually took ownership in 1868. He was both a baseball fan and player. In the early 1860s, Sleeman formed an amateur factory team at the Silver Creek Brewery and covered the cost of the team's equipment and travelling expenses. He even pitched for some of the team's games. Competitive by nature, when he found "his own employees inadequate, he provided jobs in the brewery for some of the better local amateurs."[19] It would be much the same after Sleeman became president and manager of the Guelph Maple Leaf Baseball Club in 1874. It didn't matter if the players on the team were from Guelph; it mattered only that the team from Guelph won.

When Sleeman took over the Maple Leafs, he began a program of importing professional American ballplayers, the first being George Keerl and Hank Myers. The brewer was determined to raise the Maple Leafs's profile and was constantly on the lookout for opportunities to do so. In July 1874, for example, Sleeman entered his team into an amateur tournament in Watertown, New York. Although advertised as an amateur affair, the tournament attracted semi-professional clubs on both sides of baseball's borderland. The admission of these teams reflected the different interpretations of what an amateur team was. At a cost of $1,250, Guelph and six other clubs entered the tournament's first-class division.[20]

Guelph, helped by a seven-run third inning, won its first game handily, defeating the Oneida team of New York — which, incredibly, was sponsored by the local chapter of the newly formed Ku Klux Klan — 13–4. Guelph's second game was a closer contest, but the Maple Leafs again prevailed, defeating the Brooklyn Nassaus 13–8. This set up a showdown with the favoured Philadelphia Eastons for the championship. With Canadian-born William Smith pitching a shutout into the fifth inning, Guelph gave him the support of an explosive 11 runs. A late push by the Eastons was too little, too late, and the Maple Leafs were crowned tournament champions — final score 13–10.

The Guelph team received national recognition. The Maple Leaf Baseball Club was, as *Harper's Weekly* reported, "famous as having for three years passed [*sic*] held the proud distinction of the Champions of Canada." In an article in the September 12 edition of *Harper's Weekly*, the magazine stated that in defeating "some of the best amateur clubs in the United States," the Maple Leafs could proudly claim "the title of the champion amateur club of the world."[21] Apart from skimming over the flagrant use of professional players in the Maple Leafs's roster, the essence of the *Harper's Weekly* report was sincere enough: Guelph had outshone the Americans.

Other Canadian teams took notice. In eastern Ontario, for instance, "virtually all members of the Kingston club," as historian Brian Martin assures, "were lured from south of the border," while Toronto recruited an American pitcher in addition to amalgamating local teams to become more competitive.[22] For a variety of reasons, not least of which would be the reality of financial constraints for Canada's small-town teams, the Canadians would soon be unable to keep up with Americans. In the end, this period introduced and, in many minds, legitimized the notion of a professional baseball player. The possibilities of the mercenary player — plying his trade to the highest bidder — would not be limited to the model that saw Americans coming to Canada to fill spaces on its various teams but would extend to include a reverse scenario. Such a scenario awaited one talented young ballplayer, and future Canadian Baseball Hall of Famer, who grew up in baseball-daft Woodstock, Ontario.

TIP AND THE BIG LEAGUES

The first team to dominate Canadian baseball was from one of the country's smallest towns. In 1860, Jim Shuttleworth moved to Woodstock, a town of fewer than 4,000 souls. Over the next two years, Shuttleworth helped create the first powerhouse baseball team in the country, the Woodstock Young Canadians.[23]

The Woodstock club, with a roster drawn primarily from the trades in the immediate area, quickly became a skilled team. Their early success encouraged them to seek competition farther from home. In order to complete this mission, the team adopted the governing rules of the New York style of ball. The *New York Clipper* reported that the Young Canadians had played "nine picked from the town of Woodstock" in June 1861 in what was "the first match that has been played there on the New York System."[24] Changing

The Metropolitan Baseball Nine 1882. O'Neill is the third player on the left, top row.

the style of play to line up with the New York rules ended any evolution of an indigenous, Canadian-specific game. Thus, Canadian baseball would soon become the hinterland for top-level American baseball until the Montreal Expos and Toronto Blue Jays emerged in the latter part of the 20th century.

Meanwhile, back in Ontario, the Woodstock nine defeated Hamilton twice in 1861 and 1863. Perhaps more impressively, they crushed the Brother Jonathans team from Detroit 29–6 in 1863. It was a heady time for the small town whose team was receiving international recognition.

As the frequency and quality of interurban competition increased, the Young Canadians developed a plan to showcase their abilities and to test their skills against a wider pool of Canadian teams. In August 1864, C.L. Wood, a New York expatriate and owner of the Royal Hotel in Woodstock, along with local organizers "invited other clubs to a meeting aimed at promoting interurban competition."[25] Perhaps unsurprisingly, all of the clubs that attended were linked to each other by the Great Western and

Grand Trunk railway lines. At the meeting, the clubs created the Canadian Association of Base Ball Players (CABBP), modelled after the NABBP.

Such was the enthusiasm for baseball in Woodstock that the town, helped by the club members, raised the money to create a "Silver Ball" trophy to be awarded to the best CABBP team. It effectively became the Canadian championship. Donations were collected, American silver dollars melted down, and a life-sized silver baseball created as the trophy for the championship. All member teams could challenge the reigning champions, who had 10 days to set up a match date — ideally on a holiday to maximize the spectators. If a team held the Silver Ball for three consecutive years, it could keep the trophy. All games were played under the rules established by the NABBP. The Silver Ball would remain in Woodstock for most of the 1860s. Playing at home in defence of the trophy, the Young Canadians would defeat Hamilton, Ingersoll, Newcastle, Dundas, Guelph, and London.

James Edward "Tip" O'Neill was born in Springfield, Ontario, in 1860, but while still a young boy, he moved with his family to the home of the Silver Ball. There he witnessed first-hand the rise of Canada's original baseball super-club. O'Neill's father, James, kept a hotel in Woodstock and was a great champion of baseball. Father was able to send son to the De La Salle Institute, a Catholic preparatory school in Toronto. Here, baseball — not cricket — was king.

During his time there, Tip showed tremendous aptitude as a pitcher. Although the world would come to know O'Neill as a fielder with the greatest batting average ever recorded in major league baseball, young Tip aspired to become a pitcher. Indeed, this was how he started his career. Back home in Woodstock, the now 18-year-old O'Neill led that town's Actives — a team that very much carried on the tradition set by the more famous Young Canadians of the previous decade — to the amateur championship of Canada in 1878. O'Neill pitched two no-hitters in the Actives's championship series.[26]

With such success, O'Neill may have been forgiven for believing that he would remain a pitcher in the major leagues. Tip did indeed debut as a pitcher with the New York Metropolitans of the League Alliance in 1882 and remained in that position with the National League's New York Gothams, with whom he played in 1883. The following season, O'Neill signed with Charlie Comiskey's St. Louis Browns of the American Association. Tip posted an impressive 2.68 earned run average (ERA) on the strength of an 11–4 record (win–loss) and actually led the National League in winning percentage. Yet, an issue with his pitching arm prompted a shift in positions. It was a fortuitous shift. For 64 games in 1884 and the rest of his career, O'Neill would be an outfielder. This move allowed O'Neill to transition into one of the greatest batters of the 19th century.

Tip had success in Missouri. O'Neill's St. Louis Browns comprised a mix of skill and grit. Baseball, like other organized sports of this era, was a much bloodier sport than it has become in more recent times. Base running could be particularly violent. Comiskey expected his players to, as the *St. Louis Post-Dispatch* explained, "run into fielders when they can make a point by it."[27] Indeed, O'Neill missed nearly half a season with a leg injury after Comiskey's imperative of merciless base running in a game in 1885.

The mood was far merrier in October of 1886 when the Browns dominated the baseball world by beating the Chicago White Stockings in the American Association's World Series. Tip was central to the Browns's victory. In the final series against the Chicago team, O'Neill led all batters in, among other categories, batting average, extra-base hits, triples, and home runs.

When the "Woodstock Wonder" returned home to Canada in the off-season, he was feted by family and friends. On its cover page, the *Woodstock Sentinel-Review* published its own best and prophetic wishes to the hometown hero: "more power to you 'Tip,' and may you go on and do better, if possible, next season!"[28] Improbably, he would.

The Browns struggled out of the gate at the beginning of the 1887 season, but the team's fortunes soon turned around. O'Neill, who started strong, was suffering something of a mid-summer slump in late July. This fact was not lost on some members of baseball's elite. As reported in the *St.*

Louis Post-Dispatch, Pete Browning, a.k.a. "the Louisville Slugger," declared that O'Neill "must stand in with the official scorers ... he hasn't made a hit in nine games and I've been hittin' the ball on the nose and yet he leads the Association." Despite Browning's cant, O'Neill was indeed leading the league in various categories, including batting average. Moreover, in the very same article that featured Browning's misgivings, O'Neill was named to the "best nine" (all-star team) in the Association as left fielder.[29] O'Neill would, that very day, emerge spectacularly from his mild slump.

From July 30 through August 2, 1887, the Browns took two of three games in a series against the Athletics in Philadelphia. In the final game of that series, they gave their opponents a 14–6 thrashing. This August 2 game took place the same day Teddy Ogden would make Canadian cricket history at Lord's in London. O'Neill capped off his brilliant return to form by going three for five.[30] Over the three-game series against Philadelphia, O'Neill scored or drove in 10 of the Browns's 21 runs.[31] The Canadian never looked back and kept up a torrid pace right through to the end of the season.

The Browns came very close to winning the championship again in 1887, but in the end, lost 4–3 in the best-of-seven world championship series against the Detroit Wolverines. It was, of course, a disappointment for the team, but O'Neill's individual achievements in 1887 were — despite the asterisk so many sports historians are wont to attach to his name — remarkable. Tip O'Neill became only the second player ever to achieve a Triple Crown (best average, most home runs, and most runs batted in); hit for the cycle (single, double, triple, and home run) twice in the same season (only one of five players ever to do so as of 2022); and hit what remains the highest single-season batting average of all time recorded in major league history.[32] Adjusted to .435 as it has been by baseball's intelligentsia, O'Neill's average slips down one spot to second highest all time, behind only the Boston Beaneaters's Hugh Duffy's .440 of the 1894 season.[33]

After his stunning output of 1887, O'Neill was able to remain a force in the majors for another couple of years. In 1888, both the National League and the American Association no longer counted a base on balls as a hit. As a result, batting averages across the two major leagues dropped significantly. O'Neill was, nevertheless, able to manage a league-leading .355 average,

Tip O'Neill in his pose as a pitcher.

good enough for his second straight batting title. It was much the same in 1889, when O'Neill finished second in batting, with a .335 average. Tip's was, on balance, a reasonable major league career punctuated by one matchless, glorious summer.

TEDDY AT LORD'S

When an English cricket team toured Canada in 1885, the results were much the same as in previous contests — with one important exception. The first-class cricketer Charles Edward Horner was one of the English XI touring

Canada. He remarked that the hosts showed his team "nothing remarkable in the way of cricket," but a young medical doctor from the Canadian team caught Horner's expert eye.[34] In his memoir of the match, Horner affords a gentlemanly nod of praise to Teddy Ogden, whom the Englishman believed had "bowled well," taking five wickets for only 59 runs. While his was hardly the most florid and unrestrained commendation, Horner saw what several North American cricket enthusiasts had already come to know: the Canadians finally had a top-notch cricketer within its ranks.

Teddy was born in Oakville in 1862 and attended UCC, where he played in that school's XI for four years, from 1876 until 1880. Ogden captained the team for three of the four years he was at UCC. Even at this young age, Teddy was beginning to garner recognition as a cricketer of uncommon ability, bowling right-handed, medium-pace, and batting left. As such, the 17-year-old schoolboy was good enough to represent his country against a touring English side led by the famous cricketer Richard Daft in 1879. In 1881, Ogden made his debut in a match against the United States with laudable results, finishing with the second-best batting average in the contest.

By that point, Teddy's father had relocated the family to Chicago, and the budding cricket star began dividing his time between Canada and the United States. The Ogdens were of Pennsylvania Loyalist stock. Teddy's great-grandfather, Joseph Ogden, had refused to take up arms against the king and so fled America after the Revolutionary War, settling near Toronto. Dr. Edward Joseph Ogden, Teddy's dad, received his medical degree in Toronto and New York. The doctor subsequently took a position as chair of surgery at Toronto's Victoria College and was later gazetted as a military surgeon during the Civil War. When the doctor moved his family to Chicago in 1876, he became the chief surgeon to the Chicago and Atlantic Railway Company and local surgeon for the Wabash Railroad Company. Importantly, at least in terms of our story, the Ogdens were more than just transplanted Canadians with a love of cricket when they arrived in Chicago: they effectively established the game in the Windy City.

It was a family affair. The senior doctor served as the first president of the Chicago Cricket Club (CCC), which began operation on May 24, 1876.[35] One of Dr. Ogden's sons, Mahlon D. Ogden, was the club's director, while his other son, Teddy, would soon be the club's captain and its most prolific "all-rounder."[36] A decade after it began operations, the CCC boasted more than 300 members and owned a park replete with clubhouse and grounds of over seven acres, all purchased at a cost of approximately $50,000.

Cricket in Chicago rose in popularity in the years after the Ogdens' move to Illinois. Other movers and shakers with means and money also took an interest in the game, including the meat packer millionaire Philip Armour, the department store millionaire Marshall Fields, and George Mortimer Pullman, the owner of the "Pullman Railcar." As a result, the Spalding Trophy was established and awarded to the champion cricket club in the Chicago area.

In 1882, Teddy moved to be with the rest of his family in Chicago and continued his pursuit of a medical degree at that city's Rush Medical College. There, the young Ogden represented the CCC and was also chosen to be one of the Western XI, which took on teams in Syracuse, New York, Pittsburgh, and cricket-crazy Philadelphia. Although he had permanently set down his roots in Illinois, Ogden continued to represent his home country in matches against the United States in 1882 and 1883.

For Canada's match at the Germantown Cricket Club in Philadelphia in 1884, Teddy was chosen captain. The young doctor rose to the position entrusted to him, bowling soundly and batting 79 runs over the two innings.[37] On the strength of Teddy's output, Canada had won its first game against the Americans since 1857. Canada, with Ogden at the helm, repeated the feat in 1885, back home.

Teddy was now regarded as a formidable cricketer in the sports world. In advance of the 1887 tour of the British Isles, *Cricket: A Weekly Record of the Game*, described Ogden:

> He has an easy delivery, bowls from very fast to very slow with a great deal of spin, and obtains an astonishing amount of break back on his slow balls. The *American Cricketer* once said editorially that Odgen was "as good a left-hander at the bat as we know." As a captain he has no superior in Canada.[38]

The ostensibly peerless Ogden and his teammates were by then ready to embark on Canada's most ambitious cricketing endeavour to date: a late-summer tour of 18 matches in the British Isles, including several against ace county cricket sides. There was a very real danger that Canada's team would suffer yet another set of embarrassing drubbings at the hands of various expert XIs. Teddy, however, had other ideas.

Principally organized by George Goldwin Smith Lindsey, the distinguished lawyer and secretary of the Toronto Cricket Club, the tour of Ireland, Scotland, and England was set for July and August 1887. A warm-up game in New York City was arranged for the Canadians before the team set sail across the Atlantic. Lindsey — whose mother, Janet, was the eldest daughter of the Upper Canadian rebel William Lyon Mackenzie King — co-wrote a useful memoir of the 1887 tour with fellow cricketing-lawyer Dyce W. Saunders in the tradition of those earlier English cricket travelogues. The two men knew well the importance of this particular tour, which they regarded as "an event of such moment in the history of the game in Canada, as to be deserving of some permanent record." Lindsey and Saunders's work, *Cricket Across the Sea, or, The Wanderings and Matches of the Gentlemen of Canada, 1887*, breaks down each of the matches and offers much in the way of anecdotal information about the various Canadian players.

Here, one finds a fundamental difference between those who were playing baseball versus those who chose cricket. The Canadians, with representation from the legal and medical professions, unanimously accepted the burden of paying their fair share — about half of the team's expenses — to embark on the British tour in the first place. It was, after all, a fundamental tenet of the English amateur code. The rest was raised through subscriptions from high-profile supporters, which included, as Lindsey and Saunders confirm:

> His Excellency the Governor-General, Sir Alexander Campbell, the Lieut.-Governor of Ontario, Hon. Matthew Richie, the Lieut.-Governor of Nova Scotia, Hon. L.F.R. Masson, the Lieut.-Governor of Quebec, and a number

> of the prominent citizens of Canada, but particularly of Toronto — among whom may be especially mentioned Mr. George Gooderham and Hon. John Macdonald.[39]

The remainder was achieved through gate receipts from the games themselves. It is unlikely that Ogden's contemporaries in baseball would countenance such a proposition or, indeed, have the necessary means or "subscribers" to make such a tour happen.

Such as it was, the Canadian team included an assemblage of UCC "Old Boys," Trinity College graduates, and two players — W.A. Henry and G.W. Jones — who attended the private Merchiston Castle School in Edinburgh, Scotland.[40] In this way, Canada was very much represented by the nation's exclusive set. The 1887 Canadian team was led by, as Canadian cricket historians Hall and McCulloch would declare nearly a decade later, "the ripe generalship and grand playing" of its captain, Dr. Edward Russell Ogden.

Canadian Gentlemen in England, 1887.

The tour attracted the attention of the cricket world. *Cricket: A Weekly Record of the Game* ran several features on the Canadians, beginning months before the first match was played. When the tour finally kicked off, the magazine kept its readers up to date with the tourists' progress: "Dr. Ogden and his men are to commence their first fixture against the Gentlemen of Ireland to-morrow, so that they will have not had much time to get their land legs."[41]

Back in Canada, readers could keep up to date with the matches in the *Globe*, which regularly published reports (likely written by Lindsey and Saunders). While there was something of a play-by-play to these missives — as was the style of the sports pages of the day — the reports added wonderful colour to the cricketers' trip to the Old Country. Among those present at the team's dinner in Surrey, for example, "were Hon. Mr. Onslow and the celebrities Dr. Jones and 'Billy Burrup.' Also Dr. Scott, the captain of last year's Australian team. This is perhaps, next to Ireland, the most enjoyable dinner we have had."[42]

Ogden — who had journeyed ahead of the rest of the XI with his wife and met up with the team when they arrived in Dublin — was named captain and, according to Dyce Saunders, "exercised his authority with excellent judgment, and throughout the tour enjoyed the entire confidence of his men."[43]

Although the Canadian XI beat the All New York and Ground team by five wickets before sailing to Ireland, the team's "confidence" seemed shaky during that first week of the tour. In their first match, the Canadians lost to Ireland by an innings and 102 runs. And although they bounced back in the rematch against the same foe, winning by five wickets, Ogden and company lost the next two matches against Scotland and Northumberland. A draw against Durham changed the mood somewhat, and the tourists followed it up with a victory over the Gentlemen of Derbyshire. There was, however, another setback with a loss to the Gentlemen of Sussex. It seemed as though Canada's historical performance in international cricket was set to repeat. Then, with the turning of a new month, a change to the Canadian cricketers commenced a string of impressive matches against some of the best cricketers in England.[44]

Next up for the tourists was the most storied club in cricket history: the MCC, which had embarrassed the Canadian XXII organized by Thomas Patteson, 15 years earlier. This new and much improved XI now found themselves at Lord's, home to MCC and hearth to English sportsmen everywhere. It was here, against that most famous team, that the colonials gallingly (for the English) grabbed glory for themselves in a match that began on August 1, 1887.

Lindsey and Saunders set the scene:

> When we rose on bank holiday morning in August, and met at breakfast, it was evident that any feeling of funk which might have existed among us at an earlier stage of our tour had quite disappeared, for on reading in the morning papers the name of the powerful team ... we were not at all dismayed. Let us hasten to explain, it was not because we were confident of making even a respectable showing against them, but because we felt that we would do our best, and from experience gained and continued practice, we were now in a position to put our best foot foremost.[45]

The venue did not disappoint the author-cricketers:

> It is, perhaps, needless to say that the pavilion and dining hall far surpass anything of the kind in England.... The scoring apparatus is a most ingenious piece of mechanism, and enables a spectator at a glance to learn, after any run has been made, not only the total number of runs, the wickets down, and the last man's score, but also the individual scores of the two batsmen, which are increased run by run till a wicket falls. The field looked level as a billiard table, and here, under as bright a sun as ever shone on old England, we were to play the most important match of our tour.[46]

And Canadian cricket, as it happened, would never shine brighter.

On August 2, the second day of the match, Teddy Ogden pulled off the single greatest achievement any Canadian had had in the sport of cricket to that point, and one that still rates among the best performances in Canadian cricket history. England had managed 306 runs to Canada's 254 during the first innings on the previous day. In the second frame, however, the hosts were stymied by the Canadian bowlers and held to only 191 runs. Certainly, Allan, Annand, and Wallace Jones batted well for the Canadians and kept them in striking distance of MCC, but it was Teddy's remarkable nine wickets for only 83 runs given up that separated him from his other countrymen. During their second innings, the Canadian batters tallied 139 for six wickets before the match was declared a draw. It was a stunning result.

Dyce W. Saunders later described the historical moment: "Canada bearded the British Lion ... in his den, at Lord's."[47] In a much more soft-pedalled review, *Cricket: A Weekly Record of the Game* gave Canadian cricket its due:

> The Gentlemen of Canada showed some good all-round cricket on their first appearance in London, playing a drawn game against a strong batting side of MCC at Lord's on Monday and Tuesday. Dr. Ogden, in the second innings of MCC, took 9 of the 10 wickets at a cost of 83 runs.[48]

The Canadians hoped in vain that dusk would hold off long enough for them to have a shot at the runs they needed for victory. Alas, a draw — spectacular as it was against the fabled men of Lord's — would have to do.

The tourists followed up their moment in the London sun with three well-earned draws against the Gentlemen of United Services, the Gentlemen of Surrey, and the Gentlemen of Hampshire.[49] Ten days after their success at Lord's, the Canadians found themselves in Gloucester, facing the most famous British cricketer of them all: W.G. Grace. This instantly recognizable, hulking figure cut a mighty swath. He was — and, for some, remains — "the Father of Cricket." His longevity in the game (he played his final first-class match in 1908 at the age of 59) and his utter domination of the sport gives credence to the claims of so many cricket historians, old and new, that Grace was one of the greatest ever to have played.

W.G. had last seen a Canadian side when he was in Canada in 1872. Back then, towering at the height of his career, he put on a clinic wherever he went. With little in the way of competition, Grace considered his tour of Canada and America as one "prolonged and happy picnic."[50] Some of the Canadians of 1887 had witnessed Grace's "picnic" and knew well what they'd be facing in Gloucester. Once again, Lindsey and Saunders set the stage: "[Grace] shook hands with us cordially, flipped up the coin which came down as Ogden said it would, and went off to make ready for the fray. There is perhaps no keener Gentleman cricketer in England than the man who stands out in bold relief as the ablest of them all."[51]

Able as he was, Grace was a complex man. He personified what has been called "shamateurism," appearing as a full-fledged amateur gentleman yet often making more money than the professionals of his day. He also had a short fuse, drank too much (sometimes before the game), and could be dangerously erratic with his bowling. Members of the 1872 Montreal Cricket Club were stopping some of Grace's bowling with their heads and stomachs.[52] A decade and a half later, the legendary Englishman was deeply impressed by this latest incarnation of Canadian cricket, as Lindsey and Saunders recounted:

> Dr. Grace was good enough to say that he was surprised at the immense improvement in our form on that which he had seen when visiting Canada in 1872, and he said he saw no reason why the success of cricket should not be as well assured from this out in Canada, as it had for some time been in the far-off sister Colony, Australia.[53]

Once again, the Canadian tourists had punched above their weight; the county team, with seven wickets remaining, needed 81 runs to beat the Canadians when the match was declared a draw.

After their match against Grace in Gloucester, the tourists finished strong: wins against the Gentlemen of Warwickshire and Mr. C.I. Thornton's XI; draws against the Gentlemen of Staffordshire, the Gentlemen of Leicestershire, and the Gentlemen of Cheshire; and only one loss against the Gentlemen of

Liverpool & District rounded out the tour.[54] All told, the Canadians played 19 matches (including the one against New York) and managed a record of five wins, five losses, and nine draws. It was quite respectable when one considers that the English counties made up the greater part of their opposition. In actuality, Ogden and company were playing some of the best cricketers in the world at that time. The *New York Times* observed: "The Canadian cricketers have at last concluded the series arranged for them in the British Isles and need not be ashamed of their record."[55] *Cricket: A Weekly Record of the Game* said of the Canadians' performance throughout the tour:

> Although in their earlier fixtures success was like X, an unknown quantity, the Gentlemen of Canada — whose appearance on English grounds … have, on the whole, no reason to be dissatisfied with their visit to the Old Country. Whether socially or as cricketers, the Canadian team have borne themselves in a way to reflect credit on the sport of the Dominion.[56]

It was, after all, the wish of the organizers that the tour would serve as something of a launch pad for the game in the Dominion. As Lindsey and Saunders hopefully opined:

> We believe that the good [the tour] has done is not interred with its bones, but will, phoenix like, rise from the ashes of the past and inaugurate a new era in Canadian Cricket. That the tour has stimulated the feeling in this country in favour of the game, we have been assured … while the coming in contact with the finished players of the game at its own home, must of itself have had a general educating effect.[57]

While the tourists had done themselves proud against the "finished players" of English county cricket, Lindsey and Saunders may have oversold the prospect of a "new era in Canadian cricket." Sustained success in international cricket was not something on which Canada would be able to rely.

Dr. Teddy Ogden, "undoubtedly the finest all-round player in Canada."

For his part, though, Teddy Ogden had had a sensational tour. Apart from his record-setting bowling exhibition, Teddy finished second among the Canadians in runs scored (701), behind only W.A. Henry (879), and third in batting average (23.37/innings), trailing only Henry (25.85) and Dyce Saunders (23.58). Ogden had several good outings in the crease, hitting 98 against Durham and 133 against Hampshire. In terms of bowling, however, it wasn't even close: after 817.3 overs (in this era, four bowls per over), Ogden claimed 91 wickets (32 more than the next Canadian, Gillespie, with 59), and posted a low runs average of only 16.7.[58] Teddy's nine wickets for 83 runs against the MCC at Lord's and his nearly-as-impressive eight for 27 against Warwickshire a fortnight later remain — more than 135 years later — fourth and fifth, respectively, on the list of the best Canadian bowling performances ever, exclusive of those records made during the relatively recent development of One Day Internationals (Canada's first was in 1979) and Twenty20 Internationals (Canada played its first in 2008), which differ from the test match format in which Ogden played.

At the end of the tour, the Canadian captain and his new wife sailed off to Rome to enjoy the rest of their "wedding tour" before returning home to Chicago, where Teddy's medical practice and yet more domestic cricket beckoned.

TIP AND TEDDY IN CHICAGO, 1890

Tip O'Neill left the St. Louis Browns after the 1889 season and would play three more seasons on three different teams in three different major leagues. Before a return to St. Louis in 1891 and his final season with the Cincinnati Reds in 1892, O'Neill spent one year with the Chicago Pirates in the newly formed Players' League. Here, Tip experienced something of a dip in his prolific output. Although he was still able to manage a respectable .302 (good for 18th overall), the sun was slowly beginning to set on the "Woodstock Wonder's" career.

As it happened, Teddy Ogden was also in Chicago, practising medicine and playing cricket for the family's Chicago Cricket Club. The two men's sporting exploits were often reported on the very same page in the sports sections of the local newspapers.[59] Although Ogden was enjoying a tremendous season with the best league batting average and was considered the best "all-rounder" in the city, O'Neill stumbled. Despite an outstanding five-year period in which O'Neill led the majors in several categories, Tip was starkly criticized in the local newspapers.[60] One uncharitable summary of a Chicago Pirates game in the *Daily Inter Ocean* surmised: "O'Neill seemed so tired in left field that one felt like going out and chasing the ball for him."[61] Tip would soon be returning home to Canada for good.

While O'Neill declined, Ogden remained strong. The CCC remained as good a side as any in America. This was largely down to its star player, Teddy Ogden. The CCC, nevertheless, struggled against its main rivals, the Pullman Cricket Club (PCC). In the span of 10 years, the Pullman side had taken seven of eight Spalding championships. In 1891, however, the CCC was finally able to get the better of the PCC. And Teddy Ogden led the league in batting average throughout the 15-game season that year. Even after 1891, and unlike his baseball counterpart's sharp decline, Ogden remained a force in his chosen sport for a good decade after his remarkable performance in 1887. As late as 1897, Ogden was still leading the Chicago circuit in averages.

Speaking of the Canadians tour of 1887, *Wisden*, the world's pre-eminent cricket magazine and almanac, revered the doctor's fine play and assured readers that Teddy Ogden "was clearly the best all-round player in the [Canadian] side."[62] Before his remarkable innings of 1887, *Cricket: A Weekly Record of the Game* hailed Ogden as "the best all-round cricketer Canada ever produced."[63] It was much the same in Spalding's *Official Cricket Guide for 1914*, which considered Ogden to be "undoubtedly the finest all-round player in Canada, and must be classed with J.B. King, G.S. Patterson, and J.A. Lester, the best which the Western continent has ever produced."[64]

After a short battle with pneumonia and heart disease, Canada's greatest cricketer of the 19th century died in Chicago on May 15, 1913.

Following his career, Tip O'Neill moved to Montreal where he was, in various capacities, involved in that city's baseball scene for decades. On New Year's Eve 1915, Canada's first baseball superstar died unexpectedly of heart failure in a Montreal drug store.

Tip and Teddy were born only 140 kilometres away from one another, less than two years apart, and died only two years apart, in their early 50s. In 1887, and for a few summers afterward, these Canadians were the best in their respective sports. Today, Tip's name is much less *forgotten* than Ogden's; each year since 1984, the Canadian Baseball Hall of Fame presents the Tip O'Neill Award to the Canadian player "judged to have excelled in individual achievement and team contribution while adhering to the highest ideals of the game of baseball."

CRICKET FAILED; BASEBALL WON

The protectionist approach to sport demonstrated by powerful men in the upper echelon of Canadian society did little to raise cricket's profile. The English game was regarded as the preserve of the country's elite. It did not invite cross-class participation. Baseball did. Several other issues spoiled the progress of cricket in Canada.

Of course, the harsh and long Canadian winters affected most outdoor sports, and cricket was no exception. There was also the fact that the new country was lacking in terms of the number of wealthy men who had the requisite amount of leisure time to actually complete a three- or sometimes five-day test match. As well, important schools, including UCC, gradually began to decrease their cricket activities within their curricula. As a result, Canada, unlike other British outposts such as Australia, the West Indies, and India, fared very poorly — with a few important exceptions, including Ogden and company's achievements in 1887 — on cricket's world stage. Many of the "new" Canadians in this era had little interest in a sport so closely identified with an elite British segment of the population. Alas, there would be no "Ashes" tournament for the Canadian national team.[65] Importantly, the relatively quick pace that baseball offered was more attractive to most working-class Canadians than was the meandering saunter of cricket. Clearly, baseball had won. And it would take nearly a century after Teddy's day at Lord's before new Canadians — most of whom were either born *in* or were descendants *of* other cricketing nations — would take to the international pitches with renewed purpose. By then, Tip had been inducted into the CSHF and had a national award named in his honour. Teddy remained out in the cold. Indeed, even when the inaugural inductees were elected to the Cricket Canada Hall of Fame in 2019, Ogden's name was absent. As of 2023, there are 13 members representing baseball in the CSHF. There is one cricketer: Frederick James Heather. He was an umpire.

It can be said with some degree of certainty that few, if any, 19th-century Canadian cricketers harboured the illusion that someday they would make a career out of their game. Teddy Ogden likely never contemplated abandoning his medical career. For those Canadians who played it, cricket was an important self-expression, an involved and all-consuming hobby, but never a career. Baseball players — at least the very best — *could* parlay the game into a profession. And for many young Canadians, the dream that baseball provided was a comfort to those who dreamt it, a chance — fleeting as it may have been — to leave the farm or the factory for some dusty diamond in the big leagues.

III

SCORCHERS AND WANDERERS: CANADA'S CYCLING CRAZE, 1883–1901

IN THE MID-1890S, THE EDITOR OF THE *FORT MCMURRAY GAZETTE* IN southern Alberta warned: "If this craze for bicycles continues much longer our livery stable men will have to close down." He believed that courting couples "will have no use whatsoever for ... a horse and buggy, and consequently the livery industry will receive a death blow."[1] The editor's grim forecast was never realized. The fascination for the bicycle, however, was very real, and the ways in which it affected the new nation reveal much about Canadian society and its economy.

As is the case today, in the first years after the introduction of bicycles, Canadians bought them for recreation and for their health benefits. Given the high cost of the early vehicles, the purchases also served as status symbols. Initially, there were the expensive "high-wheelers" or "penny farthings," which were as impressively large and costly as they were difficult to master. These were followed by the "safeties." The emergence of this safer, improved bicycle — with pneumatic tires, lighter and more rigid construction, and a special drop-frame version for women — triggered a second wave of bike-buying among the nation's urban consumers. Consequently,

Two riders racing their "penny farthing," or high-wheel bicycles, on ice.

high-wheelers became obsolete long before they were worn out — a situation that presaged a pattern that has become prevalent since then.

From the outset, some riders were attracted by the racing side of cycling, at both the amateur and professional levels. High-wheelers provided a few Canadians with an opportunity to eke out a precarious living as professional racers. They afforded female athletes such as Louise Armaindo the space in which to challenge the prevailing attitudes about women and sport common in late-19th-century Canada. An even greater number of Canadians acquired bicycles for leisure touring. It was — for many men, at least — a way to live out their romantic Men of the North ideals. And for Karl Creelman, a would-be wanderer from Truro, Nova Scotia, it was a way to see the world. Whichever imagination it was satisfying, the bicycle soon became the first mass-market luxury item in Canada. Its economic and social impact sped across the nation's roads for decades to come.

• • •

Canada underwent a period of dramatic change in the decades after Confederation. Between 1871 and 1911, the population more than doubled. This fuelled urban growth and rapid industrialization and triggered technological innovations. It was a time when change was expected. A railroad linked the nation, the telephone offered instant trans-Canadian communication, and major scientific discoveries generally demanded new ways of thinking. A measure of the widespread popular interest in new technological innovations was the public appetite for industrial exhibitions. One such example was the Toronto Industrial Exhibition, which ran annually from its founding in 1879 until it expanded into the Canadian National Exhibition (CNE) in 1903. Such exhibitions fed public expectation regarding new labour-saving devices that so epitomized the modern society.

Soon, Canadians and Americans would be caught up in the excitement of a new form of transportation: the bicycle. The first, unwieldy variations of bicycles, or "velocipedes," brought to Canada in the 1870s (including the aptly named "boneshakers") were made *in* and imported *from* Britain. They were heavy, costly, slow, and uncomfortable. Some, such as the quasi-bicycle that Arthur Jenkins rode across the Niagara River Falls, were one-offs with limited use. By the mid-1870s, however, new styles of bicycles had become popular among riders in North America. Some riders opted for the tricycle, but the vast majority chose the high-wheel bicycle, commonly called the "penny farthing" after its very large front wheel and small back wheel that seemed to mimic the eponymous coinage. Indeed, the penny farthing so dominated the early cycling market that many people referred to it as the "ordinary" bicycle.

To operate it, the rider sat directly over the front wheel and pedals, about 5' above the road. Although it was a major improvement on the earlier boneshakers, its very large front wheel made it a difficult bike to ride on anything but a hard and smooth road. Riding downhill provided its own special excitement; as a fixed-gear, high-wheeler with no brakes, the penny farthing could be quite dangerous. An unseen rut or a momentary lack of attention could result in the rider being sent hurtling headfirst over the front wheel.

Face-plants and broken wrists were common. Mark Twain captured his own painful experience of learning to ride the penny farthing in one humorous story. Twain's conclusion was simple: "Get a bicycle. You will not regret it, if you live."[2] *Canadian Wheelman* also poked fun at the difficulties of learning to ride:

> *Wife* had indicated to *Father* that their son wanted them to buy him a bike. *Indulgent Father* (who once had ambitions himself) responded, "Bicycle? Nonsense: The boy can't have it. Tell him to go up in the attic and fall down two flights of stairs. It will be just about the same thing and will save me $100."[3]

Despite the difficulty in mastering the high-wheeler and its substantial cost, the penny farthing became one of the most iconic symbols of late-19th-century North America. Available as it was to those who were adventurous and wealthy enough, the bike could raise one's status. Numerous sportsmen became interested in what seemed like an exciting and modern way to travel. Perhaps unsurprisingly — given the numerous sporting organizations that emerged out of that city at this time — the Montreal Bicycle Club was formed in 1878. The Montreal club was soon followed by others in many of Canada's urban centres: London (1881), Winnipeg (1883), and Halifax, Toronto, and Calgary (1891). As the number of cyclists grew, the Canadian Wheelmen's Association (CWA) was created in 1882.[4] The clubs were, by and large, hierarchical male organizations with a strong military flavour, as reflected in the adoption of club uniforms and officers.[5] Because membership fees could range from $100 to $150, the social status of the members was ensured.[6]

Just as other organized sports were finding fans, high-wheel racing begin to draw a paying audience. In September 1887, a financially successful meet was held in Brantford. Co-hosted by the local cycling club and the CWA, the meet's gate receipts were over $800, while another $100 was earned from the rental of booths and the sale of sundry goods. The profit after costs was $400. The money was evenly split between the Brantford club and the CWA.

Bicycle Club at the Athletic Park, Stratford, Ontario, 1895. By now, women were fully participating in the cycling craze.

Not everyone, of course, had the opportunity to ride. The structure of the bike, the difficulties of riding it, and Victorian attitudes toward correct dress for women precluded most, but not all, women from riding the high-wheeler. Yet, manufacturers were keen to tap into the potential market of female riders. As an alternative to the high-wheeler, the safety bicycle was introduced in the 1890s. With two wheels of equal size powered by a chain-driven rear wheel, the safety was much less dangerous and was easier to ride than the high-wheel bicycle. Although the first of the safeties was heavy and slow, inventors quickly found ways to make the frame, wheels, transmission, and brakes lighter and stronger. The development of pneumatic tires softened the ride. Consequently, overall consumer demand grew, and women quickly became a significant part of the bicycle market. Building on this development, manufacturers offered buyers a drop-frame model that allowed women in dresses to ride. Safeties soon came to dominate the cycling world, which made the high-wheeler an early victim of modern obsolescence, abandoned as it was by Canadian cyclists.

Although demand for them increased, safeties remained expensive and a status symbol. In 1893, Winnipeg's Timothy Eaton Company, for example, offered a "Gent's New Rapid" for $165 on an instalment plan, or $110 if paid in cash. For a labourer working for the Canadian Pacific Railroad earning $0.125 an hour, the bicycle was beyond their means. It was not, however, beyond the means of the merchants, managers, and established tradesmen who increasingly made up club membership. And soon these fraternities expanded to include those middle-class women interested in joining club rides. By the summer of 1896, for instance, the Winnipeg Bicycle Club had 125 to 150 riders turning out for its rides, and a "large number" were female cyclists.[7] As women became full or associated members, the dynamics of the clubs changed: now there were fewer club races and more club socials.[8]

SPECTATOR SPORT

As cycling became a spectator sport as well as an activity, events would gain traction with an enthusiastic crowd already intoxicated with "pedestrianism," a form of competitive walking. After the American Civil War, it had become a popular spectator sport in both North America and Britain. A growing number of professional walkers travelled around the country, competing against each other or against local favourites. Sometimes the challenge was to walk a certain distance in a certain number of days. Increasingly common were races that stretched over six days, starting early on Monday and ending Saturday night to avoid racing on the Sabbath. Holding the races indoors in large structures such as storage barns, exhibition halls, or roller rinks ensured that the audience paid the organizers and that distances claimed by racers were accurate. Gambling on the results of these matches fuelled local interest and brought in even more paying customers. Newspapers, covering the races to sell more copies, quickly created national celebrities.

Pedestrianism offered young working-class athletes a more appealing, if usually unrealistic, source of income to that which could be made in the factory. Spectators were attracted by the dangerously hard terms of the contests. In 1879, Exilda Lachapelle, a French-Canadian walker, successfully completed the amazing challenge of walking 2,700 quarter miles for

Starting a Bicycle Race, Manitoba, 1895.

2,700 consecutive quarter hours. Every 15 minutes, she set out on the track, walked a quarter mile in 3 or 4 minutes, then used the remaining 11 or 12 minutes to rest, eat, or doze. She walked four times an hour, day and night, for a month and covered 675 miles.[9] While spectators applauded her, the *Chicago Tribune* reported on her discomfort and privations: "someone is making money out of this half-dead woman, whose suffering and hardship would excite the keenest pity."[10]

Competitors *could* earn significant prize money, but ultimately, on balance, racewalkers were precariously paid hired help. Racewalkers, like those earlier athletes who performed feats of strength and endurance, were part of a long tradition. Working-class men and women entered these entertainment-athletic activities, rife as they were with gambling and dishonest promoters, with the hope of improving their lives. As Lachapelle's case revealed, it was all too often an exploitive environment, both physically and financially.

By 1880, high-wheel racing had replaced pedestrianism as the public's favourite spectacle. Impromptu races gave way to more formalized competition. The newly formed bike clubs, for example, put on races at local fairs and attracted a great number of fairgoers. In 1883 the Woodstock Amateur Athletic Association built Canada's first asphalt quarter-mile cycling track, and one of its cyclists, Herbert William Clark, went on to become the amateur cycling champion of Canada. High-wheel competition was added to horse racing at Peterborough's Morrow Park racetrack in 1885. Interest in cycling was also high in the West, and in 1898, large crowds in Winnipeg filled the Exhibition Grounds to watch two days of cycling races, which offered $1,000 in prizes.[11] In 1898, when Peterborough held the CWA's first national meet, 7,000 cyclists, representing 93 clubs across the country, took part.[12]

Perhaps the most prestigious bicycling event held in 19th-century Canada was the World Track Cycling Championships in Montreal in August 1899. The international contest — open only to male cyclists — was covered by newspapers across Canada. The event attracted riders from Britain, Europe, South Africa, Australia, and the United States, and the opening day was declared a civic holiday in Montreal. The championship drew a crowd of 30,000. Preparation for the event had involved six months of hard work and the construction of a new track that was reported to be as fast as any ever built. Hotels were full and railroads across Canada and the United States were offering return tickets to Montreal at the price of regular one-way tickets. And spectators, particularly local ones, would not be disappointed: Henry Gibson, a professional rider, won Canada's first track world championship in the men's motor-pace event, while two other Canadians won bronze in other events.

WOMEN ON WHEELS

Whether for sport or leisure, many men *and* women rode during the last quarter of the 19th century. Photographic evidence, however, suggests that their activities remained quite gendered. The bicycle clubs continued to be a male domain. Most of the staged photographs of Canadian bicycle clubs and organizations, and their formal rides, show only men. By contrast, most of the photographs that do include female cyclists were taken during informal social or family gatherings. Women's participation in sports, however, has traditionally been underreported.[13]

Contemporary writers — mostly men — questioned whether cycling was appropriate or even healthy for women. Both critics and supporters claimed "science" in support of their arguments. Anti-cyclists claimed that cycling would ruin women's health, compromise proper gender distinctions, and promote masturbation among those who did not ride slowly and in the correct, ladylike upright position. Champions of women's participation countered that it was a safe and healthy activity that would strengthen women's bodies and make them healthier to raise children.

Historians have argued over the extent *of* and reason *for* the physical emancipation of women during the last decade of the 19th century and the role played by cycling.[14] Colin Howell, for instance, argues that the bicycle "had the greatest impact on women's physical activities."[15] Cycling provided women with an outdoor activity that was easily learned, enjoyable, robust, and healthy, all while not contravening the age's standards for proper decorum.[16] In the end, women rode for a spectrum of reasons, and the pleasure ride could sometimes double as a conscious challenge to the constraints of Victorianism. The bicycle was, at the very least, a major accelerator of social change that had already begun.

One female who directly challenged societal norms through riding was Louise Brisebois, or Brisbois (both spellings can be found). Born just outside of Montreal sometime between 1857 and 1861, Brisebois was a petite but muscular young French Canadian, whose mother had been a weightlifter. Brisebois herself turned professional at age 14.[17] By the late 1870s, she was working in a Chicago circus as a trapeze artist and strongwoman — she could lift 760 pounds deadweight. In March 1879, she competed in her first pedestrian race and finished third out of 12 walkers. Pedestrianism, it seemed, offered a better life than the circus. As a result, Brisebois left Chicago and, accompanied by another Canadian, Thomas Eck, began travelling around small towns, giving exhibitions of her endurance or racing against local walkers. Although Eck was a fellow competitive walker and later cyclist, he did not offer competition to Brisebois; rather, he acted primarily as a coach, manager, and promoter. Given the social attitudes of the time, they were perceived, incorrectly, to be a married couple.[18]

By 1880, the money offered in pedestrian races had greatly declined and many walkers simply disappeared. In that very same year and performing under the pseudonym she would retain for the rest of her life, Louise Armaindo competed as a pedestrian in Canada for the last time before reinventing herself as a high-wheel racer. Given the limited number of female high-wheel cyclists and her intimidating talent, Armaindo raced primarily against men and, sometimes, extraordinarily, against horses. At other times, she gave exhibitions of her riding skills and endurance, as in the Horticultural Gardens Pavilion in Toronto in March 1882. She followed that up by winning a 10-mile race against Eck before travelling to Montreal, where she won another 10-mile race, crossing the finish line in just over 40 minutes.

Given her early success and her outgoing and brash personality, Armaindo soon developed a large fan following. In a highly publicized race in April 1882, Armaindo competed against John S. Prince, arguably the best cyclist of the period. The race, which Prince narrowly won, covered 50 miles, with Armaindo being given a 5-mile head start. Although Prince managed to catch her in the last miles, Armaindo's near-victory catapulted her into national prominence and established her as a "scorcher," a fast-riding female cyclist. The newspapers covering the race reported that the audience was full of women fans wearing Armaindo's trademark crimson and white colours and holding banners to support her. This particular scorcher was a star.

Promoters read the numbers and well understood the interest that a race between Armaindo and the most prominent female cyclist of the age, the American Elsa von Blumen (a.k.a. the "White Fawn"), might generate. Although von Blumen's manager resisted the challenge, public demand for it was too hard to ignore. In July 1882, the two met in a series of races in Philadelphia. The two riders would compete in two 5-mile races every afternoon for six straight days. In hindsight, von Blumen's manager was perhaps correct in resisting: winning two-thirds of the races, Armaindo dominated her opponent so badly that von Blumen withdrew from racing for several years. For the remainder of the decade, Armaindo would be recognized, rightly, as North America's greatest female cyclist.[19]

After the thrashing of her American counterpart, Armaindo set about racing against men and that very small number of professional women who had taken to riding high-wheelers. In a six-day bike race at the Battery D Armory in Chicago in May 1883, Armaindo raced against William Woodside and William Morgan in what might be considered the first true long-distance race for the U.S. championship. The track was 13 laps to the mile and the cyclists raced 12 hours a day, from noon to midnight, resting when they so wanted. By the end of the fourth day, Armaindo had covered 561 miles to Morgan's 559 and Woodside's 558. With many women in the audience cheering her on, Armaindo had, at race's end, covered 843 miles to Morgan's 820 and Woodside's 723. The French Canadian had, for anyone who had seen her ride, destroyed prevailing sentiments about the "weaker sex."

In April 1884, Armaindo and John Prince teamed up in a six-day race in San Francisco against a noted Western horseman, Charles Anderson, and his stable of 15 mustangs. Under the terms of the competition, they would race 12 hours a day, from noon to midnight. The cyclists would change every hour while Anderson could change horses at will. The race was held in the city's new Mechanics' Institute. The horses did not handle the indoor track and noisy crowds well. At the end of the 72 hours of racing, the cyclists had covered 1,073 miles, 1.5 miles farther than Anderson and his horses.[20] The *National Police Gazette*, a paper supportive of working-class women's activities, carried a full-page account of the race with a flattering picture of Armaindo.[21] Profitable as it had been, the race had attracted enough attention in the North American newspapers that it was repeated in August of the same year. This time, Armaindo and Prince won by six miles.[22]

ON THE BASIS OF SEX

Armaindo and other record-setting Canadian female racers, such as Mary Marshall and Exilda Lachapelle, were socially significant not because they were numerous, but rather because they directly challenged the dominant medical argument of the day that strenuous exercise was dangerous to a woman's health. These women's accomplishments, although covered by the *National Police Gazette* or even *Sporting Life*, were largely ignored by more conservative journals like *Scribner's Magazine* and *Outing*. Yet, even if they received only partial press coverage, Armaindo's successes were important in that they helped to refute the belief in female weakness. She was, after all, beating proven male competitors.

Women's racing drew large crowds because of its novelty as a challenge to accepted gender values. Not surprisingly, Armaindo and company had both avid supporters and vehement critics. The League of American Wheelmen (LAW), for example, largely ignored women competing in high-wheel racing. And when more women began competing, LAW simply doubled down and officially excluded any race that "has upon its schedule any event which is open to women competitors." Upon hearing that Armaindo had married (she hadn't yet), *Bicycling World*, openly hostile to female cyclists, trumpeted: "The sooner the female bicycle rider is hooted off the race track, the better for our sport." Everyone, apparently, had wives, sisters, and mothers who would "instinctively blush to be seen at a race meeting where ex-trapeze performers and variety queens rode against time and morality in an unbecoming and unwomanly position."[23]

Female cyclists were heavily dependent on male managers and promoters to get into profitable contests. This dependency reaped, perhaps unsurprisingly, its own set of negative repercussions and patterns. In 1883, for instance, the *Peoria Journal* announced that Armaindo and Eck had separated. At an exhibition race in Peoria, they had quarrelled repeatedly. That night at the hotel, he beat her so badly that a doctor had to be called. The fallout from the incident reflected the power imbalance facing a female athlete on the racing circuit at this time. After she left Eck, Armaindo found it increasingly difficult to book herself into any races or exhibitions. With no alternative, and given the fact that he, too, needed her talent for his own success, Armaindo turned back to Eck. Within a few months, they were performing together again, along with Prince, Morgan, and Woodside.

By the end of 1886, Armaindo was showing some weakness in long endurance races, perhaps the result of an accumulation of injuries on the track. A year before, she had told a reporter that she had "had plenty of falls, some so hard I thought I should be killed." In October 1886, however, she was still able to set a 24-hour record riding tandem with William Morgan. They covered 250 miles with some minutes to spare.

Still, when a new crop of female cyclists was being groomed by promoters, Armaindo's time left on the track was limited. After dropping out of a race because of illness, Armaindo explained to a female reporter that she had been involved in 13 six-day races in the past three years. It had been too much, and she no longer had the same strength.

Her vulnerability became crystal clear in February 1889, during a six-day race in New York. Of the 12 women cyclists who started the race, 10 were new racers. Although Armaindo led for much of the first day, she fainted around midnight, crashed, and had to be carried off the track. The *Saint Joseph Daily Gazette* reported that the "deathly pale" Armaindo requested a physician for "she felt she was going to die."[24] The paper also claimed that she had not been well for some time and had not eaten for several days. Armaindo started the next day, rode an hour, and had to withdraw. It was a pattern repeated over the next four days before she finished a disappointing tenth. Lottie Stanley, an 18-year-old from Pittsburgh, won the race by 20 miles and emerged as the new dominant female racer.

Although Armaindo continued to race into 1890, she was a shadow of her former self. Reports from races in 1889 suggest that Armaindo was past her prime and that, as her competitive career was near an end, her husband had gone through most of her savings. She continued racing through 1891, and while she did not win, she podiumed several times. Her last recorded race was in Chicago in May 1893 where she finished third, behind Helen Baldwin and Lillie Williams.

As Armaindo's stardom faded, a new generation of women riders competing on safeties had emerged to fill the void. The best of the new racers to emerge was Swedish Tillie "the Terrible Swede" Anderson, who had arrived in Chicago as a teen in 1891. She soon left her job as a two-dollar-a-week seamstress and was reportedly making thousands of dollars racing her bike. By 1895, she was being referred to as the "second Louise Armaindo."

The amount of money available to a successful bike racer might have seemed unfathomable to a late-19th-century factory worker, but competitive

A rare photograph of Louise Armaindo with her Yale high-wheel bicycle, 1883.

riding was, for the most part, gruelling and thankless. Armaindo's career provides a stark illustration of the extreme difficulties facing professional athletes at the turn of the century. All too often, the talented riders — and especially the talented female riders — who could earn real money, in part thanks to the widespread gambling on races, would see their money vanish into the pockets of agents, managers, and event organizers. To be a woman racing high-wheelers and travelling with a man not her husband was to invite public odium. Moreover, too many of the long endurance races, such as the six-day races, broke down athletes' bodies, while coaches were all too quick to provide sketchy stimulants.[25]

After Armaindo's departure from the limelight, female cyclists enjoyed fewer opportunities. There were, of course, some events. In June 1896, Ben Gordon promoted Canada's first professional women's six-day races, held at Fort Garry Park in Winnipeg. Interest was strong from the start and built up during the week.[26] By the final night, the grandstand was packed.[27] With no Canadian racing in the five-woman field, the crowd favourite was a British rider, May Allen, who finished third. The event attracted approximately 6,000 paying spectators and another race was planned for August.[28] Here was that rare occasion, afforded to only a handful of professional female riders by a well-connected male promoter. The Fort Garry Park experience, however, stood in sharp contrast to the dearth of chances that would be afforded to the majority of Canada's female cyclists for decades to come.

To be sure, there were fleeting moments of glory for the most exceptional riders. Peterborough's Lottie Brandon entered a six-day race in Brooklyn, New York, in November 1900. Riding alone, the diminutive rider covered 475 miles before finishing second, short by only one lap to Marguerite Gast.[29] Six months later, Brandon was the star of the Revere Beach Carnival as a member of Thomas Eck's Motor Cycle Whirl.[30] Once again, success for women riders seemed to be meted out by men.

It would be different for amateur racers in Canada's reported "Golden Age of Women's Sports," which followed the First World War. Nora Young, for example, did much of her racing against female cyclists in the 1930s on a dirt track at the CNE or at Mimico Bowl. It was at the CNE that Young set a national record and won a national championship in the quarter mile, but there were few national and no international events for amateur female cyclists. In keeping with the values of the time, there was a separate competition for the most attractive woman cyclist at the CNE. When Young and several other women cyclists took part in a demonstration race during a men's six-day race at Maple Leaf Gardens, however, the women were suspended 30 days for competing in a race at which professionals competed.[31] The hurdles faced by female cyclists, both professional and amateur, were many.

The lack of recognized official races for women meant a lack of general recognition of their talents. Women could not compete in Canada's national cycling championships until 1974. Unsurprisingly, it was not until 2010 that the first female cyclist (and speed skater), Clara Hughes, was inducted into the CSHF.

THE BIKE CRAZE

Across time and place, sports have contributed to the fluid issue of national identity. The growth of Canada's cycling community raised issues of nationalism and resistance to American expansion. It is no surprise, then, that the CWA had to deal with a related issue almost immediately after its founding in 1883: should it allow itself to be absorbed into a much larger American organization, the LAW, or should it remain as a national entity, free to enforce its own rules? The issue was, of course, not exclusive to cycling, and it exemplified the cultural tightrope so many Canadians had to walk in the late 19th century. It was a tightrope anchored at one end to the traditions of the mother country, Britain, and at the other to the culturally explosive (and often more exciting) neighbour to the south, the United States.

The country's proximity to the larger American cycling community caused some Canadians to advocate for the CWA's assimilation into the American organization.[32] The pro-American sentiment of some Canadian cyclists was reflected in an 1884 letter that appeared in the *Wheel*, the voice of the LAW: "There exists no reason," the writer claimed, "for a separate organization in Canada." Given that there were only 500 CWA members at that time — scarcely enough to form a single state chapter — the advocate called for the union of the two associations. There was sufficiently strong pushback from angry Canadian wheelmen, however, that the author of the letter quickly recanted his position in a letter to *Canadian Wheelman*. In it, he wrote that he had meant "affiliation," not "amalgamation," and claimed that "as young Canadians we should not relinquish our national feelings by taking a secondary place." Not everyone was convinced.

In early 1885, the *Wheel* claimed, incorrectly, that the Toronto Wanderers Club was about to join LAW. In fact, there had been a vote to join LAW and withdraw from the CWA, but most club officials had opposed the motion. *Canadian Wheelman* claimed that the LAW's appeal to CWA members to join had failed and that there was not even "a fractional feeling" for amalgamation. It concluded by depicting the *Wheel* as "a Yankee cycling journal with an anti-Canadian tendency." The Wanderers remained in the CWA and Canadian cyclists, as a group, remained outside of the LAW.

During the 1890s, Canadian bicycle makers also publicly opposed American expansionism and played on nationalistic pride. Relatively few high-wheel bicycles had been manufactured in Canada, but the growing market demand for the safety bicycle created an opportunity for small firms to begin production. By 1895, for instance, there were at least 13 firms manufacturing or assembling bicycles in Toronto alone. These companies sold approximately 18,000 bikes at a time when the population of Toronto was less than 200,000.[33] The large number of new firms reflected the early scramble of small producers to get a share of the expanding bicycle market.

Fierce competition followed, which led to consolidation among Canadian producers. The same thing had occurred in the United States, where in 1898, forty-two small firms merged to form the American Bicycle Company (ABC).[34] That year, ABC announced that it would build a bicycle factory in Hamilton, thereby avoiding the high tariffs imposed on bicycles imported from the United States. Canadian firms were quick to follow the American consolidation. In 1899, the five largest Canadian bicycle manufacturers — Massey-Harris, H.A. Lozier, Welland Vale, Goold Bicycle, and Gendron — joined to form a company that would remain intact across the next nine decades: the Canada Cycle & Motor Company (CCM).

The firm had a shaky beginning. CCM was formed at almost exactly the same time that the Canadian bicycle market began to contract.

The company responded in several ways. The first was a direct appeal to Canadian nationalism; the new company claimed its primary goal was "to defend Canada's bicycle industry against foreign competition." The second strategy was to exploit the benefits of being part of the British Empire, both as an opportunity to tap into a larger market and as a symbol of CCM's commitment to queen and flag.[35] Both strategies deflected attention away from American bike makers. It worked.

CCM sold bicycles to consumers in other parts of the Empire. With the outbreak of the South African War, CCM portrayed its sale of bicycles to the Australian military as a sign of support in a time of war. Meanwhile, at home, CCM and other North American bicycle manufacturers were looking to drum up more consumers. To achieve this end, companies such as CCM became trailblazers in their use of magazine advertisements.[36] At the outset, advertisements targeted the social elites who could afford expensive bicycles. As the cost of bicycles came down, however, the ads were increasingly directed at youngsters and working-class adults who continued to want and need bicycles. Indeed, as more and more attention and money were lavished on children in middle-class Canadian families, the bicycle became the symbol of parental love and care.[37]

INNOVATIONS

By 1900, the safety bicycle was both a product and driver of new techniques in metallurgy and milling. It was likewise central to improved quality rubber, to the efficiency of interchangeable parts, and to dozens of other innovations and improvements. The production of thin-wall metal tubing, combined with the diamond frame construction, made the frame lighter and more rigid. Improved steel-making allowed for lighter and stronger spokes. Ball bearings became stronger and lighter, benefiting not only the bicycle but almost all forms of modern transportation. The rear-drive chain of the safety bicycle allowed riders to go faster with less effort, while work on the tricycle led to the English inventor James Starley's development of the differential gear, now part of the rear axle of every car. Integrated assembly plants developed for bicycles would offer a template for future automobile assembly plants. All these improvements made in the bicycle industry had a much wider impact as they were adopted into other sectors of the economy. As journalist-historian Carlton Reid argues: "No proceeding technology — not even the internal combustion engine — was as important to the development of the automobile as the bicycle."[38]

For CCM, the causal relationship between car and bike transcended technology. In a reaction to the sharp decline in bicycle sales in 1901 and the financial fallout from poor decision-making, CCM began to explore the development of other products. The new manager, Thomas A. Russell, quickly consolidated CCM's assets, restored financial stability, and became an enthusiast of the motor car. His goal was to produce a car suited to the particular Canadian driving conditions. The first CCM-designed vehicle, the Russell, was introduced in 1905. It was marketed as "the thoroughly Canadian car, with Canadian material, Canadian labour, and Canadian capital."[39] While the product may have been different, CCM remained steadfast in its use of Canadian nationalism as a marketing device.

Whether they were the beneficiaries of a strong sense of patriotism or not, various sectors of the nation's economy reverberated with the bicycle boom. Buying a bicycle required the purchase of a range of accessories and set of services to go with it. High-wheeler club members were expected to purchase a tailor-made club uniform for club rides. Indeed, because of club rules and seasonal needs, riders usually needed three outfits — four, if they raced. Although not all new cyclists donned uniforms, they did wear new "cycling-appropriate" outfits. With the introduction of the safety bicycle, far more women rode, and they chose "modern" styles of dress to suit their new "modern" bicycle. To be sure, manufacturers encouraged female participation and, through advertising, countered the idea that cycling was a male-only activity.

There were also the "bells and whistles" needed for all fashionable and well-prepared cyclists. This meant owning a range of tools and accessories to make repairs on the road. All told, the cost of the clothes, accessories, and services likely matched that of the bicycle itself.[40]

BICYCLE TOURISM

Bicycle ownership was largely an urban phenomenon, but the cyclist's area of activity was increasingly the countryside. This informed the approach entrepreneurs would use to best exploit the bike boom. Bicycle liveries, for instance, advertised their willingness to store and service bicycles during the winter.[41] Photographers, too, came into greater demand by cyclists who wanted a permanent record of their new activity. Touring literature and bike maps also became available across Canada as more cyclists planned leisure trips to the country. These cycling-related industries could not be ignored.

Newspapers began to pay attention to cycling activities, often carrying a regular cycling column. On a Sunday afternoon in 1896, the *Toronto Evening Star* conducted a census of cyclists leaving the city for the country. On that one afternoon, 6,000 cyclists spent part of the day in the countryside and almost one-third were girls and young women. It made clear the growing number of women who had taken up cycling in the 1890s.

It also highlighted the economic impact that cycling was having on various sectors. Presumably, many of the cyclists who left Toronto that day spent money during their rambles. Prudently, hotels and tea rooms around urban centres took these cues and began to cater to the cyclists as a new source of income. And the impact could be large: the 106 members of the Hamilton Bike Club, as an example, booked hotels in Niagara Falls and St. Catharines to ensure accommodation during club rides in that area.[42] The trend was not limited to Ontario. To promote cycling tourism across Canada, in 1895 the CWA began publishing its *Wheel Outing in Canada* with a guide to hotels that were cyclist friendly. By the 1890s, there were more than 70 establishments across Canada that offered special rates for cyclists.[43]

Not everyone cared to cater to the growing number of bicycle owners. The appearance of bicycles on city streets and sidewalks led to early conflicts with traditional users, who argued against the presence of speeders and scorchers. Some things, it would seem, never change. There were also those who took a dim view of those who dared cycle on the Sabbath. *Canadian Wheelman* assured readers in 1887 that pious Toronto, with its recognizable profusion of church spires, had passed an ordinance that had prohibited Sunday cycling.[44] The conflict over road usage was as much a problem in small towns as in large cities. For example, Tillsonburg's police chief, Archie Pow, repeatedly warned female cyclists that if they did not stop riding on the sidewalk, he would take them before the magistrate. Similarly, Ingersoll banned cyclists from using sidewalks throughout the township and threatened violators with a fine of up to $20 or 30 days in jail.[45] It is not clear that either threat was effective.

Yet, some acknowledgement of the arrival of the scorchers on Canadian streets was necessary. In Ontario, cyclists were able to persuade the provincial government to recognize the bicycle as a vehicle with rights to travel on Ontario's highways, despite county bylaws that prohibited cyclists on some roads.[46] Likewise, in Manitoba, cycling advocates persuaded the provincial government to give Winnipeg the authority to establish a Bicycle Path Board with the power to create and maintain a system of bike paths in and around the city limits.[47]

More importantly, cyclists also became early advocates and boosters of the "Good Roads Movement." This was, for the cycling community, a necessity. By the last half of the 19th century, North American railroads had taken over much of the haulage of goods and freight that had earlier been moved over roads by horse and wagon. The maintenance of roads near the end of the 19th century had lost priority and rural roads were often in bad condition. For cyclists, good roads — at least near urban centres — were a priority for comfortable and safe cycling. In 1891 the CWA joined farm groups and others in a campaign already under way to improve roads.[48] Cyclists, while numerically a small group, were able to muster a disproportionate influence on the upkeep and improvement of Canadian roads. This is perhaps less remarkable when we recall that a great many members of the country's social and political elite were themselves bike daft.

KARL CREELMAN

By 1900, cheap bicycles were readily available, and, with the advent of the early automobile, the bicycle was no longer the "new" machine coveted by the social elite. The bicycle nevertheless retained its ability to hold out the romantic promise of freedom and adventure. It was this promise that summoned Karl Creelman, a young man living in Truro, Nova Scotia. Creelman would become the first Canadian to circle the world on a bicycle.[49] This accomplishment was all the more astonishing because Creelman had never ridden a bicycle before he bought one second-hand in 1899.

After taking a riding lesson, Creelman left Nova Scotia and headed west. Although he had planned to tour the world by ship, Creelman became fully intoxicated by stories of other cyclists who had travelled the world.[50] Yet, while these stories were full of romance and adventure, there was also the prospect of danger. Creelman would have known the fate of Frank Lenz, an American cyclist who attempted to circle the world in 1892 only to disappear in 1894, somewhere in Turkey. A group of bandits there was subsequently charged with his murder and convicted in absentia. It was a case covered widely in the North American press, but it clearly did not discourage Creelman. Indeed, the willingness to take risks was a core tenet for those cyclists, like Creelman, who believed that travel on two wheels would offer a deeper knowledge of humanity and the experience of true freedom.

Creelman made extensive travel plans, although he had limited knowledge of conditions in those countries he planned to visit. After cycling across Canada, Creelman's plan was to sail to Japan, cross over to China, then head south and cycle in the Philippines and Borneo, before a visit to Australia and New Zealand.[51] From there, Creelman would sail to South Africa and cycle north to Europe, setting up an eventual return home to Canada from Ireland. He expected his trips would take four years.

Things did not go quite as planned. Emerging conflict along his proposed travel route ensured that he would never see Japan, China, or South Africa. More, Creelman's itinerary was predicated on his ability to work and make money aboard those ships heading to his ports of call. This proved more difficult than first anticipated. His belief that he would be able to support himself financially by working during his trip resulted in him deciding that there was no need for him to obtain even modest funding prior to his trip. Indeed, he purposefully left Truro with no money to cover his expenses and was armed only with supporting letters from Prime Minister Sir Wilfred Laurier, Premier G.H. Murray of Nova Scotia, Creelman's pastor, and a few others.[52] It was a bold set of conditions.

The decision to leave penniless split the citizens of Creelman's hometown. The idea of a healthy young man travelling merely for pleasure and depending upon the charity of others offended many people. Their feelings did not deter Creelman, but the uncharitable designation of "tramp" would follow him for years. To be fair, while Creelman seldom turned down the hospitality of strangers, he did indeed earn money along the way by writing articles for newspapers, giving public lectures, and endorsing and selling products.[53] To maximize his income and local support, he contacted local newspaper and bike clubs well ahead of his arrival.

Typical of his tour, Creelman notified the local Brandon, Manitoba, paper of his imminent appearance *before* he left Winnipeg. The Brandon paper then announced his coming, which drummed up support for the young man's ambitious endeavour: "Creelman rides a famous 'Red Bird,' manufactured by the Goold Bicycle company of Brantford, Ont., which he will have on exhibition at Johnson and Co.'s store, where he will sell souvenir buttons, which is the only way he makes expenses en route."[54]

When he was going to be staying anywhere for more than a few days, Creelman found short-term jobs. While in Canada, his membership in the CWA earned him a discount in some hotels.

When Creelman left Truro on May 11, 1899, he headed north through Amherst into New Brunswick and then Quebec. Among the precious few things he carried on his bicycle were headache powder, salve, a change of clothes, a pencil, 250 envelopes, and an odometer. At Saint John, he could report to the Truro paper that of the first 231 miles covered, 25 had been on excellent roads, 75 on fairly good roads, and 131 on bad roads. In the six months it took him to reach Vancouver, Creelman travelled 5,320 miles, much of it on railroad rights-of-way because of the lack of usable roads. He walked some 700 of the miles.

Road conditions were a great concern for Creelman. By the time he reached Brantford in July, his second-hand bicycle was breaking down. He knew that a mechanical failure in a remote area of the world could be catastrophic. Fortunately, the Goold Bicycle Company was based in Brantford and, after some perseverance, Creelman reached a sponsorship agreement with the firm. The company provided him with a new Red Bird

Special, Model 55, at no cost.[55] In return, he promised to promote the brand throughout his travels.

Creelman was as good as his word. Someone who had helped the cyclist in Scotland later wrote the Goold Company to describe "the tremendous praise that Karl had heaped on his trusty wheel."[56] As it turned out, the Goold sponsorship brought new opportunities to Creelman; in Australia and Britain, for example, the cyclist received assistance and encouragement from Red Bird distributors and from the cycling community at large. At stops along his route, Creelman found work in bicycle shops, where he earned money and was able to do maintenance on his Red Bird.[57]

From Windsor, Creelman went south of the Great Lakes, through Chicago and Minneapolis and then up to Winnipeg. He found support from a surprising number of former Nova Scotians he met along the way. One of them, John Christie, a deputy sheriff in Minneapolis, warned Creelman of the dangers of the road and gave him a revolver for his protection. Before Creelman left the state, he encountered gangs of tramps who were believed to have committed violent crimes, but he rode past them without a problem. In actuality, Creelman was probably at greater risk from the extreme weather he would encounter. In one particularly bad snowstorm, he lost his way several times and wound up taking a 300-mile detour south to Seattle before getting up to Vancouver.[58]

Creelman would experience different but perhaps equally frustrating issues upon arriving in Vancouver. After weeks of futile attempts to get a berth on an Asia-bound ship, Creelman changed his plans and signed on to a ship that was heading for Melbourne, Australia. According to Creelman, the old American lumber schooner "leaked like a basket." Bullied and mistreated by an indifferent captain and a hostile first mate, Creelman described the 87-day passage as the worst experience of his life.

Once in Australia, Creelman regained his independence on his Red Bird and spent six months cycling through Victoria and New South Wales. Fortunately for the tourist, Australia was in the midst of its own bicycle craze, and Creelman — with assistance from Red Bird distributors — captured the imagination of Australians.[59]

Karl Creelman and his Red Bird bicycle having reached Vancouver.

When Creelman left Australia in September, he abandoned plans of cycling in China and Japan because of unrest in the former. Improvising once again, he signed on to a boat going to India, working as one of the hostlers looking after 230 horses being shipped to the Bengal Lancers. Despite the occasional bite or kick from the horses, Creelman's trip was enjoyable. When the ship made a brief stop at Ceylon (now Sri Lanka), Creelman took the opportunity to cycle around the island. In the middle of October 1900, Creelman and his equine charges finally arrived outside Calcutta (now Kolkata). He sent back articles to North American papers that wanted to follow his adventures.[60]

It would take Creelman six months to cycle across India from Kolkata to Bombay (now Mumbai), in part because he ignored his serious bouts of malaria. A week after leaving Kolkata, he collapsed on the road near Benares. A local doctor diagnosed his disease and told him he needed prolonged rest. Eleven days on, however, the bored and restless Canadian set off again. It was a poor decision. An agonizing mile later, Creelman met soldiers from the Black Watch Regiment who recognized the seriousness of his condition even if he did not. The soldiers took him back to their barracks, where he stayed in the Sergeants' Mess for several weeks. Although he thought himself recovered, when he set out once more, he lasted only five miles, collapsing again by the roadside. Once again, he was forced to return.

Finally, in mid-January 1901, two and a half months after first being diagnosed with malaria, Creelman set off for Mumbai. It was a hard and difficult trip to the coast. The failure of the summer monsoons over western and central India in 1899 had produced a severe drought, resulting in widespread famine and death. Creelman wrote from western India, and well south of Agra, that it was not "altogether pleasant travelling in some parts of the interior, where the famine had killed the people off and where tigers roamed, for the people who were left wanted my money and the tigers wanted my life."[61] Although he escaped the tigers, Creelman could not escape malarial relapses, and the first doctor he saw in Mumbai urged him to leave India.

To his great dismay, Creelman found that there were no regular shipping connections between Mumbai and Cape Town. Grudgingly, but with thanks to the aid of another Nova Scotian, the cyclist accepted free passage on a steamer bound for the Suez Canal. In Egypt, where the sandy roads and temperature melted the patches on his tires, he was forced to tour the pyramids and catacombs by camel, *not* bicycle. After almost a month exploring Cairo and vicinity, he rode to Alexandria, hoping to get a ship heading to Italy. Foiled again by the shipping schedules, he left Alexandria on a ship to Hull, England. Because of a bubonic plague outbreak in Alexandria, Creelman began his journey hiding in the ship's hold as a stowaway in order to escape Egyptian officials.

Once in Hull, he headed north, spending a month and a half touring Scotland. Creelman made sure to take time to visit the Glasgow

International Exhibition, where he could be photographed with his bicycle. In Scotland, he was slowed down by recurring bouts of malaria, but by the middle of June, he and his Red Bird were in Ireland. After three weeks circling the island, he returned to England and then made a quick trip through Belgium, Holland, and northern Germany, where anti-British sentiment caused him to once again return to England.[62] After a few days in London, he set off for Wales, where he suffered yet another relapse. When he recovered, Creelman rode to Manchester. There he was able to sign on as a bosun's mate on a steamer heading to Saint John, New Brunswick. On September 4, 1901, he arrived home in Truro to a welcoming gathering of friends and family.

Creelman's trip had taken him almost two and a half years. Always with an aim to amuse, he was happy to share his colourful story. In Australia, Creelman assured his audience that he was almost eaten by an alligator; in Sri Lanka, it was a boa constrictor; and then there were the Indian tigers.[63] However close he had been to being the supper of another, Creelman had covered 51,283 miles, the majority of which had been done by sea. On land, he had cycled 15,125 miles and had walked another 1,600, pushing or carrying his bicycle. He had also gone through five pairs of tires, three bicycle chains, and 15 pairs of shoes. While the Red Bird had held up, its rear tire collapsed just outside Truro. With $1.65 in his pocket, Creelman rode the last four miles into town on the Red Bird's rim.

Creelman's relationship with the bicycle reflected an important aspect of the bicycle craze. He had given up his first plan of travelling around the world by boat because of the promise of the new safety bicycle. The Red Bird offered him the freedom and independence to go where he wanted and on his own schedule and terms. It also allowed the readers who followed his travels in the newspapers the opportunity to relive his adventures vicariously through the cyclist's own reporting. His story was widely read. Big-city papers such as the *Montreal Star* and the *Vancouver World*, as well as small-town daily papers such as the *Minnedosa Tribune* and the *Brantford Courier*, had all brought the Canadian wanderer's stories back to North America.

FLEETING FAME

In November 1896, Louise Armaindo was living in Buffalo's Carlino Hotel when a fire broke out below her room. She was forced to jump out of a window, landing on a shed below. She broke her hip and suffered internal injuries. She would remain in the Buffalo General Hospital for five months. She never raced again and disappeared from the public memory. Perhaps as a result of her lingering injuries, Armaindo died in Montreal on September 2, 1900. She was buried in Notre-Dame-des-Neiges Cemetery. There was no gravestone.

Armaindo was both famous *and* forgotten because she reflected transgressive femininity. As a scorcher, she was a woman riding fast and on the rivet at a time when "proper ladies" rode leisurely and upright. The high-wheeler, far more than the safety bicycle, had been a male preserve, and it was in this environment that she competed and thrived. Importantly, she not only mastered the bike, but she also conquered men on bikes. Working in a circus, lifting weights, travelling with a man not her husband, and besting men physically, she seemed free from the passive domesticity depicted in much of the Victorian literature. If there were only limited criticisms directed at her, it was because she was perceived as working class, and expectations were therefore much lower. Openly challenging gender norms, Armaindo captured public attention and earned a loyal following while she raced. It followed that after she stopped racing and lost public prominence, she was soon and cruelly forgotten.

In many ways, it was the same for the wanderer. Early owners of the bicycle had achieved status through its purchase. By the time Karl Creelman bought his second-hand bicycle in Truro, though, that phase had passed. Creelman had ridden his trusty Red Bird across Canada, the United States, Australia, Sri Lanka, India, Egypt, Europe, and Great Britain. In 1902, Creelman was living and working in parts of the American Southwest. That summer, he returned to Canada. This time, it was by train. Had he cycled again, it is likely that few would have taken notice. To be sure, he was remembered by many of his generation. When he visited Brandon almost two decades after the fact, he was feted as a celebrity. Yet, cycling no longer meant the same thing. Soon after Creelman's world tour, the bicycle transcended the domain of the elite and became a two-wheeled workhorse of the poor and a tool or toy of children. Creelman's was a novel use of the bike that was far more Jules Verne than Clara Hughes, but it had given him a level of fame that he would never have achieved otherwise.[64]

Creelman returned to Canada from the United States in 1905, settling in Winnipeg. The cyclist married in 1907. Plagued by poor health, Karl Creelman died in Vancouver in 1924 at age 42 after a lengthy illness. Few Canadians were aware of his passing, and Creelman would make no sports hall of fame.

IV

"THE GREATEST ALL-ROUND ATHLETIC MACHINE OF MODERN TIMES": WALTER KNOX

FROM 1906 TO 1908, CANADIANS WITNESSED THE CULMINATION OF a struggle between two amateur sports organizations: the Toronto-based Canadian Amateur Athletic Union (CAAU) and the Montreal-based Amateur Athletic Federation of Canada (AAF of C). The struggle is commonly referred to as the Athletic War. It was ostensibly driven by the contentious issue of allowing amateurs and professionals to play *together* in certain team sports — specifically, lacrosse and hockey — while attempting to defend and enshrine an amateur ideal. As we've seen in earlier chapters, many 19th-century Canadian sports clubs acted as gatekeepers for a British social hierarchy. One such club was the Montreal Pedestrian Club, which, like so many other clubs at the time, used the concept of "professional" to exclude groups considered undesirable — groups defined by class and race. The club's concept of a professional, someone to be excluded from membership, included anyone who had benefited financially from a sport or who was "a labourer or an Indian."[1]

It was, of course, an increasingly anachronistic distinction. The growing popularity of team sports drew a paying audience that demanded their

Walter Knox about to take flight.

teams pay the best players. This reality troubled those who argued for the lily-white amateur ideal. However, attempts to stop, or at least limit, the growth of professionalism varied from sport to sport. Efforts to do so were often chaotic and always mutable. At times, such as when the AAF of C and the Amateur Athletic Union of the United States (AAU) unsuccessfully protested the famous Onondaga distance runner and Boston Marathon winner Tom Longboat's amateur eligibility just days before he was to run in the Olympics, the relations between supporters of "amateurs" or "professionals" became vitriolic. It was in this environment that the nation's "Greatest All-Round Athletic Machine of Modern Times" made his mark.[2]

Walter Knox is perhaps Canada's greatest forgotten athlete. His career sheds light on the complex interaction between amateur and professional athletes in the early 20th century. It also reveals the strong and widespread ties that existed between Canadian sports and gambling. Knox had a Janus-faced career that saw him compete as an amateur track and field star and, at times, participate in opaque ventures involving match-race hustling across

Canada and the United States. Knox yearned for the public acknowledgement of his exceptional talents that could only come from competing in amateur events. Yet he also wanted to maximize his success in professional match-racing. In trying to do both, he sometimes competed anonymously and often resorted to the use of aliases. Given the parameters of "professional" and "amateur" as dictated by the two sporting bodies that engaged in "Athletic War," and his often-questionable moral code and personal belief structure, it would be hard for Knox to reconcile profit with fame, both during his career *and* after he had retired.

ONE DAY IN TORONTO

Walter Knox was determined to prove to Canadians what he had long believed: he was the best "all-round athlete" in Canada, and perhaps the world. His physical appearance did little to support this conviction; he was only 5'8" tall and weighed 147 pounds. Knox, though, never lacked confidence. As a planned showcase, he chose the one-day Canadian Track and Field Championships held in Toronto on June 8, 1907. Competing as part of Toronto's Central Young Men's Christian Association (YMCA) team, Knox entered six events that had hitherto been dominated by established Canadian champions, men in their prime who were competing in only one or two events. Knox was aware that earlier decisions he had made might result in his amateur status being suspended, but he remained unfazed. This was not the first time he had run this risk before, and it certainly wouldn't be the last.

Knox had just finished coaching a semester at the Montana Agricultural College in Bozeman, Montana. Coaching violated the CAAU's amateur code. Knox knew this but believed there was little chance that his work at Bozeman, such a faraway place, would be discovered. He was wrong. A Montana player had sent a photograph of the winning college baseball team and its coach to a friend in Toronto. The friend happened to be a member of the West End Y, a fierce rival of Knox's Central Y team. The "coach" was soon identified.[3]

The afternoon before the meet, the coach of the Central Y confidentially informed Knox that the president of the West End Y, N.J. Stevenson, was going to challenge his amateur status the next morning. Until he had his hearing, Knox could compete "under protest"; however, no medals would be awarded. It was clear that no matter the results, this was likely going to be Knox's last chance to compete as an amateur. Knowing that, Knox gave his brother, Will, a substantial sum of money to bet on *all* of his events.[4]

The weather for the meet was perfect. As Knox prepared for his first heat in the 100-yard dash, news spread of the West End Y's challenge to his status. Bobby Kerr, who would be a gold medallist at the 1908 Olympics, was favoured to win the sprint. Kerr had come into the championships having won 39 straight races, although his last loss had been to Knox. Kerr was, Knox believed, "the idol of Canadian sprinting fans." Fans of Kerr saw Knox's win as an aberration. It wasn't.

As the sprinters settled into their start, Knox, in an act more suited to the ring or the rink, looked across at Kerr and announced that he was going to win. And he did, beating Kerr by a full yard. He then went on to beat Cal Bricker, an Olympic medallist and one of the West End Y's stars, in the running long jump. Knox won by almost a foot. The third event, a crowd favourite, was the pole vault, which happened to be Knox's specialty. Here, his major competitor was Ed Archibald, another East Ender. The next year, he would serve as captain of the Canadian Olympic team and win a bronze in London. To Knox's great irritation, the press called Archibald "Canada's best vaulter." Knox showed them up by winning and was the only competitor to clear 11 feet that day.

The fourth event was the shot put, where Knox faced Tim O'Rourke, another Canadian champion and a man six inches taller and 80 pounds heavier. Knox drew on his memory of the Irishman's attempt to embarrass him six years earlier. This day, O'Rourke underperformed. Knox did not, making a throw of 41'1", a half-dozen feet farther than O'Rourke could manage. O'Rourke saved face a little, winning the next event, the hammer throw, when Knox fouled out in all three of his attempts.

The sixth and final event for Knox was the discus. This was not one of his stronger events and, it must be remembered, Knox had expended considerable energy in the previous events. It apparently mattered little. He threw the discus 105'1", 6 feet farther than the runner-up. He had proven himself to be the best athlete in five very different events. Knox's wins against this impressive collection of Canadian champions and Olympians were even more extraordinary, given the fact that none of his tallies that day matched his personal bests.

The following day, newspapers were full of accolades of Knox's achievements. He was described as Canada's greatest all-round athlete. The tune would soon change. Just a few days later, the papers carried reports from the hearing held by the YMCA League of Canada, the organization that hosted the championships. Stevenson, the man who had brought forth the challenge, presided over the hearing, armed with a letter from Montana Agricultural College's president. The evidence was irrefutable. Knox was given a lifetime ban from all amateur sports. While he accepted the punishment, Knox did not go quietly into the night. The newly christened pariah shared with the press examples of West End athletes who had also competed for money, as well as team officials who offered good athletes "soft jobs" to join the West End Y.[5] Although it changed little, it highlighted the hypocrisy of the age and just how hollow the term "amateur" was in 1907.

A few months later, the *Bozeman Chronicle*, a newspaper sympathetic to the Canadian athlete, carried an account of Knox's victories and disqualification. The paper explained that he had had little difficulty winning his events against Canada's best athletes and that he had been disqualified only because of his tenure as coach at the Montana Agricultural College. The paper claimed that while in Bozeman, Knox had been "a true sportsman in every respect" and, as an exponent of clean athleticism, had used his influence to elevate collegiate sports.[6] His behaviour, it seemed, had not been that of a win-at-all-costs coach, and the paper was pleased that, despite his disqualification, his demonstration of his superiority over his former rivals would be a source of personal satisfaction.

Closer to home, the *Toronto News* offered a reason for why Knox would compete in the championships despite knowing he might be discovered. The paper claimed that in the previous year, "a good deal of hard feelings arose between Knox and Kerr, Bricker, and Archibald and he was determined to give them all a beating and he did each in their own specialty."[7] Publicly besting his closest rivals and showing his dominance seemed more important to

Knox than trophies and prizes, or even his amateur status — something that he had risked before. It was, nevertheless, costly. Knox would miss the American all-round amateur competition held in Jamestown and, more importantly, would be ineligible for the 1908 Olympics. He abandoned the idea of an appeal, for the CAAU rules required a waiting period of at least two years.[8] The ramifications of Knox's spectacular day in Toronto would be, for him, as profound as they were long-lasting.

BEING AMATEUR

At the start of the 20th century, the controversy over amateurism and professionalism in sports — a quarrel involving issues of both race and class — was reaching its zenith. It was rooted in a difference of social values, ethos, and attitudes between rural and working-class communities and the urban middle-class and wealthy elites. The gatekeepers — amateur athletics associations and clubs — expected amateurs to be "lily white." And these gatekeepers held the whip hand. They could, through a variety of measures, force athletes wanting or needing to make a living from their physical talents into the murky world of match-racing, gambling, and hustlers.

The matched competitions of smaller communities stood in stark contrast to the events hosted by the athletic clubs of Canada's big centres. Unable to host regular and organized track and field meets, these towns and villages instead chose matched competitions between two competitors as the logical way to manage inflated athletic egos. This choice also satisfied the widespread desire of male spectators to wager money on contests. Prize money for the successful contestant and gambling among the observers would ultimately form the bedrock of professional sports.

Amateurs, on the other hand, were expressly *forbidden* to compete for cash. However, the amateur spirit could be corrupted by some of the "prizes" on offer. These prizes could be quickly turned into cash. It was something that the sometimes-vigilant gatekeepers guarded against. For example, the same CAAU meeting that ruled Knox a professional in 1907 for earning $350 as a coach had reversed the intention of awarding two prizes to winners at the Canadian championships. This was, in all likelihood, a decision based on the optics of the situation Knox had created. It was a good call; one prize was a thoroughbred horse donated by the Waterloo Dominion Day organizers, while the other was "an unset diamond."[9]

Professional status carried with it great stigma and came replete with a whole set of preconceived notions. The elites saw professionals as people who were easily corrupted by gamblers, match fixers, and unscrupulous handlers. In reality, professionals were often just working-class athletes with an eye on a better life. Baseball's Tip O'Neill and hockey's Fred "Cyclone" Taylor were able to fight the gatekeepers' castigations and were lauded for it. In 1909, as a member of the Renfrew Millionaires, Taylor made $5,250. It was more than Prime Minister Wilfrid Laurier's salary, and Cyclone became hockey's first and much-loved superstar. It would be different for Knox.

Much as O'Neill and Taylor — his contemporary — were doing, the working-class Knox too wanted to use his exceptional athletic talent to achieve a better financial life and greater personal status. Throughout his career, he witnessed how the latent hypocrisy in amateurism operated. As Knox recalled, "The professional clung to his amateur status as long as it was humanly possible, with officials and the public [winking] at his cash rewards, which under the rules would have barred him from competition."[10] Knox would be afforded no such grace.

Certainly, Knox was involved in affairs that he himself would later characterize as "shady." In an autobiography written decades after his athletic career had ended, Knox confessed as much, but explained that in the confusing era known as the Athletic War, amateur athletes could obtain only "meagre returns" on their talents. If, as Knox wrote, he chose "to accept hazards to that mercurial quality known as 'reputation,' it was my choice and thereon I must stand or fall."[11] And there would be many hazards.

Knox had a lengthy, if somewhat duplicitous athletic career. At once, competing under his own name, he gained recognition as the best "all-round" amateur track and field man of his day, with trophies and records to prove it. Then there were other times, when Knox toured North America using aliases and competing as an itinerant professional athlete and match-race hustler. Knox took to the life of a "vagabond athlete," challenging local runners to match-races and generating betting and public interest to increase the stakes. Beyond "shady," this endeavour was dangerous. Knox, nevertheless, believed he was a man with sufficient athletic talent, cunning, and audacity to best anyone.

BEGINNINGS

Walter Renwick Knox was born in Listowel, Ontario, on January 27, 1878, but was raised in Toronto. A decade later, his father, a timber mill manager, moved the family out to Ontario's timber frontier. In 1887 the family located first to Fesserton, and then to Coldwater, before settling in Orillia. Violence was a common feature of the town during this time. As Knox remembered, "there was no closed season on fist fights."[12] Indeed, while in Orillia, Knox was a member of one of the young street gangs that clashed over urban territory and animated local sporting competitions.

At age 12, Knox started to work after school and in the summer at the local timber mill, cutting shingles. As a self-declared "haphazard" student, he left school after grade eight to help support his family. Fortunately for Knox, Orillia and nearby Coldwater enjoyed remarkable sporting traditions that produced world-champion athletes. Shot putter George Gray and all-round athlete Harry Gill, for example, both came from adjacent Coldwater, while the sculler Jake Gaudaur — the successor to Canada's first international sports star, rower Ned Hanlan — was from Orillia.[13] Gray and Gill both played key roles in Knox's development as an athlete and taught him the importance of technique and preparation. Specifically, Gray taught Knox a technique to out-throw much bigger athletes, while Gill polished the young athlete's sprinting and all-round skills.

After honing his talent under the tutelage of the two, Knox was ready to try his luck outside of Orillia. Most towns in Ontario held athletic events on Victoria Day, Dominion Day (Canada Day), and the August civic holiday. The prestige of winning a sporting contest in front of a local crowd far exceeded the small prize money normally offered.

As a result of participating in such events, however, the teenage Knox found himself in many sticky situations. Outsiders — especially successful outsiders — were unwelcome in the small towns. Whether it was in Washago,

Jarratt, Hawkestone, or Sebright, the unknown Knox invariably beat the local favourite, often at his own peril. He would not, however, be dissuaded.

In 1898 Knox had a job that he liked, splitting shingles at Ebenezer Long's Manufacturing Company in Orillia.[14] It was employment that paid him more than a dollar a day, but he also had sporting ambitions that he wanted to live out. He realized he had an innate talent for jumping events, and he was driven by a need to match or surpass his older brother's achievements. In September 1894, Jack Knox had won the gold medal in the pole vault at the provincial championships and a year later had finished second in the Canadian Pole Vault Championship. In September 1899, Walter Knox headed south to the Canadian championships in Toronto to test his skills and to improve his techniques in the pole vault. Above all, he wanted to beat his brother's achievements. At the meet, he jumped 10'6", a personal best, and finished second, losing by only 2 inches to Irving Baxter, an American champion jumper.[15] Having come tantalizingly close to winning, Knox was motivated.

A year later, in 1900, Knox was working for Long in Parry Sound. Training when he could, Knox planned to compete again at the Ontario championships. His behaviour on his way south to Toronto to compete revealed much, however. Knox, like many of his friends and competitors, had little concern for the newly formed CAAU's amateur code. When passing through Midland on July 12, just before the Toronto meet, he saw a notice for an Orangemen's track meet that offered cash prizes. He interrupted his journey to compete in three events, despite knowing that in doing so, he was violating the CAAU's amateur code. It could have cost him his amateur status, making him ineligible for the Ontario championships. His solution was to enter under the alias of "Johnson" and hope that no one would recognize and report him. Although he was recognized by spectators from Orillia, they shared the same attitude toward the CAAU code that he did. Instead of turning on Knox, they took the opportunity to lay down bets on his performance.[16]

Two days later, "Johnson" was in Toronto to compete — as himself — in the pole vault. There was an anxious moment before the start of competition when the names of several athletes who were deemed to have competed for money were read out. Knox's name was not among those mentioned and, thus, he retained his amateur status. Looking back, he believed it only served to encourage him to make his forays into professionalism more brazen. Despite poor jumping conditions, Knox won his event, clearing 10'6", 4 inches higher than brother Jack had jumped.

That fall, Harry Gill persuaded Knox to enter the Canadian championships with him in Montreal. Although Knox could barely scrape enough money together to afford a cheap train ticket and a cheaper hotel room, he agreed. When they arrived at the meet, Knox overheard Baxter, his jumping rival from Toronto who had just won gold at the summer Olympics, tell others that it should be easy to beat "that fellow Knox from Orillia." It was all the incentive Knox needed, and in wet and cool conditions, he outjumped Baxter for the gold medal.[17] It was the only Canadian championship Knox ever won.

Gill, by contrast, won only a couple of silver medals. Discouraged by his performance, Gill decided to take up a coaching position offered him in the United States, an act that would make him a professional.

Despite his success, Knox was uncertain about his future. He had achieved one of his early athletic goals: winning the national gold medal in the pole vault denied his brother. Although he had confidence in his athletic abilities, he liked his steady job. Moreover, his employer wanted him to manage new shingle machines being set up in his mill in Newfoundland. Knox did not stay long in Newfoundland, but he did make a commitment to himself to focus on his career in the wood industry. Indeed, throughout 1902 he competed in only two track meets, in Parry Sound and Orillia. It appeared as though he was giving up athletics. This would all change when he was pulled back into the game by his old friend, Harry Gill.

BELOIT

Back in 1902, Harry Gill had taken up a coaching job at Beloit College, a small Christian college in Wisconsin. After failing to recruit some Orillia sprinters, Gill called on Knox, who was then working up north in Verner, Ontario. The 25-year-old Knox was dubious. First, he was happily employed, and second, he had never even attended high school. Moreover, he was not sure he wanted to be in a small Christian college in an out-of-the-way American town. He knew that the Beloit track team competed in the Big 9 Conference but had never been good enough to be included in the conference championships. Gill, however, persisted and finally persuaded Knox to at least visit Beloit, with the college covering all the costs of his trip.[18] The trip would forever change Knox's life.

Knox reached Beloit in January 1903. Once there, he had a long talk with Jack Hollister, the college's head coach. After their discussion, Hollister offered Knox a full scholarship with free room and board, plus free tuition and books. The issue of having never attended high school was solved with Knox being enrolled in Beloit's preparatory school, which was geared for men forced to drop out of school while young but who wanted to return.

There was, however, the matter of employment. Understandably, Knox had reservations about leaving his job in the shingle mill to become a student with no income. Hollister once again came up with a creative solution, one that revealed much about amateur athletics in American colleges. All college athletes could have their expenses reimbursed by the college, Hollister explained — even trips away from the campus. It was possible, and even expected by the alumni association, for athletes to show creativity in compiling their expenses by adding a few extra digits or altering things here and there. Knox stated that he initially had a twinge of conscience, but with time, he admitted in his autobiography, "I got real careless with the way I could throw those digits around."[19] If an athlete was meeting team expectations, expenses were never examined too closely.

Knox knew what was expected and was confident in the guidance he was receiving from his friend and coach. After a semester of training with Gill, Knox was reaching his potential. With Gill's guidance, Knox became much more than just a good leaper. Now, he was a first-class sprinter and an excellent all-rounder. Soon, Knox was the pride of Beloit's track team. In a meet against Lawrence University in May 1903, Knox won the 100-yard dash, the discus, and shot put before injuring himself while winning the pole vault. The *New York Times* believed that Knox was "the most promising athlete in Wisconsin at present" and thought he would "take rank with the best College athletes of the entire country."[20]

As Knox's stock began to rise, his bio was subtly altered in the American press. Knox was now younger — 23, not 25. He was also less Canadian, as his family had apparently just moved to Michigan. And his talent was of the wild, untamed nature. It was reported that he had never trained a day before he came to Beloit. The mythology, as constructed by the *Milwaukee Sentinel*, was that Knox had not been long at Beloit before "the quick eye of Coach Hollister recognized a diamond in the rough" and paid him particular attention. The article made no mention of Gill's role in recruiting or training Knox.

The Milwaukee Athletic Club was sufficiently impressed by Knox's performances that, with the permission of Beloit, they had him compete as a member of their club during the winter season. Besides keeping him busy most weekends, the move earned Knox an AAU amateur card. Competing with Milwaukee at an indoor meet in Chicago, Knox cleared 11'2" in the pole vault. It would have been a world record, but the bar was dislodged during a remeasurement.[21]

Despite his success with the Beloit track team, Knox did not return to Beloit the next year. He had earned his high-school equivalency and, under Gill's coaching, he blossomed as an athlete. Knox now saw himself as a true all-rounder with financial potential. He was not wrong. Moreover, his experience in the U.S. college athletic world might have left him convinced that amateur athletes were being used in self-serving and exploitative ways by many in the athletic community. Knox believed that if anyone was going to profit from his physical talents and ingenuity, it should be him.

When Knox left Beloit at the end of the college season, he had to choose between two athletic opportunities. Milwaukee had invited him to join its team in New York for the U.S. All-Round Championships. It was a title he had always coveted. At the same time, a friend recommended that he attend the July 1 Caledonia Games in Sault Ste. Marie. The town had a long sporting and betting tradition, although the competition there had been dominated recently by two local athletes, Sandy and Harry Quinn. There was considerable prize money at stake at these games, and plenty of local bettors who would put money on the Quinns against any outsiders. For Knox, it was irresistible. He decided against New York and headed north.

GAMBLING

Gambling, it seems, has always been a part of athletics. In Indigenous communities, betting predated the arrival of Europeans. Efforts to discourage gambling — whether among early colonists or within Indigenous communities — were unsuccessful. Gambling was so widespread in Canada that some have argued it was more popular than the sporting contests themselves and reflected the speculative nature of frontier existence.[22] In small towns, gambling offered men with limited finances and few forms of entertainment the attractive possibility, however unlikely, of winning big. Where there was sport in Canada, there was gambling.[23]

It must be remembered that, even after the establishment of the Criminal Code of Canada in 1892, private betting on a sporting event was never, by itself, a crime. It became a crime only when it had been organized by a bookmaker or another third party who made money from the transaction. Gambling was also very much a gendered activity. Males had easier access to the public places, such as pool halls and taverns, where illegal betting took place.

The possibilities for men to partake in gambling were ubiquitous. The *Guelph Mercury*, for instance, reported on one particular 150-yard race in 1881. The contest was between a local runner, Charles McIvor, and an unknown runner from California. The race followed a typical match-race format. Each runner purportedly put up $4,000 and the winner took it all. The race was allowed to take place only after James Sutherland, the mayor of Woodstock and a supporter of McIvor, had contacted the other runner and received assurance that he could pay if he lost. The paper estimated that there was an additional — and, given the era, incredible — $12,000 to $13,000 being wagered on the race. The first race was declared a tie. After an hour's rest, they raced again. This time, the paper reported, McIvor beat "his opponent by eight inches in, we understand, the unprecedented time of 14 seconds."[24]

Yet, Guelph was not unique in terms of such high-stakes events. And men with talent and a mercenary spirit knew where to go to get in the game.

The main haunts of the professional gambler during Knox's era were, as historian Nancy Bouchier has outlined, on "the fringes of fairs, festivals and horse-racing."[25] There were places in the Canadian West, Knox claimed, that "men would bet on anything — even to spitting at a crack."[26] Knox recounted one incident that reflected the pervasive nature of gambling. The secretary of the miners' union in Frank, Alberta, had invited him to be part of a benefit track meet for striking miners. After discussing the events in which he would compete, Knox asked if the secretary could recommend "someone I could trust to do some betting for me." Knox was introduced to the town's bank manager, who welcomed him with open arms. He then introduced Knox to two bank tellers, who were "so well educated" in betting that "they needed no instructions."[27] Knox was more than pleased with their efforts.

WINNINGS

The hundreds of spectators at the Caledonia Games saw Knox, now competing under the alias "Bailey," put on one of his greatest performances. In five hours, he won 11 events, including the 100-yard dash and the 16-pound shot put. He would claim that he finished second in the 12th event, the 200-yard dash, only after a plea from Harry Quinn to let one of the brothers win one event. Knox won most of the prize money and assorted trophies, but more than that, he earned a very large but undisclosed amount from betting. His priorities were set. For the next decade, Knox spent much of his life as a transient professional athlete and match-race hustler, ever on the lookout for money-making opportunities. It was a decision that would take him through British Columbia, Alberta, New England, Illinois, and California, and eventually to Scotland.

In 1904, on the advice of friends, Knox headed out to the interior of British Columbia, where there were athletic hot spots with eager bettors. He also knew he could find work there as a shingle splitter. Importantly, Knox understood that thousands of dollars were wagered on individual races. On this particular trip, he competed under his middle name, "Renwick" — Walter Knox was too well known in British Columbia. His decision to use an alias also reflected the extent to which "sportsmen" across Canada were aware of the dominant athletes in other parts of the country. Typically, an athlete's promoter put up the stakes for the races and laid the bets, with the winnings being split 50–50 between the runner and his backers. It was dangerous — less because it was illegal, more because of the amount of money involved. During his competition out west, Knox faced threatening gunmen, bribed referees, crooked backers, and irate losers who wanted to beat him up. He took it all in stride and saw it as part of the challenge. While match-racing had its risks, it was exciting and, for some, very lucrative.

A typical race was the one held in Nelson between Knox and Fred Mitchel of Fernie for a declared purse of $500, with each sprinter putting up $100 in forfeit money. The race was arranged by Colin Murchison, a well-known hotel owner living in Fernie, and was fuelled by local boosters in both towns. Press coverage indicated that Murchison planned to wager $3,000 on Mitchel if he could raise the money. Despite being threatened by Fernie gunmen to throw the race, Knox won, secure in the fact that most of the attending Nelson police had bet on him. Irate Fernie bettors claimed the judges were corrupt, and they drugged the man they thought, incorrectly, held the prize money. Knox took the precaution of changing hotels until the police forced the Fernie supporters to leave Nelson.[28]

A similar match sprint was held in Slocan in October. It would be, the local press announced with more flair than accuracy, "the most important foot race ever run in the interior of British Columbia." Walter Renwick, now described as "the local champion," would race W.W. Smith in a 100-yard dash down Main Street, with each man putting up $500.[29] Knox believed he had won the race by a foot, and two of the three judges initially agreed with him. Then one of the pro-Knox judges reversed his decision, giving Smith the win. Apparently, he had belatedly remembered that he had money on Smith. Such were the kaleidoscopic conditions that hustlers like Walter Knox had to negotiate.

In early 1905, Gill again contacted Knox, who was now finding fewer willing competitors in the British Columbia interior. Gill was then coaching a mediocre track team at the University of Illinois. Although he was well aware of Knox's race hustling, Gill wanted him to join the team for the winter semester. Perhaps looking for some semblance of stability, Knox was up for it. After an interview with complicit university officials, Knox was admitted partway through the term. It was an unusual act by a sympathetic dean, familiar with the athlete's exploits at Beloit. Despite Knox's long history of earning money from his participation in athletic competitions, he received an amateur card from the college.

The Urbana paper described Knox as a "note-worthy acquisition" with an exceptional record in the shot put, broad jump, and pole vault. Although Knox was willing to compete with the university team, he was less committed to his university courses; that is to say, not at all. His professors, who understood explicitly why he had been admitted, let him, as Knox later confessed, "get by with murder." At the conference championships, Knox did well enough to earn his team valuable points (one win and three second places), but without the kind of performance that would attract too much press coverage.

In the summer, "Walter Renwick" was again out west, racing against Tom Morris, an older sprinter in Spokane, Washington. In a touch of irony, the terms of the race — including the $250 cash prize — were negotiated inside the Spokane Amateur Athletic Clubhouse, and the club held the forfeit money. Although Knox won the race, despite being offered $500 to lose, the wagering had fallen off after the local newspaper correctly identified him as Walter Knox.[30] At this juncture, Knox then headed off to western Canada to find events with serious prize money, heavy betting, and crowds with little knowledge of his name.

A race in Lethbridge, in early August, yielded him a $50 cash prize. This was small change, really. His stop at Michel, British Columbia, was more fruitful. After Knox checked into the hotel as "Walter K. Wilson," the owner appeared and wanted advance payment. Someone had recognized Knox and told the owner. Knox's response was to admit to having used aliases. He then asked the owner to hold $1,200 — his wagering money — for him in the hotel safe. The owner not only let him stay, but became Knox's backer for local betting, placing several hundred dollars of side bets for Knox. After "Wilson" won in Michel, he was off to Blairmore, outside Crowsnest Pass, where he beat a cocky and very large shot putter on a $200 wager.

Throughout the summer, Knox sought out races across the Prairies. In Maple Creek, Saskatchewan — which was, according to Knox, "the bettingest town I ever got into" — he entered a race as W.R. Wilson of Winnipeg. He then deliberately lost to the local sprinter, Regan, only to immediately and loudly protest that he had been cut off. Knox told a gathering crowd that he could give Regan a handicap and still win easily. He then "allowed" himself to be talked into a $250 bet, while giving Regan a nine-yard advantage. After a few discreet side bets, Knox won despite the handicap.

Despite continued success in the hustling game, Knox was equally driven to have the public understand how good an athlete he really was. In January 1906, he was angered by a Toronto paper touting Ed Archibald as the premier pole vaulter in Canada. Knox wrote the Toronto Central Y, which Archibald represented, and issued a vaulting challenge. He wanted to prove he was the best vaulter and, if his challenge was accepted, he would know his amateur status was still good. Three days later, he was invited to the Central Y's indoor meet. At the meet, Knox easily out-vaulted Archibald. The Central Y then invited Knox to join its team and issued him its amateur card. For his part, Archibald saw it as a personal insult and left Central Y to join the West End Y. These were the birth pangs of the infamous 1907 Canadian championships. Knox, having beaten Archibald as an "amateur," headed back west to make money as a professional.

In May 1906, Knox entered a race in Nanaimo, British Columbia, once again under the alias W. Wilson. Here, the dangers of hustling would be rendered most apparent. Following a familiar script, Knox let the local favourite, a Vancouver runner named H.W. Ferguson, whom he had beaten before, win the race. Knox then loudly complained about how the race had been run and immediately challenged the top two finishers to a match-race, with each racer putting up $50. Knox knew that the real money would be made in betting. Before the race, he stayed mainly in his hotel to avoid being recognized. Something, though, was not quite right. Knox began to feel unwell and the night before the race, he thought he was dying. He received little help from the hotel people, who first thought he was drunk. When he finally got to see a doctor in the early morning, the frightful diagnosis was iodine poisoning.

As it turned out, one of Ferguson's supporters worked in the hotel kitchen. It was, to be sure, a dirty trick. Knox's anger and willpower, though, overcame his nausea, tremors, and dizziness. Despite feeling "wobbly" from the poisoning, Knox won convincingly.[31] He collected his winnings and headed back to his hotel to recover. The event, however, was not quite done. Ferguson's supporters had realized he was a ringer, using an alias. They were waiting for him at the hotel, where he was beaten up. Knox came to on the steps of the hotel with a pounding head, scraped knuckles, and a black eye.[32] He left on the next boat for Vancouver.

PRELUDE TO TORONTO

On Knox's way back home to compete in the Penman Games in August, his brother Jack persuaded him to take a side trip 100 miles north of North Bay to Earlton, Ontario. Jack had land in Earlton, near to where silver and gold deposits had been found. Jack's gold fever quickly infected Walter. The brothers' proposed remedy was for Jack to start prospecting. Walter would continue race hustling to raise operating capital for their venture, and when race season was over, Walter would join Jack in the field. It was settled: Walter would run in summer and mine in winter.

It would not be all hustle; Walter Knox would partake in some legitimate races. The Penman Games, for instance, had become an annual event in Orillia, exclusively for YMCA teams. It offered impressive trophies to the highest-scoring individual and team over 10 events. Archibald and Bobby Kerr, as well as many other very good athletes, were there. Both Kerr and Walter Knox won their heats to advance to the finals and then, as Knox later claimed, Kerr made him an offer to throw the race. If Knox let Kerr win at Orillia, Knox could win in Hamilton a month later, at the YMCA Athletic League Championships. The odds would be against Knox and the two sprinters could make serious money betting. Whether Kerr had made the offer or not, Knox finished second at Orillia, just behind Kerr, and later claimed that he had been paid to do so. In other events, Knox had not been bought and set new Canadian records in the pole vault (11') and the 12-pound shot put (49'6") as well as winning the individual championship.[33] He then headed south to raise mining money from his match-racing enterprise.

Walter Knox and no soft landing, Scotland, 1911.

In September, he was in Corry, Pennsylvania, to run in a high-stakes race against a very good local Black runner named Henry Batson. The local paper reported that the new challenger called himself W. Wilson (an alias Knox frequently used) from Batavia, New York, but rumours spread that he was probably Arthur Duffy, the world champion of short distances. Another rumour was that he was really the great college sprinter, Archie Hahn. When Knox discovered that his training was secretly being watched by Batson supporters, he faked an injury and then acted as if he were trying to hide it. Once a flurry of big bets was placed on Batson, Knox knew the impressive ruse was working.

Knox faced a problem the night before the race, when Corry's chief of police visited him to explain that he was going to bet $300 — his down payment on a house — and wanted to know if Knox was healthy. Knox decided to tell the truth, thinking that if things got ugly after the race, having the police on his side would be useful. Knox had also found out that Batson was himself an experienced match-hustler.

Apart from being something of a master deceiver, Knox also demonstrated his inherent racism at times. While Batson called Knox a "white boy," Knox responded using a racist slur when referring to the Black sprinter. It wasn't the first time. Earlier, when competing against George Poage, an African American sprinter who held the Wisconsin state 100-yard record, Knox asked himself, as he later explained, "Am I going to be beaten by a coloured fellow?" His answer, both on the track and in his mind, was, "No coloured fellow can beat me."[34] As far as the race against Batson went, Knox won easily and the police ensured there was no violence. He returned to Canada with $1,500.

His winnings may have been paying the bills and financing the prospecting business he had with his brother Jack, but they could not buy him out of trouble with the governing bodies of amateur athletics in Canada. Only a few months after his race with Batson, Knox had the day of his life in Toronto. The fallout, however, was profound. There would be no 1908 Olympics. And Walter Knox's name would be forever tainted.

BEING PROFESSIONAL

After Knox lost his amateur status in 1907, he doubled down and became even more focused on professional match-racing. During 1908 and 1909, Knox competed on the American West Coast, where he was less recognizable. Starting in Seattle, he worked his way south, looking for match-races or events with large cash prizes. He spent much of his time in San Francisco and other parts of California, but he also raced in Mexicali, Mexico.

Bizarrely, for part of the time, he ran for the Olympic Club of San Francisco, the oldest American amateur athletic club. The club had approached him to join its team. After some discussion, Knox admitted that he was a professional and had been competing under the alias "Kennedy." The recruiter assured Knox that there would be no questions and the club could issue him an amateur card.

Emboldened, Knox began participating under his own name.[35] The Olympic Club, however, had less power on the West Coast than it perhaps thought. In time, his professional status was revealed. AAU president James Sullivan identified Knox as a professional who had been "masquerading" as both amateur and professional, and noted that Knox's prizes had been pawned to cover his expenses. Knox did not cower, and instead acknowledged that he was a professional. He claimed that he had admitted as such to the club's track captain, Andrew Glarner, *before* he joined the club.[36] His attempt at playing both sides failed, however. He could not escape his past.

Yet, the hustler did not curb his hustling. He saw any track and field athlete as an opponent who could be bested. Celebrities were no exception. Knox was in San Francisco in September 1909 when he met Jack Johnson, the powerful Black world-champion boxer. Johnson, as we shall see a little later, was something of an impediment to the careers of more than one Black Canadian boxer and was set to square off against Al Kaufman in only a few days. Knox found out that Johnson thought himself a runner and was a man who might be hustled.

The Canadian hung around the pool hall where Johnson was training. Aptly, Knox played the role of a pool shark who thought he could also run. Eventually Johnson confronted Knox: "What's all this talk, white boy, about you being able to beat me in a foot race?" Knox said he was sure he could take Johnson for $200 over 200 yards, but before he could get his forfeit money down, Billie Little, Johnson's manager, forbade the fighter from running before the fight.

After Johnson turned down the race, Knox taunted the fighter: "You're a quitter." As Johnson got angrier, Knox added, "You always were a quitter and if it wasn't only three days until you fight Kaufman, I'd bat you one myself." As Johnson came over the table after him, Knox flew out the door. The Canadian explained, "I could always run better than I could fight."[37]

Later that year, and after being away for two years, Knox returned to northern Ontario to help his brother at Elk Lake, where Jack had found silver tracings.[38] The discovery of silver in 1903 at Cobalt, about 50 miles to the south, had ushered in a feverish period of prospecting and mining across Canada's Precambrian Shield. At its peak — between 1903 and 1926 — more value was extracted from the ground around Cobalt than had been taken in the form of gold from the Klondike.[39] Prospectors often sold their claims to larger mining concerns at the first sign of gold or silver. The Knox brothers held a longer view. During the fall and winter, they worked their various claims. Walter Knox found he could keep in good shape by "swinging a pick" and "tramping through snow, belly deep." With spring breakup, the brothers headed to the nearest village, Gowganda, for some human contact before Walter started serious training for the summer competition.

He was back on the road by July, first to local track meets to get his edge back, and then to the Caledonia Games outside Boston to make serious money. After three quick victories and an apparent fourth in the 100-yard dash, he was placed second by officials who believed, but could not prove, that he was a "ringer." In the fall, Knox returned to Elk Lake with substantial prize money, plus his gambling winnings.

SCOTS WHA HAE

During the next winter, Knox overheard visiting prospectors talking about competing in Scotland. The more he heard about Highland gatherings and the Scottish games, the more attractive things sounded to him. During the summer, more than 50 Highland gatherings were held across Scotland, all with cash prizes and legalized betting. Knox was drawn to the idea of competitions intended primarily for professionals, where good athletes could make a decent living by touring the games. Around this time, Jack's "holes in the ground" had begun paying out. Yet, Walter was not going to resist making some cash from competing.[40] At 33, he was nearing the end of his competitive career. If he was going to test the Scottish waters, now was the time. After several weeks of strenuous training and competing in two Ontario games to prove he was ready, he sailed from Montreal on June 17, 1911.

In Scotland, Knox found competition that suited his abilities. In his very first competition at Shotts, he competed under the alias A.R. Stearns. Knox, however, fared poorly because of an intestinal problem. It was all for the best that he was below par and under the radar, for he found out that any athlete using an alias would face criminal charges. It was the first and last time he used an alias in Scotland. As his health improved, so did his results. From

July until the last game at Girvan at the end of September, Knox competed in 37 meets, winning 63 events, placing second in 37 and third in 31. On his final day, he won the 100-yard dash, the pole vault, the shot put, and standing jump, and placed second in the hammer and broad jump. The Highland Games were clearly an environment in which Knox — a multi-talented athlete with huge endurance — could thrive. As local historian David Town estimated, Knox's prize money amounted to almost $1,300, not counting what he won by betting on himself.

As Knox set out for home, the Scottish press was full of praise for his performances. One article, "Knox Beat Every Weight Man in Old Scotland," claimed the Canadian was "the most scientific Ball-Putter in Scotland." Another stressed his complete domination among pole vaulters. Having won the championship of Scotland by clearing 11'6", Knox's performance was reported as "the absolute best ever done in the history of Scottish games." Yet another paper described him as "one of the best all-round men that ever competed in the Scottish games." With such successes, Knox responded with a resounding yes to Lady Nairne's famous query, "Will Ye No Come Back Again?"

TEAM CANADA

Although a return to Scotland may have been on top of Knox's to-do list in 1912, it was a very long list. Sailing back across the Atlantic after a winter of mining was the plan, but he became intrigued by the Canadian Olympic Committee's (COC) call for potential managers to lead the team headed to Stockholm. The successful applicant would be responsible for the athletes in *all* Olympic events. The press carried a short list of possible candidates that included Tom Flanagan, former manager of Tom Longboat; Bobby Kerr, the sprinter; Dr. Barton, a Toronto varsity coach; and Walter Knox.

In late May, Knox emerged successful. It was a measure of his reputation. The committee judged that his ability to pass on technical knowledge was paramount, but his contract specified that he start only on June 8, the day of the Dominion Trials. This left him little time for any effective coaching or, indeed, to get to know the athletes that would be in his charge. Popular if difficult (at least for 21st-century sensibilities) sportswriter Lou Marsh thought this was unfortunate, for he believed Knox to be "the cleverest all-round athlete Canada ever produced."[41]

Despite his character flaws and, at times, unlikeability, Knox certainly had plenty of knowledge to pass on to team members. Even Flanagan, who had lost out to Knox, believed the manager to be "a past master in all and every branch of athletics and knows from long experience how to impart his knowledge."[42] Knox's efforts to mentor some athletes, however, would be hampered by his personality. He was a stubborn man, not a little racist, and held a belief that a coach's word was law.

One potential star on the team was John "Army" Howard, Canada's first Black Olympian. The day before Knox took over the team, he predicted to the press that Howard would win gold in the 200 metres. Knox was confident because he believed he could significantly improve Howard's start, which was his one perceived weakness. Controversies over discipline and training, however, culminated in a fist fight between Knox and Howard, whom Knox — and, it must be said, the press — referred to as "that coloured boy." The fight occurred after Knox had accused Howard of insubordination, rebelliousness, and lack of effort. Knox wanted two practices a day. Howard believed that he knew best how much training he needed, and that two-a-days were too much.

Howard also resented Knox's claims that his start resembled that of a raw novice and Knox could improve it substantially. Knox compounded the problems by embarrassing Howard, winning a 50-yard dash on board the boat. And while Knox threatened to remove him from the team, Howard remained put. This was largely through the efforts of the Amateur Athletic Union of Canada.[43] However, it cannot be said that Howard, despite being allowed to remain on the team, was truly respected. Howard's presence on the Olympic team highlighted the ugly racism of the time, something that was particularly evident in the press coverage of the team. Even commercial establishments reflected that racism: Howard was excluded from the same Montreal hotel used by his white teammates.

Unfortunately, Howard suffered health issues upon arrival in Sweden and did not qualify for any of the finals in his events. It can be said that

Knox's Olympics were a success — the track and field team picked up five of Canada's eight medals. It was not, however, an unqualified one: the Stockholm experience was marred by Knox's open clash with Howard and his supporters.

BACK AGAIN

When the Olympic track and field events ended on July 17, Knox set off across the North Sea for a return to Scotland and another Highland Games. If Knox's Olympics had had mixed results, his second Scottish tour was an undeniable triumph. In just over two months, he competed in 23 various games, winning 41 events and never finishing less than third place. In the process, he set 20 new pole-vault records and another with the shot.[44] Finally, at the end of September, Knox returned to Elk Lake to work once again with his brother in their joint venture.

Before Knox returned to Scotland for another successful and final tour in 1913, he achieved another of his long-term goals: winning the North American All-Round Championship. By now, Jim Thorpe, the dominant American all-rounder, was focused on professional baseball. Thorpe's title then went to John A. MacDonald, athletic instructor at Tufts College. Knox wanted to compete against Jim Thorpe, but when he issued a public challenge to all and sundry, it was MacDonald who accepted the challenge. The match, involving 10 separate events, was scheduled at Hanlan's Point, Toronto, on June 25, 1913.

Lou Marsh covered the event. He noted that all previous champions, including MacDonald, were big men, while Knox was only 150 pounds. Marsh also explained that the championship was now decided not simply by wins and losses, but by performance in all 10 events, each scored out of a possible 1,000 points. Despite his size, Knox took seven of the events and outscored MacDonald by 6,498 points to 5,339.[45] It was a compelling victory and one that should have secured Walter Knox as an enduring household name in Canada, as it marked the end of his competitive career as an athlete. For a variety of reasons, not least of which was his difficult personality, it did not turn out that way.

TEAM BRITAIN

The 1912 Games left the British athletic establishment with serious concerns about its nation's performance. The British team fell to third at Stockholm, behind the United States and Sweden. By all accounts, it appeared that Germany was also poised to better Britain at the next Olympiad. After months of debate and criticism, the British Amateur Athletic Association (BAAA) decided that a new way forward was needed. In August 1913, the British Olympic Financial Committee was formed with the goal of raising £100,000 to support the creation of a British team for the 1916 Olympics.[46] Supporters saw it as a modernization effort necessary in a period of fierce international competition, athletic and otherwise.

The man selected to revolutionize the British Olympic effort was Walter Knox. In February 1914, the BAAA offered him the position of national head coach for a three-year term at £400 a year.[47] It was, unquestionably, a measure of his international reputation. From February to August, he worked to create a sports structure that could generate winning Olympians. He identified and appointed 22 assistant coaches and set up coaching centres across Britain. Travelling widely, Knox gave clinics on techniques, met with coaches, and identified those athletes with exceptional potential. The Canadian had the skills and a plan to transform the British Olympic team.[48]

However, Knox was not quite finished competing himself. That year, with permission from the BAAA, he competed in what was billed as the World All-Round Championship. In early August, Knox faced Findlay Cramb, a man more than a decade his junior. Knox won the title handily, beating Cramb in six of the eight events.[49] Now, having won more than a few prestigious competitions and having been given the helm of the British Olympic Team, Knox was riding high and seemed to have jettisoned much of the stigma of his earlier, shady dealings.

With the beginning of the First World War, Knox effectively lost his job, and plans to transform Britain's Olympic efforts were abandoned. By the end of October, Walter Knox was back in Elk Lake.

TEAM CANADA AGAIN

Knox did not volunteer for military service during the war, although he was younger than the maximum enlistment age. Instead, he spent much of the next five years working as a "mine manager" and "mine broker" in Ontario and Quebec. He periodically announced his retirement from athletic activity but could never fully abandon sports.[50] After the war, he was offered a chance to manage Canada's 1920 Olympic team. Knox quickly accepted but was pessimistic about Canada's chances.

Knox knew that Earl "Tommy" Thomson was a threat for several medals, although his focus was the 110-metre hurdles. George Goulding, a gold medallist in Stockholm, was Canada's other significant threat, but he had been declared a professional for coaching in the YMCA during the war. Attempts by the Amateur Athletic Union of Canada (AAU of C) to get him reinstated failed. Thomson won gold in his specialty, Canada's only athletic medal, but refused to enter other events, to avoid fatigue. Only the Canadian boxers' haul of five medals provided national solace. As far as Knox was concerned, the poor showing was a result of the lack of organization and coaching at the grassroots level. The following year, he was offered an opportunity to address the situation.

In 1920, the E.C. Drury coalition government in Ontario injected new money into high-school recreation and athletics. It passed legislation to control a spectrum of professional sports and, in doing so, raise revenue to benefit amateur sports. The Ontario Athletic Commission (OAC) Act of 1920 regulated professional sports; licensed professional athletes, trainers, and promoters; and imposed a 5 percent tax on the gate receipts of professional sports to fund the OAC's activities. Besides eliminating some of the worst abuses among professional athletics, the Act created a financial windfall for the province, which it used to support amateur sports and recreation in schools. The primary goals of the OAC were to facilitate the physical development of students, encourage an interest in sports (and avoid idleness), and, lastly, produce elite athletes.

The OAC used the funds to increase physical education in schools, develop coaches, subsidize amateur organizations, and create a training centre near Orillia. The man hired to oversee all of these efforts was Walter Knox, who became the OAC's travelling coach in February 1921. Knox immediately employed the use of slow-motion films, using Canada's best-known athletes to illustrate their technical skills in different events. The films became part of his province-wide clinics, which also included two hours of demonstration followed by a practice period. In his first few years as coach, Knox spent about a hundred days on the road, running clinics at public schools, the vast majority of which were outside Toronto.

His activities in the late summer of 1923 were typical: after four days of teaching high-school teachers in Orillia how to coach, he was off to the Niagara Peninsula for a week, making appearances in the schools of 16 towns and cities, where he conferred with school board members. He then visited a great many towns from Orillia to Sault Ste. Marie and as far north as Cochrane to promote a provincial track and field championship.[51] Ending his tour in Cobalt, Knox had held clinics for, shown films to, and coached nearly 3,500 boys and girls in the towns he visited. The *Sault Weekly Star* only echoed what so many Ontarians already believed: Walter Knox was "Canada's Greatest Athlete."[52]

Knox established a system of regional competition for Ontario's young athletes, and in 1925 the first Provincial Schoolboy Championships were held. It marked a shift of OAC emphasis toward elite competition. By 1928, more than 5,000 students were competing in regional meets, with the finals being held in Toronto. The following year, the OAC established the Ontario Athletic Camp near Orillia to provide three-week summer training camps for high-school male athletes. The camp was also made available to amateur sports associations and, more reluctantly, to the Women's Amateur Athletic Association of Ontario, for the upgrading of physical-education teachers. Ultimately, it led to a clash of priorities: the creation of elite athletes versus the promoting of mass participation for enjoyment and health. Funds directed toward the camp and amateur associations left little revenue for the travelling coach program. It was consequently cancelled in 1931.[53]

The ground for Olympic success, however, had been tilled. And many saw a correlation between Knox's work with the OAC to develop elite competitors and Canada's later success on the world stage. The evidence

Walter Knox, a master of many events.

supports this observation. In the two Olympics before OAC athletes were old enough for selection to the nation's track and field teams (1920 and 1924), Canada managed a single medal in athletics. In the next three Olympics, after the OAC and Knox had identified and prepared young track and field athletes for the bigger stage, Canada won 21 medals, including 5 golds. OAC members were able to boast that 90 percent of the athletes on the 1928 team had benefited from OAC coaches. That team's haul was 14 medals.[54] Alas, after the Second World War, the OAC summer program was shut down, effectively ending promotional support for track and field. In the next seven Olympic Games, Canada won a total of four track and field medals. None were gold.

FOREVER IN THE SHADE

During the 1920s, Knox's reputation and influence as an athletic coach grew. The OAC's focus was on male amateur sports, but starting in 1922, Knox included girls in his programs. He also played an important role in the athletic success of Canadian women outside the school system. In June 1922, Knox held a tryout at Dufferin Park in Toronto to organize a team of young women to attend a track meet at Philadelphia. The team had considerable success at the meet. The following year, he began to coach the woman's relay team of Myrtle Cook, Rosa Grosse, Bobbie Rosenfeld, and Grace Conacher. In July 1926, functioning as coach and manager — and with his wife serving as chaperone — he took a group of eight female athletes to Philadelphia's Sesquicentennial Games. The 440-yard relay team won its event, beating 12 American teams and matching the world record.[55]

Female athletes knew of Knox's reputation as something of a champion of women's sports. As a result, sports organizations and clubs sought his services. In 1927 the Parkdale Ladies' Athletic Club hired him as its coach at the request of its athletic star.[56] In 1929, Knox became one of the specialist coaches at the Toronto Central YMCA. And during the 1930s, he became a head coach of the large, new Beaches Olympic Club. In addition, Knox served as the coach of the Queen's University track team. He had become as acclaimed a coach as he had been as an athlete.

In 1950, sports writers selected Canada's outstanding track and field performer of the half century. They placed Walter Knox third, behind Percy Williams and Bob McFarlane. Knox was disappointed and said as much to his friend Fred Steel: "I guess they've forgotten me."[57]

How could the "greatest all-round athlete" be forgotten? The issue was in how he was remembered. Knox's athletic achievements had been scattered across time and space. He won championships in Canada, the United States, Scotland, and England, but few people were aware of the totality of his accomplishments. This was, in part, because he sometimes competed under an alias. More, his accomplishments on that one glorious day in Toronto in 1907 — which, arguably, was his single greatest athletic opus — were soon regarded as illegitimate by most, and particularly so by those who wielded power during the unforgiving Athletic War. The pejorative label of being a professional stuck with him long after his hustling years were over. When Knox's name was brought up, there was a residue of the stigma from those earlier times, even among people who could no longer remember exactly what he had done. The dodgy, if sometimes unmemorable, aspects of his career meant that the legacy of Walter Knox — one of Canada's greatest all-time athletes — would forever remain in the shade.

V

BARE-KNUCKLE BRAWLERS AND MEN OF MEANS: BOXING, 1881–1908

AT THE TURN OF THE 20TH CENTURY, BOXING IN NORTH AMERICA underwent a transformation. What had been a violent, working-class, hyper-masculine, and generally illegal activity played out before crowds numbering in the dozens was refurbished into a respectable, "scientific" form of sport *and* entertainment, capturing the imagination of thousands of well-heeled spectators. While the "sweet science" provided the underprivileged in society with an opportunity to escape poverty and anonymity, fighters were often exploited by uncaring promoters and managers whose primary interest was making money.

Going hand in hand with this transformation was the pervasiveness of the racism that marked America's Jim Crow era, tenets of which enjoyed great currency among many Canadians. Although boxing had been one of the few sports where athletes could compete together regardless of their skin colour, this situation was altered at the end of the 19th century, when boxing became a lucrative commercial endeavour and the stakes were much higher.

Such was the case in September 1881, when two men stood ready to fight in a Boston barroom that had been temporarily converted into a boxing ring. The bar was jam-packed with spectators paying $2 a head to watch the match scheduled as a bare-knuckle, fight-to-the-finish contest.

In one corner was George Godfrey, a Black man from Prince Edward Island later called "Old Chocolate" by Boston fans. Never bigger than a light heavyweight, at 170 pounds he often fought much larger opponents. Facing Godfrey in the opposite corner was the famous John L. Sullivan, a ferocious 200-pound Irish American nicknamed the "Boston Strong Boy," who was then just at the very start of a dominating, violent career. Both fighters had stripped down and were about to begin when Sullivan suddenly pulled out of the fight.[1] The boxer had decided not to fight the Black boxer— or, perhaps more accurately, had been persuaded against it by an intervening police officer. It was a policy that Sullivan would observe for years to come after he won the heavyweight boxing crown in 1882.[2] Over the next 10 years, Sullivan ignored Godfrey's numerous challenges and taunts for a title bout. In response to Godfrey's incessant appeals, Sullivan, at least once, retorted acerbically, in highly racist fashion.[3]

Sullivan never faced a Black fighter in the ring; nor would the next four heavyweight champions. The colour line — set at the heavyweight level — reflected a pervasive racism that was present throughout North America. When a white boxer from Canada finally broke the colour line, his reward was the anger and scorn of millions of white fans. Three Black Canadian boxers fought their way to the top levels of the sport and would, as a result, enjoy international renown.

These were unfathomable expectations for Black men during this period. Still, they were never given the chance to truly summit the boxing world, blocked as they were first by white boxers' dogmatic observance of the colour bar, and then, ironically, by the first Black man to wrest the title away from a white Canadian.

THE BARE-KNUCKLE BRAWL

Both Godfrey and Sullivan began their careers in the era of bare-knuckle fighting. As the name implies, the fighters wore no gloves. The matches generally followed the Broughton Rules that had been imported from England.

Apart from punches, these rules also allowed for a range of throws and holds, but prohibited strangling, hitting below the waist, or hitting an opponent when he was down. A round ended when a man was downed by a punch or throw and resumed after 30 seconds, when each man "toed" the scratch line in the centre of the ring.[4] Unless a number of rounds had been agreed on before the fight, the match continued until one fighter could no longer come "up to scratch." Some fights could last a hundred rounds, urged on by large crowds of spectators, "sporting men," and eager gamblers.

This style of fighting was primarily a pre-modern working-class activity and was run by saloonkeepers, ward bosses, and gamblers to make money. For the fighting men, it was an act of survival in a society that emphasized strength, violence, fortitude, and personal status. It offered a way, however limited, for some poor men to rise out of their social conditions. With skill and a bit of luck, it was a way to earn quick money and get some recognition.

Each province in Canada had the power to regulate or even ban bare-knuckle prizefighting. Indeed, most legislative bodies outlawed what at the time was seen as a barbaric activity run by undesirable elements of society. As was often the case, exceptions were made, depending on the class and social status of the combatants. Gloved "boxing" or "sparring" was perceived as a skill-based, rule-governed contest between respectable fighters. With this change, the sport became increasingly popular. And many men from the upper- and middle-class — especially those in garrison towns or those who were members of urban athletic clubs — were drawn to boxing. Some clubs, such as the "Gentlemen's Sparring Club of Ottawa," for instance, won a degree of respectability within that city's upper echelons during the 1880s.

As respectable gloved fighting rose in popularity, crude bare-knuckle fighting — associated as it was with gangsters and gamblers — was on the ropes. In time, those forces driving boxing in the country were able to remove the worst of the rowdy and criminal elements in the sport, while at the same time retaining its hyper-masculinity. Dressed up with amateur rules, boxing became regarded as something that could build better character in a nation that still thought itself in the midst of a crisis in masculinity.

Canada's own cradle of boxing was in the Maritimes. Here, during the late 1880s, organized fighting emerged out of extant and violent rivalries between lumbermen, fishermen, and miners in towns such as Glace Bay, Sydney, and Baie-Sainte-Anne. It was in these areas that the Marquess of Queensberry Rules were formally adopted for the first time in Canada.[5] Under the Queensberry Rules, gloves were mandatory, but could vary in size; wrestling, grappling, or throwing were no longer allowed; rounds were three minutes long, with one-minute breaks between rounds; and a boxer on one knee was considered down and could not be hit. In many ways, these rules made boxing more palatable for some and, more generally, gave the sport an air of respectability.

Celebrities added positively to the perception of boxing. The writer Ernest Hemingway, for example, was a devotee of the ring and boasted that he had sparred with Sam Langford and other professional boxers. He also claimed, "My writing is nothing. My boxing is everything."[6] Baron Rothschild, one of the world's richest men, was a great fan of Tommy Burns, with whom he shadowboxed before inviting Burns and his wife to a lavish garden party.[7]

Riding this wave of respectability, amateur fighters took to the sport in great number. These refined pugilists could spar with light gloves and were motivated, they claimed, by the love of sport and not money. This was, after all, "scientific" boxing. As proof of this, specific weight classes were introduced during this period in an attempt to ensure fairer fights between more evenly matched opponents. By 1903, there were eight generally accepted divisions. Yet, then as now, it was the heavyweight class that generated the greatest interest and publicity. It followed, then, that the purses offered for the heavyweights were commensurate with the popularity of their fights.

"THREE 'COLOURED' ACES"

Around the turn of the century, three Black Canadian boxers from poor communities in the Maritimes were able to carve out successful careers fighting in the American boxing centres. Professional fighting offered Black boxers more than just the possibility of a large payday. The combination of the very public act of prizefighting and the extensive publicity that it generated could give a Black man, facing civil and economic rights diminished by the virulent racism of the era, the rare opportunity to assert his masculinity in the ring and his intelligence through the press. All three men would be international celebrities during their lifetimes.

GEORGE GODFREY

George Godfrey was born on March 30, 1853, in a poor part of Charlottetown, Prince Edward Island. He grew up in the city's "Bog," an area noted for petty crime and poverty. Godfrey, like many other residents of the Bog, was a descendant of slaves who had been brought to the colony by American Loyalists fleeing the American Revolution. In his late teens, Godfrey sought out a better life, leaving Prince Edward Island and moving to Boston. His decision to move to the United States was part of a trend among Black residents across Canada in the post–Civil War era. Some of the migrants were African Americans who had left the United States and moved to Canada before the war to escape slavery and were now returning home. Others were Black Canadians who moved south looking for better economic and social opportunities. Indeed, Godfrey was followed to Boston by other Black boxers from the Bog, including his cousin, George Byers, who would enjoy a successful career as a boxer and trainer.

When he got to Massachusetts, Godfrey worked as a porter for a silk-importing firm and later as a meat carrier in a Boston market.[8] When he wasn't working, Godfrey kept in shape at the Hub City Gym. In 1878, he began taking boxing lessons from the gym's Black owner, John B. Bailey, a man with a reputation as an excellent trainer. Bailey found in his pupil a fighter of exceptional talent, and Godfrey found in his trainer an opportunity. In 1879, after winning the heavyweight division in a local boxing tournament, Godfrey decided to become a prize fighter. By then, he was 26 and married, with six children. Godfrey capitalized on the life that boxing could offer a skilled Black fighter like himself.[9] In an environment full of manipulating white promoters and managers and recklessly spending athletes, the pragmatic Godfrey carefully attended to his own interests and matches. For the transplanted Maritimer, boxing was all business.

Godfrey's status as a Black champion in a white world made him a favourite in Boston's Black community. His legendary fights with the "Minneapolis Star," McHenry Johnson — a Black boxer who outweighed him by 20 pounds — drew up to 500 spectators. His matches against white fighters, such as Canadian Joe "the Hammer" Lannon, among others, drew even more paying customers.[10]

Godfrey's most famous fight, discussed earlier, was one that never happened. In September 1881, Godfrey and John L. Sullivan agreed to a fight to the finish. Precisely why Sullivan walked out of the fight has been debated for years. For his part, Godfrey claimed that Sullivan had conspired with the police to stop the fight because he feared he might lose to the Black boxer. Sullivan's claim that he would never fight any Black boxer begs the question of why he was stripped down and ready to fight Godfrey on that September night.[11] The *Chicago Defender* offered a different reason for the cancellation. The Godfrey–Sullivan match generated tremendous interest and drew fans from as far away as New York and Philadelphia. On fight night, fans with and without tickets rushed the door and, according to the *Defender*, it took "every policeman in Boston to quiet down the gang."[12] Whether it was the police's fear of general mayhem or Sullivan's fear of losing to a Black man that persuaded Sullivan not to fight that night, boxing fans left that Boston barroom disappointed.

Two years later, Godfrey was invited to a tournament sponsored by Richard K. Fox, a boxing fan and publisher of the *National Police Gazette*. The tournament winner would receive the *National Police Gazette* belt representing the "Colored Heavyweight Champion." Nat Fleischer, a noted boxing writer and founder of *Ring Magazine*, called it the "heavyweight championship of the colored race."[13] In February 1883, Godfrey, fighting only his ninth fight, knocked out Charles Hadley in the sixth round to win the belt. In no small touch of irony, the referee of Godfrey's championship match was John L. Sullivan. The title Godfrey won — and held for five years — made his future bouts more profitable, but the existence of a "coloured" championship also served to legitimize the segregationist mentality of men like Sullivan.

Respect for Godfrey increased even as his boxing abilities began to decline. Even in defeat, though, Godfrey's display of courage, endurance, and sportsmanship won him admirers. When the celebrated Black Australian

George Godfrey.

boxer Peter Jackson came to California, promoters tried and failed to get him a fight with Sullivan. It was a measure of Godfrey's reputation that when Sullivan refused, promoters turned to him next. The fight with Jackson, however, seemed like a mismatch from the outset. And it was. After all, Jackson was eight years younger, three inches taller, and 25 pounds heavier. After the fifth round, there was little doubt who would win, but Godfrey fought on. By then, Jackson's gloves were soaked in blood. In the 12th round, Jackson caught Godfrey up against the ropes and "beat him to a pulp."[14] Solely out of fortitude and courage, Godfrey lasted until the 19th round before he admitted defeat.

Not all of Godfrey's opponents were Black, as not all white fighters followed Sullivan's example to avoid good Black fighters. One obvious reason was that racially mixed fights were extremely popular with the paying public, and promoters — then as now — followed the money. Of the white boxers whom Godfrey did face, at least two were Canadians. In March 1890, he knocked out Patsy Cardiff after 16 rounds in a fight in Providence, Rhode Island.[15] Godfrey also had at least three bouts with another fighter from Prince Edward Island, Joe "the Hammer" Lannon: a win, a loss, and a 16-round draw. Regardless of the result, Godfrey's most profitable fights were against white opponents. He won $1,200 beating Jake Ashton (1889), $1,500 against Cardiff (1890), $1,500 facing "Denver" Ed Smith (1890), and $2,200 from Lannon (1894).[16] Such unimaginable sums for a former meat carrier validated the business decision Godfrey had made those many years earlier.

By the 1890s, though, Godfrey was doing less fighting and had instead turned to giving exhibitions and demonstration bouts. He even had Peter Jackson do a series of exhibitions with him. To be sure, Black boxers still faced prejudice, unscrupulous white promoters, and a hostile society at large. Godfrey, however, believed they could use their bodies as a commodity over which they now had some control and could begin to set their price for its use. The Black Maritimer was very much in charge of his own career.

When John B. Bailey died, George Godfrey took over running his gymnasium in Boston.[17] Godfrey himself died of "dropsy" in October 1901, just five years after his last fight against Nick Burley. By the time of his death, he had acquired significant real-estate holdings around Boston, the result of his prudence with his winnings. He left, as he had hoped, a very sizable estate to his children.

GEORGE DIXON

George Godfrey urged one of his impressive young Black protégés to ignore the incessant racist taunts he heard around the ring and concentrate on the opponent facing him. "Race," the older boxer advised, was "nothing more than a barrier to opportunity — find a way around it."[18] George Dixon would.

Born on July 29, 1870, in Africville, a district in northern Halifax on the shore of Bedford Basin, Dixon was the descendant of a family that had fled the United States during the War of 1812 and settled in Nova Scotia. As with Godfrey, the district in which Dixon grew up was poor and racialized. By 1881, the family had joined other Black residents of Halifax who had made the move to Boston. Here, in boxing's mecca, George quickly became enamoured with the ring. As a young boy, he was apprenticed to a well-known photographer, Elmer Chickering, who produced publicity photographs for many of the city's boxers. Dixon's existing interest in boxing was further stimulated by conversations with these boxers. The sweet science, it seemed, enveloped the young Nova Scotian.

Although only about 5'3" tall, Dixon has been described as one of the all-time great fighters, holding, as he did, the world featherweight title for more than seven years.[19] In 1888, Dixon claimed the 105-pound championship of America. By 1890, he held the bantamweight title. The fighter made up for his diminutive size with fast hands, aggressiveness, and quickness in the ring. His professional career would be a mixture of extreme success, adulation, and tragedy.

Dixon spent 18 years as a fighter, during which time he introduced the use of shadowboxing and the heavy bag. He became world famous and one of North America's richest and most popular Black men. His successes were possible because there was less popular resistance to interracial bouts in the lighter weight classes. This relaxation of the colour line allowed

Dixon to fight some of the best white fighters. And he won, earning titles from paperweight to bantamweight and the big paycheques that came with each victory.

Dixon fought and won his first fight against Young Johnson in Halifax when he was only 16. In March 1888, in only his second year of boxing, Dixon fought Patrick Kelly, an unremarkable local fighter, in a 15-round match. The contest was ruled a draw, although most agreed that Dixon had taken the greatest punishment. In the crowd was Tom O'Rourke, then a plasterer but soon to be Dixon's white manager. He saw in Dixon's raw skill and speed and his uncanny fighting instincts the stuff of champions, a champion that he could mould. Boxing connoisseurs have argued about whether Dixon made O'Rourke or the other way around. Regardless, the two formed a formidable combination.

Despite that, O'Rourke, as trainer, was a callous character who treated his fighters well only as long as they had value to him.[20] Complicating their partnership was George's marriage to Tom's sister, Catherine "Katie" O'Rourke. An attractive, intelligent, and thrifty woman, she had announced that she had married Dixon for love and would share all his joys and sorrows to the last.[21] The popular and celebratory reporting of their marriage in the Boston press — even in this era of increasing prejudice — was a measure of the widespread respect that Dixon commanded.[22]

One of the white fighters whom Dixon fought in 1889, Eugene Hornbacher, was the American 115-pound champion. The match was held in a second-floor hotel room in New London, Connecticut. It took Dixon only two rounds to knock Hornbacher out. That fight set up one of Dixon's legendary bouts. In January 1890, Dixon fought a white boxer, Cal McCarthy, to a draw in a hall above a Boston bank for the featherweight championship of America.[23] The fight lasted 70 rounds. Five hundred spectators had crowded in to watch a contest that took four hours and 40 minutes. It was, according to the *Brooklyn Daily Eagle,* "one of the greatest battles ever fought between Featherweights."[24] Despite the accolades, many in attendance felt that the referee — aware of all the money wagered on McCarthy — had stolen a victory from Dixon. However, the draw and its ensuing controversy allowed O'Rourke to claim part of the title for his fighter.[25]

International fight between Nunc Wallace and George Dixon for the bantamweight championship

The Great Nova Scotian George Dixon Knocking Out the English Champion.

Five months later, Dixon was in London, England, where he defeated Edwin "Nunc" Wallace by a knockout in the 18th round to win the Featherweight Championship of the World. In so doing, Dixon became the first North American boxer to go to Britain and win an international title. Dixon and Wallace then toured England in July for a series of exhibition bouts.

Although many in the press praised Dixon as a hero for beating the British fighter, the *National Police Gazette* took the position that Wallace had been an overrated fighter.[26] In this way, the featherweight championship remained a disputed title.

At home, Dixon continued to face racism when he fought a white fighter. His next fight, in Providence, Rhode Island, in October 1890, was against Johnny Murphy, with the featherweight championship at stake. Although Dixon won the bout after 40 rounds, he had to limit much of his fighting to the centre of the ring. If he got close to the ropes, Murphy's supporters would hit at his legs with blackjacks and canes.[27] At times, it felt as though the referee was fighting Dixon as well. In his title defence against Cal McCarthy in 1891, Dixon put the white boxer down with a flurry of punches, but as the referee was counting the downed fighter, McCarthy's cornermen pulled him over to the corner and looked after him. When O'Rourke screamed for a disqualification, the referee told him to be quiet. Unaffected, Dixon knocked McCarthy out in the next round.

Over the next year, Dixon took on other claimants to the featherweight crown. In July 1891, he fought Abe Willis, the Australian boxer. In front of 8,000 fans in San Francisco's Athletic Club, Dixon knocked out Willis in five rounds. Eleven months and about 30 exhibition fights later, Dixon took on the latest British featherweight claimant, Fred Johnson, and knocked him out in the 14th round. Dixon — now dubbed "Little Chocolate" in the press — seemed unstoppable.

In 1892, the Canadian took part in a three-day event called the Carnival of Champions. It was a watershed moment in boxing history. Hosted by the Olympic Club in New Orleans, the carnival featured world-title bouts in the lightweight, featherweight, and heavyweight division. The club wanted to show that the era of violent, working-class, bare-knuckle prizefighting was over and that a new era of respectable "gloved contests" had begun. Although three-quarters of each night's audience was made up of doctors, lawyers, bankers, and successful merchants, the club had enlarged its arena to accommodate 10,000 fans, and Dixon himself had negotiated a block of 850 tickets in the upper gallery for Black fans. Organizers made sure there were enough police in attendance to limit any disturbance by roughs and keep out the few female fans who, dressing as men, attempted to get in to watch the boxers.

While the heavyweight match between John L. Sullivan and "Gentleman" Jim Corbett generated the greatest publicity, Dixon's bout, the day before, resulted in even greater emotion. In that fight, Dixon had beaten the badly overmatched white boxer, Jack Skelly, in his defence of the featherweight title. In a rare Southern mixed-race fight, Dixon put Skelly down four times and dominated the match before it was stopped in the eighth round. Despite the best intentions of the Olympic Club, the use of four-ounce gloves did little to remove the bloody nature of the sport. Unhappy at Skelly's comprehensive defeat, one New Orleans paper assured readers that even "the most blasé fans at the ringside were heard to shudder, and some even turned their heads in disgust as they saw Dixon savagely chopping away at that face already disfigured beyond recognition and heard the ugly half-splashing sound as his blood-soaked glove again and again revisited the bleeding wounds."[28] Unsurprisingly, the symbolism of a Black man crushing a white opponent fired up Southern racism.

Certainly, interracial contests had been controversial before the bout, especially in the South. There, limited Reconstruction efforts to improve the lives of Black citizens after the Civil War had given way to a new era of Southern-imposed segregation and vigilante law. The increased numbers of lynchings of Black men by white mobs reflected the growth of the Jim Crow era.[29] Skelly's loss fed the rising intolerance. No other interracial fight would be permitted in New Orleans until well into the next century.

For his part, Dixon believed that he had to be dominant in the ring so that racist judges could not rob him of a decision and, importantly, the $17,500, winner-take-all purse. Dixon retained his featherweight championship for another seven years, but he never fought south of Kentucky again.[30]

When Dixon defeated Eddie Pierce at Coney Island in 1883, he was at the peak of his career, with a streak of 14 wins, 5 draws, and 3 no-decisions. During the height of popularity, Dixon also starred in his own vaudeville road show. It was a profitable venture that brought in up to $20,000 a year.[31] Yet, the schedule Dixon was forced to keep was taking its toll. Touring the country and fighting exhibition bouts or "come-all" challenges with local toughs placed consistent wear and tear on his body and, specifically, on his hands.[32] On some tours, Dixon took on up to 15 locals. In the year he beat Pierce, Dixon had fought — excluding any of the road-show fights — more than 40 times.[33]

Adding to this untenable workload was Dixon's overindulgence in New York's Black Bohemian lifestyle. A part of the older Tenderloin District, the Black Bohemia district was a mixture of Black vitality and vice, replete with flourishing nightclubs full of Black celebrities, actors, artists, writers, and, of course, posers. Scattered throughout the district were saloons, gambling parlours, dubious hotels, and brothels. For a man with a fondness for alcohol, gambling, and conspicuous consumption, it was a very dangerous place. By 1896, friends and fans alike noticed and were concerned about Dixon's intemperance and physical decline. John L. Sullivan, who had become a friend to Dixon, was likewise concerned. Sullivan observed that the Canadian "got rid of his money faster than any fighter I ever knew, except myself."[34] Sullivan and Dixon were fighting the same personal demons.

Still, Dixon managed to dominate his weight class during the mid-1890s. Although he may have lost the title several times — usually in very dubious decisions — he would often regain it within months. He won the title for the last time in November 1898, beating Dave Sullivan in the 10th round. Dixon defended the title half a dozen more times. His successes in the ring at this twilight period of his career were all the more remarkable given that Dixon was now an alcoholic and Katie O'Rourke had divorced him on the grounds of cruelty.[35] His hard living and out-of-ring problems caught up with him in January 1900, when he lost his title for the last time to Terry McGovern. By then, Dixon's drinking and public behaviour had begun to erode his good public image. In May 1895, he had to be taken off a train in New York Central Station and was charged with being drunk and disorderly.[36]

Dixon fought for smaller purses for six years after losing his title. Hoping to find better opportunities across the Atlantic, he spent two years in Britain, where he showed that even a compromised Dixon was dangerous. In April 1904, he fought "Spike" Robson in a bout in Newcastle, England. The fight was scheduled to last 20 rounds but was stopped by the referee after 11. In it, Dixon had dominated Robson but, as the *National Police Gazette* reported, "knowing the condition of his opponent [Dixon] did not try to finish him."[37]

By May 1905, Dixon had left England, and a year and a half later he was out of boxing and destitute. His appeal to O'Rourke for funds ended with the little boxer being thrown out of the Irishman's saloon. On January 4, 1908, two unidentified men, one white and one Black, carried George Dixon into the Bellevue Hospital in New York City. He told doctors that he had fought his last bout with "John Barleycorn" and had lost. Only two days after having been admitted to Bellevue, George Dixon died of acute alcoholism and inflammatory rheumatism.

SAM LANGFORD

As good as Godfrey and Dixon were, the best boxer to come out of the Maritimes was one who never won a world championship. Sam Langford was born in 1896 in Weymouth Falls, Nova Scotia, a small Black community settled originally by Black Loyalists. Fed up with an abusive, alcoholic father, Sam ran away at the age of 12. During the next few years, he worked in logging camps, as a farmhand, and on a ship as a cabin boy before moving to Boston to live with his sister. In 1901, Langford got a job as a janitor with Joe Woodman, a druggist who was also the operator of the Lennox Athletic Club.[38] Working in the gym under the boxing-savvy Woodman, as he did, Langford was quickly intoxicated with the sport. Soon, the skinny Maritimer would emerge as a boxer himself, one with serious ambitions.

When Langford informed Woodman of his desire to be a professional fighter, the latter suggested that the young man first refine his game against amateurs. Although there were some areas for improvement, Langford was already a formidable combatant; he could take punishment and had a long reach for his size and tremendous power in both fists. Also working in his favour was the crouched fighting style he adopted, a style that made him an elusive opponent.

After three successful amateur fights, Langford won his first professional bout in the spring of 1902, when he knocked out Jack McVicker in five rounds. In 1903, as he built up weight and experience, Langford fought a remarkable two dozen fights against fighters of various races, with only one loss. The 17-year-old then faced Joe Gans, the world lightweight champion in December, less than two weeks after his previous fight. Although the young Canadian shocked boxing fans by beating Gans in 15 rounds — leaving no doubt that he was the better boxer — he did not win the lightweight title.[39] As it happened, both fighters had weighed in just *over* the 135-pound division limit. It was not the last time Langford would miss out on a world title. Adding salt to the wound, a pre-arranged agreement gave Gans $750 for the fight while Langford, the winner, received only $250.

The following year, Langford moved up a weight division and fought Joe Walcott, the world welterweight champion then managed by Tom O'Rourke, in a 15-round match. The referee ruled the fight a draw, but spectators disagreed. The editor of the *New York Illustrated News* believed that Langford had clearly won the fight and should indeed have been crowned the welterweight champion. Once again, Langford missed out.

In April 1910, the Canadian fought the world middleweight champion, Stanley "the Michigan Assassin" Ketchel, in a pre-arranged, no-decision, six-round match in Philadelphia. Although Langford "stunned" Ketchel in the third round, he did not follow up on his advantage; nor did Ketchel when he had Langford briefly in trouble. It was widely assumed that their fight was a preview to a big-money title bout later that year. Before that could happen, however, Ketchel was shot and killed.[40] While his career would last another 16 years, Langford would never get another chance to fight for a recognized world championship.

One factor that kept him from summiting the boxing world was that he had become *too* good; some fighters simply avoided him. In 1906, and weighing just 151 pounds, he had fought the great Jack Johnson, perhaps the most feared boxer then fighting and a man 30-odd pounds heavier than Langford. After 15 unrelenting rounds, the Canadian, with broken nose to prove it, had clearly lost, but he had knocked Johnson down twice during the fight.

Two years later, Johnson became the first Black heavyweight champion of the world. In the years that followed, Johnson refused any rematch with a mature Langford, observing, perhaps correctly, that on any given night, "Sam is just liable to beat me or make it close, and what's the sense of that for the money we'd draw."[41] Johnson knew he could make more money fighting white opponents who were less skilled and much less dangerous. He boasted that he would be the only Black world heavyweight champion. In taking this position, Johnson was almost as controversial a figure in the Black community as in the white. Even during his reign as a world champion, local fans in Boston had their own popular and earnest hero in Sam Langford.[42]

Johnson's refusal as champion to fight Langford was more than a personal affront: it actually violated an agreement that the champion had made earlier and highlighted a problem facing "contenders." Two and a half years after fighting Langford, Johnson found himself in London and out of money as he followed Tommy Burns around the globe, trying to force a title match. The National Sporting Club (NSC) offered Johnson the necessary money to follow Burns to Australia, on one condition: if Johnson fought Burns and won the world heavyweight championship, then his first title defence would be at the club and against Sam Langford.

Johnson defeated Burns but refused to honour his agreement, claiming his manager had signed the letter without Johnson's knowledge and the purse was too small. After the club produced the document with Johnson's signature, the champion simply reneged. Johnson claimed that Langford could not meet his $30,000 appearance fee. In response, the NSC announced that Langford's claim to the world heavyweight title would be recognized in England. This was, according to the NSC, because Johnson had failed "to live up to the articles of agreement that he had signed."[43] In 1908, however, there was no recognized international regulatory organization in professional boxing. As a result, a world champion could decide himself where, when, and who he would fight (or not fight). Pride, purses, and self-interest would decide if or when a champion took on a contender. Breathing that rarefied air as a Black world heavyweight champion in 1908, Johnson had no interest in fighting other Black boxers.

Jack Johnson's behaviour after winning the title had a negative impact on other Black boxers in several ways. His flamboyant lifestyle and refusal to act as subservient to the white establishment fuelled white hostility toward any mixed-race fights. Johnson's unwillingness to meet the top Black contenders, such as Langford, Sam McVey, and Joe Jeanette, led the International Boxing Union in November 1913 to declare the heavyweight championship vacant. The following month, Johnson's choice of a Black opponent to meet the Union's demands was "Battling" Jim Johnson, a journeyman fighter. The poorly fought bout ended in a draw and Jack Johnson retained his title until his loss to Jess Willard in 1915. After that, the white establishment would not entertain another Black contender until Joe Louis won the title in 1937.

American promoters began to bar Black boxers from title fights in all divisions. Black fighters were likewise barred from interracial bouts among leading contenders. As a result, men like Langford had to fight the same Black boxers repeatedly, for modest purses. In fact, he fought five different Black opponents (Harry Wills, Sam McVey, Joe Jeanette, Jeff Clark, and Jim Barry) a total of 72 times. These were all excellent boxers and big men.[44] Still, frequent fights between the same opponents in the same venues along the famous "Chitlin' Circuit" (noted for its Black music, theatres, and culture) meant less excitement and, unsurprisingly, less money. One solution was for the boxers to take their fights outside of the United States to places such as England, France, and Australia. With far more receptive and at least *less* racist audiences, the boxers were able to fight for different national titles.

Benefiting from European interest in the American style of boxing, Langford was invited to fight in front of the NSC in London in April 1907. It was advertised as a fight for the vacant British and Commonwealth middleweight championship of the world. His opponent was Tiger Smith, a Welsh fighter, whom Langford knocked out in the 4th round of a 20-round match for $2,000.[45] The Canadian fought at the club again in a June bout held as part of a boxing carnival. He knocked out Geoff Thome in the first round.[46] Langford would return to the club a year later, where he defeated William "Iron" Hague and claimed the British heavyweight title. It seemed that distant shores offered Black boxers much more than their own domestic boxing scene did.

Other Black boxers were able to capitalize on French interest in American boxing. Sam McVey, for instance, fought more than 30 matches, primarily in Paris, with additional bouts in England, Belgium, and Portugal. It was much the same for Joe Jeanette, who in 1909 fought in Paris nine times and on four other occasions in London. Although these sojourns may have been somewhat satisfying, the quest for a world heavyweight championship was over for these Black fighters. Their competitors would now be any Black boxer not named Jack Johnson, or the few second-level white boxers willing to cross the colour line.

This meant more travel. At the end of 1911, for example, Langford, McVey, Jim Barry, Dan "Porky" Flynn, and several other North American

Joe Hartnet and Sam Langford with Bill Lynch's travelling circus.

boxers headed to Australia. Over an 18-month stretch, Langford fought 11 matches, 6 against McVey and 3 against Barry, often defending or reclaiming his "colored heavyweight championship of the world" title while adding the Australian heavyweight crown to his résumé.

In the years after the Australian tour, Langford continued a heavy schedule of fights. The Canadian fought between 10 and 20 matches a year against the best Black boxers and some of the earlier "great white hopes" — those white boxers whom the public envisioned as capable of beating Jack Johnson. The punishment of such a schedule took its toll.

In June 1917, Langford lost sight in his left eye when his opponent, Fred Fulton, landed a right hook to his head that Langford said felt "like a thousand needles shoved into his skull."[47] The punch had detached his retina at a time when doctors could do little for him. Two months later, though, he fought and *beat* Andre Anderson, a boxer who had knocked down Jack Dempsey. And he didn't stop there. Remarkably, with no sight in his left eye and a cataract emerging in the right, Langford fought over a hundred more times.

Not unlike Dixon, Sullivan, and so many other pugilists of his time, Langford went through money as quickly as he earned it. This meant that he had to continue fighting lesser-known opponents for smaller purses. Physically, the Canadian was breaking down. This was certainly the case when he fought Kid Savage for the heavyweight championship of Mexico in 1923. Despite seeing only shadows out of his one good eye, Langford still managed to knock out Savage in the first round. Incredibly, a month after beating Savage, he knocked out Andres Balsas front of a crowd of 20,000 in Mexico City's bullring to win the heavyweight championship of Spain.[48] It would be Langford's last title.

The 43-year-old Langford retired from boxing in August 1925. Many years later, in 1944, the *New York Herald Tribune's* sportswriter Al Laney found him living in a cheap room in Harlem. Langford was completely blind, penniless, and very much alone. Laney's sympathetic article on Langford, titled "A Dark Man Laughs," hastened the establishment of a charitable fund for the old fighter. Approximately $10,000 was raised to fund successful eye surgery for the forgotten boxer.

For his part, however, Langford never felt sorry for himself. When Laney visited his once-famous friend one Christmas Eve, Langford cheerfully surmised, "I got a geetar and a bottle of gin, and money in my pocket to buy Christmas dinner. No millionaire in the world got more than that, or anyhow they can't use more."[49]

Although comparing fighters from across eras and categories may be a hopeless task, Langford's name was remembered for a time by those who had seen him fight. Hype Igoe, the famous boxing writer of the *New York Journal*, believed that Langford was the greatest fighter, pound for pound, who ever lived. Joe Woodman, Langford's manager, was even more certain and thought that Langford would have eaten Joe Louis.[50] In 1955, Langford was enshrined in the CSHF. He died the following year in a nursing home in Cambridge, Massachusetts. In 2007, ESPN's boxing aficionado, Kieran Mulvaney, wrote that Langford was "the greatest fighter almost nobody knows."[51]

TOMMY BURNS

Gentleman Jim Jeffries fought his last world-title defence in 1904 against Canadian Jack Munro, after which he announced his retirement. Jeffries suggested a tournament to find his successor, but he insisted that the two best Black fighters — Jack Johnson and Sam Langford — not be allowed to participate. White heavyweight champions, like Jeffries and John L. Sullivan before him, continued the racist custom of refusing to fight Black boxers. The man who finally broke that policy, and would be hated for doing so, was Canadian Noah Brusso — better known as Tommy Burns.

At 5'7" and seldom fighting over 175 pounds, Burns was the smallest fighter to win the world heavyweight title. Over an eight-year period, from 1901 to 1909, Burns won and defended five separate titles, including said world heavyweight championship.[52] He was also the only world champion never to have a manager.

Noah Brusso was born into a large, poor, German Canadian family near Hanover, Ontario. The 12th of 13 children, he grew up in a four-room log cabin. Brusso left school at 10 after an incident that revealed much about the young boy and his environment. Noah and Sam Hill, a larger boy, were finalists in an unofficial bare-knuckle tournament at his school. Their fight was watched by dozens of students and local adults, who cheered on the fighters and gambled on the results. After an hour of boxing, Brusso finally knocked Hill down for good. Brusso was delighted. His parents were less so and were furious that the school would condone children fighting. Brusso's mother, Sophia, decided to home-school him while he worked part time.

Two years later, the recently widowed Sophia Brusso remarried, choosing an abusive alcoholic as her new husband. At 17, Noah Brusso decided it was time to leave his troubled home. He found work in a Hespeler wool mill and played professional lacrosse for Galt. Brusso was an exceptional goalie and a willing fighter. With the number of fighting ejections, however, he became something of a liability for his team. As a result, on top of the $20 per game that players received, Brusso earned a $50 bonus for every game in which he was not ejected. With Brusso's temper under check, Galt won the 1898 Canadian junior lacrosse championship.

It was while playing lacrosse that Brusso took his first public stand against racial intolerance. Galt had lined up an exhibition game with an Indigenous club, the "Seneca Indians," only to have its players refuse to play against an Indigenous team. Brusso disagreed. He argued that Indigenous players had invented the game and were the best in the world, and that the Galt players could learn much. Brusso was even prepared to play alone, if necessary. Embarrassed by their goalie, the rest of the Galt team grudgingly took the field for what turned out to be one of the best games of the season. The *Galt Weekly Reporter* claimed that the "Indians were gentlemanly through their visit and we will welcome them again."

The next year, Brusso played for the Woodstock Beavers, using an equally abrasive style. When the lacrosse season was over, he drifted down to Sarnia where, at 130 pounds, he got a job as a bouncer in a riverside tavern. That he was an efficient bouncer spoke to his ability as a fighter who could control larger men. Then, while working as a baggage handler on a Great Lake steamer, he had a fight with the ship's steward and jumped ship when it docked at Detroit. It was a decision that changed his life.

By 1900, he had met Sam Biddle, a former Canadian lightweight champion and bare-knuckle fighter with a ruthless disposition. Under Biddle's guidance, Brusso became a puncher, although with limited defensive skills. His first fight against a professional boxer, Freddie "Thunderbolt" Thornton, a Black fighter from Windsor, was unplanned. Brusso and friends went to watch Thornton fight, only to find out that his opponent was unavailable. A call was made to the audience for a replacement, and Brusso's friends persuaded him to take up the challenge. He knocked Thornton out in five rounds and received $1.25 for his efforts, enough to buy his friends cigars. The fight, as Brusso recalled, gave him "a much-needed boxing lesson for the first two rounds."[53] Still, the Canadian knew he needed to develop better defensive skills and ring management. He also quickly learned that by fighting a Black boxer, he would anger many white fans.

In 1902, Brusso won a dozen times, fighting in Detroit against local Michigan fighters, including African American boxers. Entry-level fighters received small purses. For nine prize fights and three exhibition matches, Brusso earned $885, more than most workers' salaries but still less than $100 a fight. Real money came to fighters who had developed credibility, a winning record, and a name. Brusso started to gain respect when in December, he knocked out Tom McCune in seven rounds to win the Middleweight Championship of Michigan.[54] He had also earned the enmity of McCune supporters, who belted out racist chants before the bout.[55]

To be clear, Brusso was a complex man with strikingly different personalities inside and outside of the ring. He used racist and demeaning language, especially when baiting his opponents in the ring, but he also defied social conventions by not only fighting Black boxers but also hiring them as sparring partners. A man easily bored, Brusso sought risks outside the ring. He filled his spare time with gambling at cards or at the track. Some claimed he made as much money gambling as fighting. He certainly lost as much. He did not, however, frequent bars and saloons, as he wanted to avoid encountering some drunk looking to make a name for himself. Brusso didn't want to hurt a hand outside the ring.

Brusso was also a clothes horse. When in public, he normally wore an expensive suit. Raised in poverty as he had been but now with some money, Brusso wanted to appear the gentleman and a man of means. He further developed this persona when he published a book on boxing.[56] In the end, though, his acute business sense would not keep him out of poverty.

The year 1903 started poorly for Brusso, with a 10-round loss to the first left-hander he faced, Mike Shreck. Brusso was able to retain his Michigan middleweight title, however, because Shreck was a heavyweight. Brusso learned well from his mistakes and would not lose another bout for two years.

During this time, Brusso underwent something of a transformation. One fight in January 1904 would change the trajectory for the Canadian fighter. His opponent that night, Ben O'Grady, came close to dying from injuries suffered at the hands of Brusso during the bout. In the third round, Brusso knocked O'Grady out. The latter's head struck the wooden floor hard when he collapsed. He suffered a severe concussion and was in a coma for four days. The police put Brusso in jail on a charge of assault pending O'Grady's outcome. If O'Grady died, Brusso was told, the boxer would face a manslaughter charge.[57] Fortunately, O'Grady recovered enough to be discharged, although he had suffered long-term brain trauma. After that tragic fight, Brusso began fighting under a pseudonym that boxing fans the world over would come to know: Tommy Burns.

Burns did not just change his name; he changed his residence. The Canadian chose Chicago because he saw it as a vibrant city with a reputation as one of the country's best fight towns. After only a few fights in the Windy City, Burns fought Tony Capponi, a tough Italian American boxer. After their first bout ended in a draw, Burns was propositioned by gangsters: if he threw the next match, he would get $1,000. If he did not, they would break his legs. Burns chose to go ahead and win the fight despite the very serious and credible threat, but he left Chicago immediately, for fights in Tacoma and Salt Lake City. Burns would never fight in Chicago again.

In a poker game after one of his Tacoma fights, Burns won the deed to a gold mine in Alaska. Perhaps because it was even farther from Chicago, he decided to head north to Nome. Once there, however, Burns quickly lost most of his money, playing poker. To get a grubstake for his mining enterprise, Burns drummed up the idea of staging a prize fight with a local fighter. This turned out to be "Klondike Mike" Mahoney, a former lumberman who had become a local hero in Alaska, carrying supplies up the Chilkoot Pass.[58]

Mike was half a foot taller and 50 pounds heavier than Burns. Moreover, he claimed home field rights to set the style they would fight — lumberjack style, with both kicking and punching allowed. After the second round, Burns told his ring man, Billy Woods, a Black boxer, that Mahoney was "going to kill me if I don't knock him out." Woods's response was that if he did, "this crowd is going to kill us both." The problem was solved in the next round when Klondike Mike planted a kick to Burns's solar plexus, putting him down and out of the fight. Burns maintained, retrospectively, that with the right trainer, Mahoney could have been a world heavyweight champion.[59]

After exploring the mine claim, driving off gunmen, and finding out that boxing was easier than mining, Burns and Woods decided to leave Alaska in the summer of 1904. Woods, from Los Angeles, convinced Burns that California was the best place for a fighter. And Burns had promised Woods a bout. So it was that one of his first fights after his Alaskan adventure was a 15-round draw with Billy Woods. This was Burns's seventh fight against a Black opponent, a commendable record for the time. Yet, during the match, Burns himself yelled racist slurs at Woods in an attempt to anger him and throw him off his game.

After the fight, Burns apologized and offered to buy Woods dinner. It was an example of how Burns could compartmentalize his behaviour. One of the people very offended by Burns's friendship with Woods was his new wife, Julia Keating, whom Burns called Jewel. He had invited the Black boxer to dinner, only to have Jewel erupt with anger. "It's okay to have *them* in the gym," she reportedly told Burns, "but there'll be no coloreds in this house."[60] Woods cut the couple's argument short by leaving. From then on, the men met socially at Burns's pub or Woods's home.

Burns fought a series of middling opponents during the summer of 1904 before he ran into a really good one in Milwaukee: "Philadelphia" Jack O'Brien, one of the best light-heavyweight boxers in America and a fan favourite. Burns had arrived in Wisconsin expecting to fight Hugo Kelly, only to find the promoter had changed the fighters. O'Brien was a great ring tactician, a polished boxer, and a devastating puncher. Burns was likely unprepared for this calibre of fighter, but the promoter assured him that it was just an exhibition and O'Brien would put on a good show. No one told O'Brien. After six rounds of dishing out punishment, O'Brien won by decision.

Burns felt that he had been double-crossed, and he would carry a grudge against O'Brien for many years. He may have ended the year with his pride hurt, but it had been a financially successful year. Burns's nine fights had earned him about $2,000.

The year 1905 began well for Burns. He knocked out the Indigenous heavyweight, "Indian Joe" Schildt. He then fought one of the best middleweights around, Jack "Twin" Sullivan. After 20 rounds, the contest was ruled a draw. The Canadian press was following Burns's improvement closely. Reporters believed Burns had "made an excellent showing in his first important go and placed himself in the first rank of his class."[61] Some fighters agreed.

One boxer who approached him for a fight was another Canadian, Dave Barry, from Montreal. Barry, who was the U.S. Pacific Coast Middleweight Champion, hoped that beating Burns could make him a contender for the world middleweight title. The two Canadians were friendly when they first met, but that ended when Barry tried to seduce Jewel. After Jewel reported this in detail to Burns, the fight took on a whole new dimension. The bad blood was evident to the fans watching the 20 rounds and seeing the punishment dished out by both men. Most observers agreed with the referee's decision in favour of Burns, but Barry was outraged and demanded a rematch. The rematch would have to wait, for Burns had other fighters lined up.

The first was Hugo Kelly, a Chicago fighter who was among the few who had defeated "Philadelphia" Jack O'Brien. Kelly and Burns fought to a draw in Chicago and then took the train to Los Angeles, where they again fought to a draw. All the while, Burns was having difficulty in getting down to the middleweight limit of 158 pounds. The effort it took him to make the limit was leaving him with little energy late in the fights. All the while, Barry was hounding Burns for a rematch, taunting him about his recent record of two wins in his last seven bouts. Burns eventually acquiesced and knocked Barry out in the 20th round, but Burns was in his last days as a middleweight. His last fight at that weight was against Jack "Twin" Sullivan, one of the two men to claim the middleweight title after the title holder, Tom Ryan, suddenly retired. Beating Sullivan could give Burns a partial claim to the title, but once again, by the time he made weight, he was running on fumes. He lasted the 20 rounds before being outpointed. Still, his fights against better boxers earned him $6,240 but his struggle making weight left him with a mediocre record. It was time to move up a division.

HEAVYWEIGHT CHAMPION OF THE WORLD

Burns's opportunity to fight for the world heavyweight championship came after Jim Jeffries, the title holder, retired in February 1905. Burns's apparent mediocrity made him seem less of a threat to other contenders, including Marvin Hart. When Hart knocked out Jack Root, he became the new, if disputed, heavyweight champion.[62] Like the previous heavyweight title holders, Hart immediately announced that he would not fight a title bout with any Black fighter. In particular, he wanted no part of Jack Johnson, whom Hart had beaten earlier in a highly controversial bout. Instead, the champion wanted a few easy fights to make money and savour the championship. After easily beating a relatively unknown boxer, Pat Callahan, Hart and his manager thought the much smaller Burns would be an easy man to beat and signed him to a bout.

Burns weighed 162 pounds; Hart 196.[63] Burns, knowing Hart's temper, baited him both before and during the fight. Taunting Hart, he claimed that "the only really rough athletes were Canadians who played lacrosse as roughly and toughly as the Mohawks ever did."[64] During the fight, Burns used his quickness and skill as a boxer to evade Hart's angry rushes. The fight went 20 rounds, but Burns was declared the clear winner. The crowd was small and Hart's share of the purse larger at 70 percent. Burns got just $750. Now, however, Burns could dictate whom he would fight.

Although Burns could claim to be the world heavyweight champion, many in the fight world remained unconvinced. As there were no governing bodies in the sport at this time to rule on who was champion, most were crowned via popular consensus, as expressed in the newspapers of the day. Burns understood that he needed to convince the many unbelievers that he was indeed the legitimate champion. His solution was to fight frequently against *all* contenders. He issued his challenge in the *National Police Gazette*: "I will defend my title as heavyweight champion of the world against all comers, none barred. By this I mean white, Black, Mexican, Indian or any other nationality without regard to colour, size, or nativity."[65] Moreover, as "world" champion, he felt the need to tour the globe, fighting the best boxers in different countries. He began in the United States where, like Dixon, and John L. Sullivan before him, he dabbled in vaudeville, appearing on stages across North America.[66]

Just over a month after beating Hart, Burns fought two challengers on the same night in a public relations event designed to show his ability and self-confidence. Neither of his two opponents, Jim O'Brien of Pittsburgh or James J. Walker of Battle Creek, made it to the second round of their bouts.[67] It was the start of an active defence of his title. During Burns's two and a half years as champion, he defended his title 13 times, almost always against men much bigger than himself. In 11 of the fights, he knocked out his opponent. The only opponent he did not knock out was "Philadelphia" Jack O'Brien, who had spent more of his time in the ring evading Burns than fighting him.

Even after Burns successfully defended his title five times, many still viewed Jim Jeffries as the legitimate champion. This was made clear when the Australian heavyweight champion, Bill Squires — a man many fight fans believed the best boxer in the world — came to California in 1907. Squires had really come to America to fight Jeffries and had dismissed Burns as a "faker."[68] However, when Jeffries refused to come out of retirement, Squires agreed to fight Burns. Although Squires might have underestimated his opponent, Burns had not. The latter had studied the films of Squires's fights, talked to people who had seen him fight, and deeply analyzed the Aussie's fighting style. Burns was ready.

The fight drew 9,000 spectators and the heavy money was on Squires. Burns knocked the Australian down three times in a fight that ended two minutes and eight seconds into the first round. Now, no respectable boxing fan could mistake Burns as a "faker."

Four months later, Sam Fitzpatrick, Jack Johnson's manager, telegraphed Burns about a potential tilt. The Canadian did not immediately say no. Instead, Burns indicated that for the right contract, he would fight Johnson. Johnson would fight Burns, Fitzpatrick declared, for 50 percent of the gate. Burns replied with his own terms: he would fight the Black boxer, provided that he got 75 percent of the gate, win, lose, or draw. It was similar to the deal Hart had given him and Burns was adamant that he would get his share. Burns was, nevertheless, prepared to break with the current custom of white heavyweights and fight a Black man. He was prepared to do so when he returned to America.[69] There were other possible white claimants whom Burns could have fought, but these plans fell through when those boxers demanded a 50 percent split. It was, for the manager-less Burns, a price too steep.

With few other options in North America — excluding Black fighters, of course — Burns's solution was to take his title to the rest of the boxing world. When he arrived in England, fight fans were underwhelmed: Burns seemed too small, too fat, and too American. After accepting the NSC's offer of £2,400 to fight the English boxer James Gunner Moir, he insulted club members by demanding to be paid in advance. The club overlooked such perceived impudence, focusing on the task at hand: crowning an Englishman as the new heavyweight champion. Most expected this result. Yet, once the fight commenced, Burns quickly took control. Burns worked inside on Moir's body and by the eighth round, Moir looked like a beaten man. Burns knocked him down and out in the 10th round. After the match, the *Sporting News* praised Burns and his American style of fighting. Others believed the fight was one-sided not because of Burns's ability, but rather because of Moir's incompetence.

After beating Moir, Burns put aside plans to return to North America. The money and the opportunities in Europe were too good to pass up. Not only was Burns earning more money in the ring than he ever had, but he was also making even more by performing in the music halls of London and going on tour with the film of his fight.

In defence of his title, Burns took on two promising fighters in 1908. Both fights went very much according to plan. He knocked out Jack Palmer, the former British heavyweight champ, in the fourth round of a fight held in a London music hall. He then crossed over to Dublin where, on St. Patrick's Day, he dropped the Irish champion, Jem Roche, in less than two minutes into the first round, for a purse of almost $12,000. A month later, he was in Paris to take on Joseph "Jewey" Smith. This fight lasted five rounds. Burns finished his European campaign with a rematch against Bill Squires. Although a more balanced match, Burns finally put him down in the eighth round. At most of these fights, Jack Johnson purportedly had a front-row seat and incessantly taunted Burns throughout the matches. Whether this was a case of romance lusting after fact, Burns must have known that there was a legitimate contender waiting for him.

In early 1908, Burns passed on the chance to fight Johnson at the NSC for a purse of £2,500 with a side stake of £3,000. Burns indicated that he wanted a purse of £7,000 with his share a guaranteed £6,000. At the same time, Burns was scornful of any suggestion that his refusal to fight Johnson left the heavyweight title vacant. As far as Burns was concerned, "Johnson's claims to the championship are just as strong as would be those of a Yankee Socialist to the throne of England."[70] Burns believed that if Johnson really wanted to fight for the heavyweight championship, he should accept any terms offered.

To be fair to Burns, despite the lopsided terms on offer, he was the only heavyweight champion who had been willing to give a Black boxer a chance. Perhaps Johnson was reluctant to accept Burns's terms because he had heard that Burns's negotiations to hold a title bout with the Black fighter Sam McVey had fallen apart when no promoter would guarantee Burns's demand of $11,000.

Burns's apparent greed when it came to fighting a Black man caught the ire of many, including Edward VII. The king believed Tommy Burns to be a "Yankee bluffer" and the terms he proffered for fighting a Black boxer outrageous. Edward declared, "I shall take every means in my power to stop the battle between him and Johnson if it is arranged with the understanding that Burns is to receive $30,000, win, lose or draw."[71] The king did not, it would appear, take counsel with the Black boxer himself.

IT TAKES A MIGHTY BIG MAN TO KNOCK JACK JOHNSON DOWN

Unknown to the public, Burns and Johnson had agreed to a fight in Australia in a match promoted by Hugh "Huge Deal" McIntosh. Burns would get $30,000, Johnson $5,000, and the fight would take place at Rushcutters Bay in Sydney on Boxing Day, 1908, when three American battleships with 4,000 sailors would be in port. McIntosh wanted Burns to fight several Australian boxers to build up interest in Burns versus Johnson. Only then would the championship bout be officially announced. The first of the preliminary bouts was a rematch against Bill Squires that almost ended Burns's title run. Burns was out of shape after his long time afloat and, more importantly, he had suffered a bout of influenza that left him seeing double. By the fifth round, Burns was in trouble. He was taking a beating and having a hard time seeing clearly. By the 11th round, Burns was staggering. Fortunately for the Canadian, Squires was even more exhausted, and Burns began to take over the fight. Two rounds later, Burns put the Australian down three times, the last one for the count. Burns was still champ but for some observers, Burns had shown important signs of weakness.

The next fight, just nine days later, was against an up-and-coming heavyweight, Billy Lang. McIntosh had been doing well promoting Burns's fights, for this bout drew a crowd of 15,000 in Melbourne. In the second round, Lang caught Burns with a solid punch that knocked him down. It was the first time he had been on the canvas since winning the title from Hart. After returning to his feet, Burns moved in close to Lang and pounded away on his body. When Lang was counted out in the sixth, it was the eighth consecutive contender knocked out by Burns in his extended title defence. The main event, however, was still to come.

The Battle of Rushcutters Bay on Boxing Day has typically been portrayed as a one-sided contest dominated by the larger, faster, and stronger Johnson. Jack London called it a "slaughter" and claimed that Burns never landed a blow. Certainly, Burns suffered the majority of the punishment and Johnson's masterful defence blocked most of Burns's punches. Throughout the fight, Johnson played the role of a predator toying with his prey. And to those ringside — whom Johnson was constantly smiling at and talking to — this was exactly how it appeared. The precious, if grainy film footage of the fight that exists also bears witness to the apparent one-sidedness of the tilt. What was not known by spectators was that in the lead-up to the fight, Burns had been bedridden for a week by something doctors felt was influenza or perhaps a form of jaundice. Although he did not postpone the fight, because of the thousands of tickets sold, by Boxing Day Burns was down to only 163 pounds, compared with Johnson's 212.[72] The police were probably correct in stepping in at the 14th round to end the match. Johnson, however, did not leave the ring unscathed.

At some point during the fight, Burns broke Johnson's ribs. After telling the post-fight press scrum that none of Burns's punches had hurt him in the least, Johnson then slipped over to Manly Hospital to have doctors treat his broken ribs. While there, he began urinating blood, and his hospital stay was close to a week. Attending doctors, however, were sworn to secrecy.

For his part, Burns stayed in Australia for the next 14 months. He did little but eat, drink, and gamble at the racetrack, where he lost all the money he had made at Rushcutters Bay. Without boxing, he lacked a tether. He fought half a dozen times in the decade after losing his title, but he did so with little conviction. He had arranged for a fight with Sam Langford in the fall of 1909. Both fighters were already looking beyond the fight and assumed that, should they win, a meeting with Johnson would surely follow.[73] Before the fight, however, Burns hurt his knee playing lacrosse, and the match was put off.

Unfortunately for Burns, in the months and years after his loss to Johnson, he was once again regarded as something of an imposter in heavyweight boxing. He was dismissed by sportswriters and historians as a mediocre champion. However, this uncharitable assessment was at odds with the facts: Burns defended his title 13 times, recording eight straight knockouts! One factor that complicates Burns's career was that he did not *look* like a heavyweight boxer. Indeed, Burns was not a true heavyweight. He was essentially a light-heavyweight boxer who fought and beat heavyweights. It must be remembered that when he fought Johnson, he gave away 50 pounds to the Black boxer. Still, Burns was a more dangerous and thoughtful fighter than his appearance may have suggested.

There was also his nationality. The sportswriter Red Wilson claimed that a lot of American reporters did not like the fact that Burns was Canadian.[74] Indeed, as of writing, Burns remains the only Canadian-born world heavyweight boxing champion. In Britain, he was disliked by many, including the British monarch, who mistook him for being American. Yet, the real albatross pinning down Burns's legacy had less to do with his size or nationality and more to do with race. Not *his*, of course, but that of his opponents.

Burns's willingness to break the colour line made him a pariah. He had broken custom from earlier American fighters such as John L. Sullivan and Jim Jeffries, who used racism as a principle. Burns's move to fight Johnson cracked open the door, ever so slightly, to allow Black boxers the ostensible opportunity of fighting for the world heavyweight championship. It was part of an ugly period of boxing that saw Jim Jeffries come out of retirement to play the "Great White Hope" who would wrest the title from Johnson. He didn't, of course. And complicating the narrative was the fact that Johnson himself enforced the colour line and refused to fight any Black boxer for his first five years as champion.[75] And so, deserving as a certain Black boxer from Weymouth Falls, Nova Scotia, was, there would be no Langford versus Johnson II.[76]

VI

PEERLESS PERCY AND THE MATCHLESS SIX: AMSTERDAM, 1928

ON AUGUST 27, 1928, 200,000 FANS GATHERED AT TORONTO'S UNION Station and along the route to Sunnyside Park to see Canada's Olympians. The crowd was particularly enthusiastic about welcoming home six young women who had done the country proud in Amsterdam.[1] Jane Bell (a.k.a. "Calamity Jane"), Ethel Catherwood, Myrtle Cook, Fanny "Bobbie" Rosenfeld, Ethel Smith, and Jean Thompson constituted Canada's women's track and field team, and their successes at the Games had captured the imagination of the nation. The press crowned them "the Matchless Six." Five of the six carried individual gold medals away from the Games. As a team, they had outscored their closest rival, the United States, by 26 to 20 points. Four received a gold medal in the 4 x 100 metres.[2] They were the best women's athletic team in the world.

The mood was much the same in Vancouver, where another equally successful, if unassuming, Olympian received a similar welcome home. Percy Williams had, despite his slender stature and relative inexperience, won the 100- and 200-metre sprints in Amsterdam. Now, "Peerless Percy" was the world's fastest human. Williams was greeted by Vancouver's mayor, L.D. Taylor, and British Columbia's premier, Simon Fraser Tolmie, who paraded him through the streets of the city. The event was broadcast on live radio. The city presented the young amateur with a new car — a sporty blue Graham-Paige coupe — and a trust fund was set up to pay for his education.[3] It was heady times for these seven young athletes who, two months earlier, were virtually unknown in Canada.

Few expected such an impressive haul. In early 1926, for instance, sportswriter H.H. Roxborough had written an article in *Maclean's Magazine* titled, "Where Are Canada's Field Athletes?" Roxborough compared the dismal record of Canadian track and field Olympic athletes in 1920 and 1924 with the international success of athletes from earlier decades. The article lauded those nearly mythological names — all men — such as Billy Sherring (gold medallist in the 1906 Olympic marathon), George Goulding (world-record race-walker), George Gray (world shot put champion for 17 years), Tom Longboat (the nation's most famous Indigenous runner), and Walter Knox (the all-rounder of track and field).[4] By contrast, Canada had won no medals in track and field in the 1924 Olympics and only one in 1920.[5] There seemed few signs that 1928 would be much better.

It was in the context of this concern about declining Canadian athletics that six remarkable young women and an unlikely male sprinter captured gold medals and Canadian hearts, drew international acclaim, and made themselves household names across Canada. Their stunning performances, in sharp contrast to the previous disappointments in earlier Olympics, help explain the huge crowd of admirers that welcomed them home. Williams, a short, skinny, shy sprinter from outside Ontario, had been continually underestimated by the Canadian press and coaches alike in the lead-up to the Games. And although women had been working for years to change the misogynistic mindset of the all-male International Olympic Committee (IOC) and allow greater female participation, Roxborough could never have anticipated what sort of success "the Matchless Six" would achieve in the Netherlands. All seven of the Canadian athletes had overcome significant social obstacles in reaching their podiums; all had to deal with forms of exclusion and athletic stereotyping.

WOMEN'S SPORTS AND THE CANADIAN NATION

A transformation in Canadian attitudes concerning the value of women's sports had been under way since the turn of the 20th century. This was, in many ways, a response to the rapid urbanization and waves of immigration that occurred in Canada's major centres. As an increasing number of young, rural Canadian women and new immigrants sought urban employment with fixed hours and a living wage, many businesses — such as department stores, railroad companies, textile mills, banks, and insurance companies — responded by providing cultural and recreational opportunities for their female employees. This transactional policy was then called "industrial recreation" (or corporate welfare practices). For instance, a young woman who started as a clerk, secretary, or salesperson could hope to trade company loyalty for career advancement, economic security, and personal enjoyment.[6] In return, her place of work became, in every way, central to her life.

This trend was accelerated with the First World War. It was, after all, a catalyst in the Women's Suffrage Movement. In 1917, the Wartime Elections Act granted some women the right to vote in federal elections. Throughout the war, women had been joining the work force en masse. Some 35,000 women, according to the Imperial Munitions Board, were working in munition factories in Ontario and Quebec. In this direct manner, the war, via munition factories, opened up opportunities for women to try new things, including engaging in team sports.

During the war, numerous Canadian firms had also begun to subsidize amateur athletics and, by extension, the growing pool of young women who participated in them. As early as 1918, for example, Eaton's had established two clubs in Toronto for its women employees, one for those older than 20 years and one for those 20 and younger. Four years later, the company joined the two clubs with other activities to form the Eaton's Girls' Club and offered members the use of a gymnasium, library, and sewing, dining, and sitting rooms.[7] For a $3 membership fee, women could, among other activities, join physical culture classes, play basketball, or use the swimming pool, all while availing themselves of the guidance of female instructors. The hiring of female instructors became more common with the influx of women into the new field of physical education.[8] Eaton's branches followed a similar practice. The Winnipeg store, founded in 1905, was rather in the vanguard; by 1913, it had already organized a women's baseball team.

Other firms in western Canada, such as the Hudson's Bay Company, adopted similar practices, providing recreational and sporting opportunities for its employees, many of whom were women. By 1915, its Winnipeg store had constructed a nearby athletic facility that included five tennis courts.[9] Other branches followed suit, in Regina, Yorkton, Edmonton, Lethbridge, Kamloops, and Vancouver. By 1924, the women's basketball team from the Hudson Bay's Edmonton store claimed to be the best "100 percent mercantile" team in the province.

Smaller firms with fewer resources began sponsoring newly emerging commercial and industrial basketball and softball leagues for women. One example was Patterson's Chocolate Company, a firm that not only funded company teams but also hired Fanny Rosenfeld and sponsored her athletic activities. Aware of the publicity she generated, the company organized a club, the Pats Athletic Club, around her.[10] With all these developments, newspapers, too, had to change their tune. Initially carrying only novelty stories on women's sports, many dailies soon dealt with the subject matter with greater respect and nuance. The *Toronto Sunday World*, for example, introduced a new "Sportswoman's Section," devoted exclusively to women's sports. Here was a regular feature aimed at the working *and* athletic woman.

WOMEN'S SPORTS IN SCHOOLS

For many Canadian females living in the early part of the 20th century, the introduction to sports began at school. Physical education had become more common in the early 1900s with the development of a syllabus for Canadian schools in 1911. By 1922, physical education had become a compulsory subject in much of western Canada.[11]

In Ontario, support for amateur athletics received a considerable boost after 1920 from the establishment of the Ontario Athletic Commission (OAC). Although the OAC was initially envisioned to address schoolboy athletics, the program quickly expanded its mandate to include schoolgirls as well. Bruce Kidd, a kinesiologist and former Olympic runner, argues that the act gave an enormous boost to male amateur sports. This was, indisputably, the goal of those who drafted the Act. As was previously described, Walter Knox — the man the Ontario government had hired to run the OAC programs — coached only schoolboys during his first year. Beginning in the fall of 1922, however, Knox included girls in his programs, although their numbers were much fewer.

Before this, Knox had also held a tryout in Toronto to organize a team of young women to attend a track meet at Philadelphia. At that meet, Jessie Glover broke the world record in the high jump, Rosa Grosse won the 100-yard dash, Dorothy O'Neil took first in the high jump, and the relay team took gold. Two things were clear: Canadian women's sports were on an upswing, and Knox was a promotor of women's participation well before it was commonly accepted in Canada.

The OAC's effort to improve amateur athletics was soon evident. After the Canadian Olympic team brought home a record 14 medals from the 1928 Games in Amsterdam, the OAC boasted that 90 percent of the Ontario athletes on the Olympic team had received assistance from OAC coaches.[17] Indeed, three of the seven athletes who came home as heroes in August 1928 were in or had just left high school.

CLUBS FOR WOMEN

Although there were signs of change in the air, before the First World War there had been limited opportunities in Canada for young women to compete in athletics. By the early 1920s, though, competition for young female athletes was opening up across Canada, and particularly in Ontario. Accelerating the emergence of Canada's world-class female athletes of the 1920s was the growth of women's athletic clubs. Ever since the establishment of the Royal Montreal Curling Club in 1807, such clubs had played a key role in the evolution of many sports in Canada, but women's roles in these clubs were always restricted or, in many cases, non-existent. The influx of working-class women into Canada's workforce after the First World War generated a grassroots movement that helped to remedy this situation, and many women's clubs and institutions were founded, organized primarily around team sports at that time. In addition to their social value, athletic clubs were important in promoting track and field by providing facilities, coaches, training time, competitions, and record-keeping. By adopting regular record-keeping, clubs allowed athletic progress to be properly measured and compared, which, necessarily, stimulated competition.[13]

The Toronto Ladies' Athletic Club (TLAC) had begun as a basketball club. By 1924, the club had approximately 40 members, participating in a range of sports. The athletes in the TLAC believed that, as Jane Bell remembered, "We were a group special unto ourselves."[14] There was good reason for this belief. Three of the club's sprinters — Rosa Grosse, Grace Conacher, and Myrtle Cook — had been part of the relay team that set the CNE record in 1924. Certainly, the TLAC was attractive to top-level female athletes. Myrtle Cook, for instance, left the Kew Beach Canoe Club where she was a war-canoe paddler to join her track-mates Grosse and Conacher at the TLAC, where they were members. Likewise, Ethel Smith, who started in the Toronto Hydro-Electric Club before moving to the Beaches Ladies' Athletic Club, was recruited by Cook to strengthen the TLAC's relay team.

Other clubs could offer female athletes their pathway to excellence. Ethel Catherwood, an impressive young high jumper from Saskatchewan, had received financial support from the Saskatoon Elks Club to attend the 1927 Canadian Women's Track and Field Championships in Toronto. After she easily won her event, she was approached by Fred "Teddy" Oke — a retired hockey player, First World War veteran, mining financier, and the wealthy sponsor of the Parkdale Ladies' Athletic Club — to join the club. Known for luring emerging stars away from other women's clubs, he invited Catherwood to join Parkdale and offered to send her and her sister, Ginger, to the Shaw Business College, after which he would give her a job in his brokerage firm. She accepted Oke's offer on one additional condition: that he hired Walter Knox as the club's coach.[15]

There were other options for female athletes with less visibility. The experiences of Rosa Grosse, a second-generation Torontonian of German descent and perhaps that city's best sprinter, reflected many of these changes to women's sports. After graduating from the Central Business College, Grosse began work as a secretary for the Dominion Bridge Company, although she remained deeply involved in sports. Her family membership in the Toronto lodge of the Royal Templars of Temperance, a temperance and benevolent society, gave Rosa the access to sports she so desired.[16] The Templars, who professed equal rights for men and women, believed in the value of physical exercise and held a regular field day each September. Perhaps more importantly, in 1912 the Templars bought the building known as the "Great Hall" on Queen Street in Toronto from the West End YMCA. The building housed a gymnasium, a raised track, and a swimming pool. The Templars then opened their gym to young women like Grosse who wanted to play basketball. It was a contrast to so many other facilities that were dominated by males. The Templars gave women like Rosa an equal chance to play.

Since 1914, the Templars had been running a women's basketball league. In a few years, though, player interest fell off. In response, in 1920 Grosse and a few of her Templar teammates, along with interested players in Hamilton and London, put together a three-team intercity league called the Ladies' Ontario Basketball Association. The following year, the Templar team — renamed the Toronto Ladies' Basketball Club (TLBC) — was joined by new players such as Alexandrine Gibb and played before a packed gymnasium. By 1922, the league had grown to 11 teams. Although the TLBC used a male coach — Gordon Fraser — its elected officers were all female.

At virtually the same time, women's hockey teams were being established, first under the Toronto Hockey League and then under the guise of the more robust and successful Ladies Ontario Hockey Association (LOHA). The LOHA was, like the TLBC, a space for women from all classes to play, attracting as it did working women from the province's urban centres. To achieve recognition, the LOHA tried to align itself with men's hockey. This produced only mixed results for a time. In its infancy, men held advisory roles within the league, yet by 1925, the LOHA was effectively a women's sport run by women.

Still, the women's hockey league met resistance from Canada's male-dominated athletic bodies. In 1923, for instance, the LOHA was denied official recognition by the Canadian Amateur Hockey Association, whose president, W.A. Fry, believed that women should stick to swimming, tennis, skating, or track and field. Fortunately, the league had enough drawing power to survive. It was clear that a variety of women's sports were becoming an increasingly attractive product for both female *and* male spectators.

THE SPECTATORS

On September 8, 1923, the CNE in Toronto held its Athletic Day and offered, for the first time, events for women athletes. Approximately 90 young women entered the various events. One event, a 4 x 100 relay, was open to international runners.[17] As a special embellishment to its program, the CNE invited the "Chicago Flyers," a prominent women's relay team from that city, to compete. The coach of the Flyers and trainer of the University of Chicago's track team was Thomas Eck who, decades before, had partnered with Louise Armaindo. Preparing to challenge the Flyers was the newly formed and untested team of Bobbie Rosenfeld, Rosa Grosse, Myrtle Cook, and Grace Conacher. The Canadian quartet had less than two weeks to train for the relay.

On the day, heavy rains delayed the relay and turned the track into mud. The 15,000 spectators were, nevertheless, delighted by the results of the 100-yard dash. In it, Rosenfeld narrowly beat out fellow Canadian Grosse. The best that the American champion Helen Filkey could do in the race was third. There was more palpable nervousness around the CNE when it came to the relay, as it would be the Canadians' first race as a team.

Aesthetically, the Chicago runners looked the part. While no doubt scandalous to some, their shorts and jerseys seemed better suited for the race than, as it was uncharitably reported, the Toronto team's "spinnaker middies and pup-tent bloomers."[18] Despite the sartorial advantage, the well-trained Flyers finished well behind the Canadians after bobbling an exchange of the baton between two runners. Women's athletics — especially in the Toronto area — received a huge boost from the victory in front of a partisan crowd. The quartet's success was widely touted by the media.

At the same time, others were cautious about what had actually been accomplished. At the annual meeting of the AAU of C, Secretary Norton Crow warned that although there had been some fine performances in women's athletics, there was "not a little difference of opinion among authorities, medical and otherwise, as to the wisdom and value of this development."[19] For promoters, however, there was less division: women sprinters drew large crowds.

The team's widely publicized success led to offers to compete in the United States, including an invitation to the Millrose Games held annually at Madison Square Gardens. Walter Knox, who had provided some rudimentary coaching before the team raced at the CNE, agreed to train the women for Millrose. Starting in October, for three times a week over three months, the relay team met at the Mutual Street Arena to practise under Knox's guidance. The women's employers supported the team by giving them time off from work and covering expenses. Unfortunately, the team finished a disappointing third, when Conacher tripped and fell during her leg of the relay. Grosse, however, won the Millrose's 50-yard sprint. Despite the mixed results, women's interest in sprinting continued to build, especially after the next CNE Athletic Day, when the same Canadian women's team not only won the relay and but also set a world record.

The new popularity of the women sprinters was one reason the AAU of C feared the creation of an independent association governing women's sport run by women and outside of AAU of C control. Now, the AAU of C took a more muscular approach and began registering the times set by Grosse, the 4 x 100-metre relay team, and other Canadian women.

FEMALE OLYMPIANS

The initial victory for women athletes in Amsterdam was winning the right to participate in the first place. Before 1926, there was little indication that women would be allowed to compete in Olympic track and field events. The presence of women in athletic events at the 1928 Olympics, however, was driven by an international women-led movement. The first of the modern Olympic Games, held in Athens in April 1896, had been a modest and strictly gendered affair. In 1896 women were allowed as observers but not participants. The role of women in the modern Games, argued Baron Pierre de Coubertin, president and driving force of the IOC, was merely to provide emotional support from the sidelines. Actual participation in the games, he and others claimed, would endanger women's health and ensure that they would never find husbands.

Despite the objections of de Coubertin, a few women participated in the 1900 Games, playing golf and lawn tennis.[20] Over the next four Olympics, women's events were expanded to include archery, fencing, figure skating, swimming, and diving. These events were, as far as the gentlemen amateurs of the Olympic Committee were concerned, compatible with women's femininity and fragility. In the years after the First World War, however, international support for women's sports grew exponentially. This movement forced a major change in the 1928 Games and allowed women to compete in a limited number of track and field events, albeit on a trial basis.

One major impediment to female involvement was removed when Pierre de Coubertin resigned as the president of the IOC in 1925. Before the First World War, there had been few international opportunities for young women to participate in athletics. Yet, global pressure for the inclusion of women in athletics dramatically increased when the Fédération Sportive Féminine Internationale (FSFI) was created in 1921. Champions of women's sports, such as the Frenchwoman Alice Milliat, advocated on behalf of women's participation in track and field, with successful results.

Not surprisingly, opposition to such progress emanated from both the IOC and the International Amateur Athletic Federation (IAAF), the body setting the rules for Olympic sports. Undeterred, Milliat and the FSFI organized "a spectacular" international track and field event in Paris. The public response to the event necessitated change. In 1924, the FSFI asked the IAAF to include women's track and field events in that year's Olympics. The IAAF refused because of time constraints but agreed to consider the request for the 1928 Olympics. To get ahead of the FSFI, the IAAF requested that its members, including Canada, take charge of women's track and field in their respective countries.[21] After extensive discussion, the AAU of C responded by creating a standing committee on women's activities. It was run by four male members.

Despite the acrimony, the struggle between the FSFI and the IAAF for control of women's athletics was finally resolved and a compromise was reached in 1928. In August 1926, the IAAF announced that women could compete in five track and field events on a trial basis. The new events included were the 100 metres, 4 x 100 metres, 800 metres, high jump, and the discus throw.[22] The most contentious of these events was the 800 metres, for many critics felt that racing that distance was far too strenuous to be safely undertaken by women and that it might damage their reproductive abilities.

It was not a foregone conclusion that Canadian women would be headed to Amsterdam. Indeed, the inclusion of the five events triggered a heated debate within the COC. In the end, though, members agreed to include some women on the Olympic athletic team.[23]

One Canadian member of the IAAF who had previously voted against admitting women's events was Dr. Arthur S. Lamb. A doctor and physical-education instructor, Lamb supported the growing participation of girls and women in modest recreational activities, but he consistently opposed including women in elite international athletic contests. His hostility to women's athletics was of particular import because in 1927 Lamb had been elected president of the AAU of C. A year later, Lamb was one of the Olympic Committee members at Amsterdam.

In the end, Lamb's opposition could not stem the tide of events. Canadian women had had a taste of international track and field competition before Amsterdam. The Women's Amateur Athletic Association of England invited the AAU of C to send a Canadian team to a three-country athletic meet at Stamford Bridge in London on August 1, 1925.[24]

Responsibility for selecting and organizing the team fell to Alexandrine Gibb, a prominent sports leader and a founder of the TLAC.[25] After the selection trials in Toronto (which limited participation from outside Ontario), Gibb took a team of 10 athletes to London. Missing some of its best female athletes, the Canadian team enjoyed only modest success.[26] Velma A. Springstead finished third in the high jump and was voted the all-round athlete of the events. Myrtle Cook picked up a bronze in the 100-yard dash and another in the relay. She would use her disappointing— at least in her eyes — performance to motivate her training over the next two years.

The Stamford Bridge meet received extensive coverage by the press, some of it quite critical. This convinced Gibb of the need for a women-run organization to oversee international competition for Canadian female athletes.

In England, Gibb had been impressed by the British Women's Amateur Athletic Association. After returning home, she immediately began working on the creation of a Women's Amateur Athletic Federation as an affiliate of the AAU of C. Advocating for the control and administration of women's sports *by women*, Gibb and others also formed the Canadian Ladies' Athletic Club. The club was to be national in scope, with branches established in important Canadian cities. The club's motto was "Girls' Sports for Girls," and all its officers were women.

MAKING THE TEAM

From the outset of the Olympic Trials, it was clear that a majority of Olympic-bound athletes would be from Ontario. This was particularly true for the female contestants. After all, the Canadian women's track and field championships of 1926 and 1927 had largely comprised those elite women athletes who were training in the Toronto area and who were associated with either the Toronto or Canadian Ladies' Athletic Clubs. The National Trials, however, were set for Halifax for July 2, 1928. For some, this was inexplicable, as the Ontario Trials of early June had already — to use a boxing reference — told the tale of the tape. As Alexandrine Gibb pointed out, all the Olympic-calibre "athletes ... are business girls, and consequently find it difficult to make arrangements for an unlimited leave of absence."[27] Those athletes selected would already be away for at least five weeks. By adding Halifax, the "business girls" would be gone for yet another week. This question of time away from work only exacerbated the major problem facing female athletes and their organizations: funding. Nevertheless, Halifax it remained.

Halifax changed little, and those identified as most likely to medal stayed much the same: Myrtle Cook, the 26-year-old veteran of the track, and Ethel Catherwood, the teenage high jumper from Saskatoon, led the group. In 1928, Cook was the best sprinter in Canada. Her long-time rival, Rosa Grosse, had married and started a family, while Bobbie Rosenfeld, the best all-round athlete in Canada, was busy with other sports and had not competed as a sprinter for more than a year. When Cook set a world record of 12 seconds even in the 100 metres at the Canadian Olympic Trials in Halifax, she became the expected winner in Amsterdam. As fast as she was, Cook was also described as being the most nervous and high-strung. These characteristics would be highlighted during the Games.[28]

Ethel Catherwood, on the other hand, was a successful multi-sport athlete raised in Saskatoon. In 1926, Catherwood's life trajectory was altered when the local paper published results of the city's high-school track and field championships. Joe Griffiths, the University of Saskatchewan's athletic director, read with amazement that she had cleared 5'. He knew it would be a new Canadian high jump record.[29] Soon, Catherwood was training with Griffiths. Within weeks, she was clearing 5'2". In the provincial championships that fall, Catherwood set a new world record of 5'2". The next year in Toronto, she became national champion in both the high jump and the javelin throw. At the Halifax Trials, Catherwood made a new record with a jump of 5'3", a Canadian record that would stand for the next quarter century.

Despite these impressive accomplishments, Catherwood was shy and somewhat aloof. Tall and statuesque, she was also as attractive as she was talented. The press hounded her. She would be, it was claimed, the most photographed woman at the Games and was nicknamed "the Saskatoon Lily" by popular sportswriter Lou Marsh.

Other strong athletes were included in the Canadian women's team. Expectations were high for Bobbie Rosenfeld, despite her recent absence from athletics. Called "Bobbie" because of her "bobbed" hair style, she was a dominant athlete in numerous team sports. She thought of herself as a "modern woman" and saw sports as a means of social integration. Born in Ekaterinoslav in the Russian Empire (now Dnipro, Ukraine), Rosenfeld, who was Jewish, captured the experience of many working-class immigrant athletes. She has been properly called "one of the most consummate female athletes of the 20th century."[30] Rosenfeld, the "all-rounder," planned to compete in the 100-metre, the 800-metre, and the discus events. This proposed itinerary was no overreach; in the 1925 Ontario Ladies Track and Field Championship, Rosenfeld entered seven events, won five, and was second in the other two.

The athlete for whom expectations were unrealistically high was 17-year-old Jean Thompson. Equal parts shy, quiet, determined, and gutsy, Thompson had something of a meteoric rise in Canadian athletics. In high school, her ability in sprints and the high jump caught the attention of the school's athletic coach, Lucien A. Wendling. In 1927, Thompson entered the Canadian Women's Track and Field Championships and finished third in both the 100-yard dash and the high jump. It was a good result for a 16-year-old, but Wendling believed that she would have greater success by focusing on the new event for women, the 800-metre run. For eight months they worked together, and in the local Huronia Trials in June 1928, Thompson not only won easily but also appeared to have set a new world record.[31] Her win made her both a candidate for the Olympic team and a target of Toronto athletic clubs, who suggested that if she were not part of a "recognized club," she would have difficulty making the Olympic team.[32] Financial support from the Penetanguishene community enabled Thompson to go to Halifax. There, Thompson's win made her an easy choice for the team.

Selecting the last two sprinters for the team proved more difficult and was not decided until after Halifax. Toronto-born Ethel Smith had been forced to leave school at 14 to help provide financial support for her family, but she maintained a passion for sports, especially running. During the mid-1920s, she became a prominent sprinter. She secured her spot on the Olympic team by her second-place finish at the Ontario Olympic Trials.

Jane Bell was the last one to join the team and was one of its youngest members. Bell joined the TLAC in 1924 and became a junior champion in 1925 and 1926. In 1927, she was still a junior and her name was seldom in the conversations about the Olympic team. At that time, she decided it was in her best interest to leave the TLAC and join the Parkdale Ladies' Athletic Club, where Knox had just been hired. Bell believed Knox was the best coach for her. She was right. Under his training, Bell made the team.

THE SPRINTER AND HIS COACH

Meanwhile, organizers of the men's track and field team had to consider the best options for the national squad. Before the Olympic Trials, few considered Percy Williams a world-level sprinter. In fact, few, if any, considered him to be very good at all. To be fair to these naysayers, Williams might not have disagreed. After all, sprinting was never his favourite sport. He much preferred rugby, tennis, target shooting, and riding. Moreover, when he was 15, it had looked like his life as an athlete was over. Williams had fallen ill with what was diagnosed as severe rheumatic fever, which damaged his heart. Although the doctor had predicted, incorrectly, that he would never be able to participate in sports again and that he should avoid strenuous exercise, within months Williams was back on the playing fields.[33]

He attended King Edward High School, a school that reflected the new importance being placed on sports. Emslie Yeo, one of Williams's teachers and the school's track coach, recognized the young man's talents. Yeo appealed, via his friends, to Williams's school spirit in order to get him to compete. Despite these efforts, Williams politely informed his coach, "I'm just not interested in track, sir."[34] Fortunately, Williams acquiesced.

Living in Vancouver, Williams was on the very margins of Canada's athletic world and ignored by the Eastern press. In 1926 and 1927, he had won the 100- and 200-yard sprints — often referred to as the "century" and the "furlong" — in the annual inter-high meet. These successes, though, won him only local notoriety. Few people east of the Rocky Mountains had even heard of him. Graduating from high school might well have ended his track career. What changed the course of his life was the recognition he received by Bob Granger, a self-trained coach and part-time janitor at King Edward High School. Their partnership would bring out the best in both men.

Initially, Granger was quite underwhelmed. Granger thought that compared with other sprinters he had trained, Percy Williams "was a runt: under 5'6", weighing no more than 110 pounds, puny and spindly." Not only did Percy have less than striking features, but Granger declared that he had never "seen such a travesty of running form. Williams ran with his arms glued to his sides." Still, Granger, with no small measure of amazement, recognized a rare ability in the skinny runner. Never in his days of watching sprinters, Granger claimed, had he seen "such a pair of legs! They moved like pistons of a gasoline engine with someone opening the throttle wider all the time."[35]

Granger himself had been a successful athlete in multiple sports. At 33, however, he now focused his considerable sporting energy into coaching athletes in a variety of sports. Granger believed, because of a series of innovations, that he could make his greatest contributions to the art of sprinting. And the innovations were plentiful.

Granger believed that massages with cocoa butter were critical to keeping muscles supple. Also, he thought sprinters should be kept warm under blankets to limit unnecessary exertions and that visualization would improve technique. Granger was also able to improvise when called upon. In Amsterdam, for instance, he had Williams practising starts in his hotel room into a mattress held against the wall. His coaching — based on intuition, observation, and extensive reading of literature on sprinting — was years ahead of most coaches. Above all, he tailored his training to Williams's personality and physiology. As his early description of Williams suggested, Granger was convinced that his new approach to sprinting could unlock Williams's real potential.[36]

Specifically, Granger sought to improve Williams's start, to use his arms more effectively, and to keep his form through the last few yards. These were things that could be taught. At Granger's invitation, Williams joined the Vancouver Athletic Club in late May 1926 and began training under his new coach. Their partnership was unique and effective. Years later, Harry Warren, a friend of Percy Williams and another sprinter, explained that "Percy's victory was a blending of these two amazing personalities."[37]

At the 1927 British Columbia Provincials, Williams qualified for the Canadian championships in both the century and furlong, only to find out that the province's Olympic Committee had only enough money to send one person to Toronto. The one man the committee sent was not an athlete but rather a local official or "badger." Although the badger travelled first class, Williams scraped together enough money for a cheap upper berth on the train. For his part, Granger got a job on the eastbound train, washing dishes.

Tired from five days on the train with little exercise, Williams reached Union Station less than six hours before his first race. He nevertheless finished second in his semifinal heat in the "century," carefully following Granger's direction to conserve his energy. Yet, because Varsity Stadium had only five and not the usual six lanes, the two second-place finishers would have to flip a coin to see who would proceed. Williams lost the coin toss. He was out of the 100-yard dash.[38] Although he had made the final in the 200-yard dash, Williams could do no better than fourth. Bitterly disappointed, he headed home. Adding to the disappointment was the eastern newspapers' assessment of the western sprinter; reporters looked at his training techniques and considered his schedule and concluded that Williams was both lazy and a prima donna.[39]

Once home, Williams had to decide whether to accept a track scholarship to the University of Washington. Olympic officials in Toronto had warned him that Canadian athletes moving south to reside and compete in the United States would be deemed ineligible to compete internationally for Canada. Also figuring into his decision was Williams's love of Vancouver. Consequently, he stayed in that city and enrolled at the High School of Commerce in a one-year business program offered to high-school graduates.

In pursuit of his running career, Williams's next target was the provincial trials at Brockton Point on June 9, 1928. Running easily, he tied the Olympic mark of 10⅗ seconds for the 110 metres.[40] He also met the Olympic standard in the 220-metre race and with that, Williams — along with Archie McDiarmid, the only other B.C. athlete participating — was off to the National Trials, which was hosted by the Hamilton Olympic Club (HOC), Canada's premier track club.

The man heading the pre-trials training camp and the coach of the Olympic team was J.R. "Cap" Cornelius. A veteran of the First World War, Cornelius was convinced of the critical need for frequent and rigorous workouts. Granger and Williams, who could at times be found sitting on the grass "visualizing" how the other sprinters worked out, were at odds with Cornelius. Fortunately for everyone involved, Cornelius saw little potential in Williams and largely left him alone.

Williams described Cornelius to his mother as "one of the Scotch men who believe in the Big 'I' and the little 'u' and he was dead set against the method of training I used."[41] Granger believed Cornelius wanted to give Williams twenty times the work he needed. Cornelius accepted that Williams was fast but believed — much like the eastern newspaper reporters — that the sprinter was lazy and lacked the endurance needed in the Olympics.

At the HOC, Williams got through his early heats in the 100 metres with the minimum effort, resting in the dressing room under blankets between races and getting massages from Granger. In the finals, the crowd favourites were the HOC sprinters Johnny Fitzpatrick, Buck Hester, and Ralph Adams. After an even start, Williams pulled into a slim lead by the halfway mark and held it to the end. The time, 10⅗ seconds, matched the Olympic record. Despite this remarkable achievement, Williams was still seen, at least in the eyes of many, as a boy among men.

Williams also ran the 200 metres, believing that the Olympic Committee wanted four sprinters who could run both sprints plus the relay. Once again, in the first heats of the furlong, Williams ran only as fast as he had to so as to make the finals. Granger had impressed on him not to run against the clock but rather against the opponents. And as it was in the 100 metres, Williams edged out the three HOC runners in the finals. While the Toronto and Hamilton press now had glowing things to say about the spindly sprinter, many still retained doubts about Williams's stamina for the much bigger tests ahead.

AMSTERDAM

On July 10, a train left Hamilton, carrying Canada's Olympic athletes. After a quick stop in Toronto to pick up the women's athletic team and one swimmer, Dorothy Prior, it was on to Montreal and the SS *Albertic*, the ship that would take the first contingent of Canadian athletes to Europe.[42] Among the 51 athletes on the Canadian team, one dapper and articulate member caught Williams's attention. It was Phil Edwards, a middle-distance runner and a member of British Guiana's Black elite. As that British colony had no Olympic team, Bobby Robinson, manager of the Canadian track team, had persuaded (or rather poached) Edwards to come north and compete for Canada. Nicknamed "the Man of Bronze" for the five bronze Olympics medals he would win in his Olympic career, Edwards won his bronze first in Amsterdam running the 4 x 400 metres.[43]

While Williams and the Olympic team were heading across the Atlantic, Granger was scrambling to fund his way to Amsterdam. He had offered to accompany Williams as trainer, but he was turned down by Olympic officials, ostensibly for lack of funds. As Granger looked for ways to get to Amsterdam, Cornelius's relationship with Williams continued to deteriorate. The manager became even more convinced that Williams was indolent and unwilling to follow the directions necessary to get a runner ready for the demands of Olympic competition. If Williams was going to make the podium, Granger had to get to Amsterdam.

Fortunately for Williams, Granger arrived at the last minute, after receiving travelling funds raised in British Columbia by Williams's mother. His arrival triggered a final clash with Cornelius, who washed his hands of Williams and claimed the sprinter's failures would be his own fault. His successes would, however, be his and Granger's.

When they finally arrived, most of Canada's male athletes were housed in the Holland Hotel, a small and seedy building in the downtown core. The women were settled some distance away at the Pension Regina, but they were closer to the stadium. When the Canadians arrived a week before the Games were to start, the stadium was unfinished, limiting practice facilities. It meant that finding suitable space to train was difficult.[44] Both Jean Thompson and Jane Bell missed the opening ceremonies because of training injuries caused or aggravated by the grounds.

The first day of the athletic events began with heats for the men's 100 metres. As a result of the number of entrants — 87 — 16 heats were required for the first round and 6 heats for the second. Getting to the finals would be a test of endurance, one that some, including Granger, felt would be too much for Williams. Nevertheless, he proved all doubters wrong, winning both of his heats easily. Only one other Canadian, Johnny Fitzpatrick, advanced with him.[45]

The following day, as Williams sat on the infield grass waiting for his semifinal heat, he watched the Canadian women in their heats of the 100 metres. They did well. Cook, Rosenfeld, and Smith all advanced to the final. Williams's own heat, however, started out poorly. He found himself having to run flat out to take second place and advance to the final. In the other heat, Fitzpatrick failed to advance. It was now, as far as the Canadian men's team was concerned, all about Percy Williams.

The favourites going into the finals that afternoon were the two Americans, Bob McAllister and Frank Wykoff. Williams, who spent his time staying warm in the dressing room under blankets, was not seen as a threat. As the runners came up to the start line, McAllister, taller and 50 pounds heavier, smiled at the Canadian and asked if he was really up to it. After two false starts, the starter's gun fired and Williams exploded out of his stance. At 25 metres, he was tied with the British runner, Jack London. At 50 metres, Williams was in the lead and running fluidly. In the next 20 metres, London clawed himself back to Williams, but he then faded. Williams hit the tape a yard ahead of London with the German, George Lammers, just behind. Percy Williams had taken the gold.

As the waves of cheering from the spectators swept over him, two teammates, Brant Little and Phil Edwards, ran out to hoist him onto their shoulders. The Canadian women's team mobbed him in the dressing room. Alexandrine Gibb was convinced that he had never been kissed so often and so fast in his life. That night, in the little pocket diary he kept for his mother, he wrote: "Well, well, well. So I'm supposed to be the World 100 M Champion. (Crushed apples.) No more fun in running now."[46]

Fans were now familiar with his name, but not his appearance. After his dinner, Williams wandered out to see why a crowd had gathered outside his hotel. One of the spectators explained to him that they were waiting to see the now famous Canadian sprinter, Percy Williams. Rather than identifying himself, Williams just chatted with the crowd. It was, for the shy man, more fun that way.

The euphoria felt by the Canadians disappeared the next day in the women's final of the 100 metres. Cook, a veteran runner who had set a world record of 12 seconds flat in the 100 metres in Halifax, was the clear favourite. In the semifinal heat, however, Betty Robinson, a young American, had beaten Cook. This left the Canadian even more concerned about the need for a fast start. Unfortunately, in trying to jump the gun, she double-faulted and was disqualified. For half an hour, she sat slumped beside the track, crying inconsolably.[47]

There was yet another false start and a German runner was disqualified. After this, the much-reduced field got away cleanly, if not quickly. Rosenfeld, Smith, and the other German were slow off the start, well behind Robinson. Rosenfeld, however, caught the American just at the finish line and set off a dispute over who had won. The judges disagreed about who had finished first and both the English and French judge claimed Robinson had broken the tape with her arm and not her body, as the rules required. Alice Milliat, president of the FSFI, was on the field at the time and was also convinced that Rosenfeld had won. Nevertheless, the chief judge, an American, declared Betty Robinson the winner. In the end, Bobbie Rosenfeld took home silver and Ethel Smith received bronze. It was another two medals for Canada.

Canadian track and field team manager Bobby Robinson was convinced that Rosenfeld had beaten his namesake. So, too, was Alexandrine Gibb. They quickly wrote out a protest. Then, Robinson, Gibb, Patrick Mulqueen of the COC, and Arthur Lamb crossed the infield and delivered it to the race judges. Gibb informed them that as manager of the Canadian women's team, she wished to file a protest. At that point, Lamb indicated that he had not known why they were seeing the judges and that he did not support the protest. He claimed it violated his perception of Olympic sportsmanship. He was, he told the judges, dissociating himself from the protest. The judges then voted three to one against Gibb's protest. Mulqueen, who disagreed with Lamb on this and other aspects of the Olympics, believed that the latter had "backed out to save face."[48]

On the same day as the women's controversial 100 metres, Williams lined up for his first heat of the men's 200 metres. Obviously, at this stage no one doubted his speed. Some, however, still doubted his endurance. After all, only twice before had a sprinter won the "double."[49] Giving credence to these misgivings was the fact that Williams had a lot of running to do. He would have to endure two more heats before the semifinals — if, of course, he made it that far.

Adding to the odds against Williams was the fact that none of the American or German sprinters he'd be facing had run in the 100 metres. They were all fresher than Williams. Still, he won his first heat easily. The next heat, though, would be far trickier. In it, Williams faced the best German, Helmut Koernig, and the American, Charley Borah. Only two runners would advance. At the start of the race, Williams trailed both men coming out of the curve, before he started to claw back some of the gap. Just before the finish, he passed Borah and almost caught Koernig. That night, he wrote in his diary: "Miracles still happen. I'm in the semifinals. Eliminated Borah. One of the nicest fellows I have ever met."[50] Williams and millions of Canadians were wondering if a second miracle was possible.

It was. Williams won his semifinals and looked comfortable doing so. Fellow Canadian Johnny Fitzpatrick had also advanced. For Williams, though, it was back under the blankets in the dressing room. As per Granger's instruction, Williams stayed warm and quiet until just before the final.

Looking at the field in the final, Williams's coach told him that Koernig was the man to beat. Granger was right. After a mediocre start, the runners were clumped together as they came around the turn. Williams was just off Koernig's shoulder. With only 30 metres to go, however, Williams began to pull away. He crossed the line a metre ahead of Koernig and the others. The young, spindly sprinter had far exceeded all expectations. Percy Williams was going home with two Olympic gold medals!

Surrounded by admirers, Williams told a teammate how, four years previously, a Vancouver doctor had told him he had "a leaky heart" and should avoid sports. It was a striking confession from the new gold medallist, who was inundated with reporters, telegrams, well-wishers, and event promoters. General Douglas MacArthur, president of the U.S. Olympic Committee, called him "the greatest sprinter the world has ever seen." For his part, Williams's self-assessment was far more modest. His diary read: "Well, it's done. Won the 200 M. Not so bad. Telegrams galore. The girls' team sent flowers to me."[51] It was a staggeringly understated diary entry. Peerless Percy was now famous.

Percy Williams winning gold in the 200-metre sprint.

WOMEN'S 800 METRES

On the morning of the 800-metre heats, Gibb was concerned about Jean Thompson's physical and emotional state. She approached Rosenfeld and asked if she would run the event to provide some moral assurance for Thompson. It was a distance that Rosenfeld had run only a few times, and she had certainly not trained for that distance. If it was to help a teammate, however, Rosenfeld would do it. As it turned out, there were only five runners in Rosenfeld's heat and three would advance to the final. Rosenfeld hung at the back for most of the heat and then accelerated into third place easily. Thompson won her larger heat, unnecessarily holding off a late attack by two runners.

In the final of the 800 metres, Thompson started off in second place but began to fade because of the leg injury she had suffered earlier in training. As Thompson dropped back into fourth, Rosenfeld, who had trailed the field, caught up with Thompson. There she remained, encouraging her friend and teammate to finish. At the very end, Rosenfeld dropped back, letting Thompson finish alone in fourth. The German Lina Radke won the race in just over 2 minutes and 16 seconds, a full 7 seconds faster than the world record.

All the women who entered the race finished it. Five finished faster than the previous world record. These facts were, however, wildly at odds with how the race was represented by the press. In numerous articles, male reporters claimed that most or all of the women had either dropped out or collapsed at the finish.[52] Knute Rockne, for instance, incorrectly claimed that only six women finished and that five of them collapsed.[53] William Shirer reported five women collapsing and that the second-place runner, Kinue Hitomi, was so exhausted that she required a 15-minute revival period.[54] In Canada, Lou Marsh's column was more balanced, but the *Montreal Daily Star* called the race a "disgrace" and stated that it was "obviously beyond women's power of endurance, and can only be injurious to them."[55]

In actuality, film footage of the final shows that *no* runners dropped out and that only one, possibly Thompson, fell after the finish. That particular runner was up within seconds; it was hardly a "collapse." Immediately after they finished, the film shows Hitomi, wrapped in a blanket, standing upright and watching other runners. There was, it would appear, no "15-minute revival period." Although they may have been competing against one another, perhaps the greater fight for these female athletes was contesting the representations and *perceived* limitations of women's sports around the world.

As for the Canadian women's team, the first two events had been somewhat disappointing. A better future was, however, in store. The first heat of the 4 x 100-metre relay was run on a wet track in cool weather, but the Canadians ran well, setting a new world record of 49⅖ seconds. It was much the same in the finals, in which the Canadians dominated. There was a brief moment when it seemed that the anchor runner, Myrtle Cook, had taken off too early, risking a team disqualification. Bell was, nevertheless, able to get her the baton, albeit in the very last foot of the transfer zone. On this day, Betty Robinson, running anchor for the American team, couldn't catch Cook. The Canadian women had their first gold medal and yet another new world record of 48⅖ seconds.

Fanny "Bobbie" Rosenfeld (second from left) and Ethel Smith (left) in the 100-metre sprint.

While the women's and men's relays were being run, Ethel Catherwood was competing in the high-jump pit. The 19 competitors who had cleared the elimination target of 4'6" began jumping for medals. Athletes had three attempts at each new height. If they failed in their attempts, they were out. After three hours, only three jumpers had cleared the bar set at 5'1⅖": Caroline Gisolf of Holland, the American Mildred Wiley, and Catherwood. Through the early jumping, Catherwood had kept her warm-up suit on, a tip from Walter Knox aimed at establishing a psychological edge on the other jumpers. Only after she missed at 5'1" did she take off her sweatpants. She made the jump on her next try. When the bar was raised to 5'3", the sweatshirt was removed, and she likewise cleared the new height on her second jump. Neither Gisolf nor Wiley could match her effort. With that, Catherwood had won the Canadian women their second gold medal.[56] Her points from the high jump also gave the Canadians the unofficial woman's track and field championship.

The high jump gold medallist, Ethel Catherwood, in action.

AFTERMATH

The day after the athletic events were finished, the Canadian track team left Amsterdam. Because this had been a trial, the IAAF met two days later to decide the future of women's track and field at the Olympics. The federation's executive council had been pleased with the performance of the women's athletic events and proposed to include them permanently.

Canada's three representatives, Lamb, Mulqueen, and Fred Marples, were all at the meeting. However, only Lamb, as president of the AAU of C, had a vote.[57] Dr. Lamb cast his vote *against* the continuation of women's athletics in the Olympics. Three months before the meeting, Lamb had sent a request for comments on this issue to the Union's Board of Governors and to all members of the COC. He had received no response. He had also invited Mulqueen and Marples to meet the night before the vote, but neither man showed up. Lamb apparently did not think to speak with Gibb and thusly felt free to vote according to his personal values.

Varied views were expressed at the IAAF meeting. The Finnish delegates, for example, saw women's participation in the Olympics as a passing fad. The Americans, by contrast, thought the experiment had been an unqualified success. In his short speech, Lamb briefly distinguished between his view that recreational sports for women were important and beneficial and his concern that the level of competition facing women at the Olympics was too severe and debilitating. Moreover, he argued that women still lacked men's sense of teamwork and ability to be good losers.

He showed his biases when he displayed little concern for the men in the 5,000-metre race who collapsed at the finish but accepted the male reporters' distorted coverage of the women's 800 metres. Lamb also claimed that Cook had violated Olympic sportsmanship by sitting near the track crying, but ignored the young American runner, Frank Wykoff, who burst into tears when he was eliminated from the 100-metre race. Nor did Lamb make mention of Rosenfeld's display of teamwork and sacrifice for Thompson in the 800-metre run. Although he saw Gibb's appeal of the 100-metre results as a gendered act, he made no mention of the quickness with which Robinson and Mulqueen had protested other actions of American athletes.

When the final motion was made to retain women's athletic events, Lamb, acting for Canada, voted against their continuance, along with Finland, Great Britain, Hungary, Italy, and Ireland. Sixteen countries, led by the United States and Greece, supported the motion and took the day. The IAAF, however, agreed to eliminate the women's 800-metre race from future games on the basis of "scientific reasoning."[58]

Although Gibb and many others were angered at Lamb's action, others agreed with his decision. The *Montreal Herald* opined that Canada's brilliant performance was marred only by the "everlasting appeals and protests" brought forward by "some members of the team."[59] Gibb located Lamb's values in the "negative attitude toward women athletes in Montreal."[60] There were almost no competitive athletics for women in Montreal, she argued. No female athletes from Montreal had attended the Halifax Trials. That reflected, Gibb claimed, the attitude in Montreal against competitive sports for women.[61] Cynical reporters from *la belle province* were hardly alone in their inflexible and unsympathetic position toward women athletes.

REMEMBERING

Sporting records and the athletes who make them have a precarious relationship with public memory. There is a tacit understanding that their achievements, while deserving of celebration, will in time be replaced and forgotten. How quickly and completely the popular memory of an individual athlete will fade is difficult to determine. This is because multiple factors dictate the shelf-life of a given athlete's fame, including personality, longevity of play, and the social import of their particular career and sport. These criteria, when one considers those Canadian athletes who captured both the hearts and imagination of Canadians on the eve of the Great Depression, produced different results for the various Olympians involved.

In 1999, the Canadian Press conducted a vote among newspaper editors and broadcasters to identify the top 10 Canadian female and male athletes of the 20th century.[62] Only one member of the 1928 women's Olympic team made the list: Bobbie Rosenfeld, who was selected sixth among the women.[63] The omission of some of the Matchless Six was understandable. Both Ethel Smith and Myrtle Cook had postponed weddings until after the Olympics and had planned to leave competitive sports. Jean Thompson and Jane Bell saw the Olympics as the culmination of a competitive career and had likewise moved on with their lives. Given Ethel Catherwood and Percy Williams's stunning individual achievements, though, their omission is less clear and demands further investigation.

The evidence suggesting that the 1999 poll was unfair to the two Canadians is rather compelling. Percy Williams would remain the only non-American male sprinter to win both the 100- and 200-metre race at a single Olympics, until Usain Bolt matched his achievement 80 years later. Ethel Catherwood remains, at the time of writing, the only Canadian female athlete to have won an individual gold medal in any Olympic track and field event. Her high-jump record stood for a quarter century.

Part of the issue came down to individual personalities. Neither Catherwood nor Williams had the social graces and PR skills of the likes of Bobbie Rosenfeld. An extrovert, Rosenfeld had friends and admirers across the sporting communities and was quite comfortable with her fame. Apart from track and field, she was well known in tennis, basketball, baseball, and hockey circles.[64] Being well known in the hockey world ensured that Rosenfeld's would be a household name for decades to come. Her status might, however, have been forever enshrined when she returned home to Toronto with the other athletes after the Olympics to take part in a four-mile celebratory parade. During it, Bell observed that the gregarious Rosenfeld seemed to know "every second person from the station to Sunnyside, every policeman and all the firemen, too."[65] After arthritis forced her early retirement from competition, Rosenfeld provided great support for women's participation in sports as coach and mentor. She was a pioneering sportswriter for the *Globe and Mail* for 20 years, from 1937 to 1957. By contrast, Catherwood and Williams neither enjoyed nor sought such attention — nor did either want continuing involvement in Canada's athletic world.

There were considerable similarities between Williams, winner of the very first event of the 1928 Games, and Catherwood, winner of the very last one. Both had been recruited in high school by charismatic coaches who urged them into a sport not necessarily their favourite. Both came from the margins of Canada's sporting world, which had been — at least in terms of track and field — Ontario-centric. Perhaps most tellingly, though, both were incredibly shy people, recoiling from the glare of the international press and clumsy in their own personal response to fame.

When Williams visited the Pension Regina, Jane Bell was struck by how shy he was: "He wouldn't talk to the girls." Once home in Vancouver, he struggled with the attention he received and became angry with the ways that advertisers were trying to profit from his name. The city also claimed ownership of the young sprinter, which became a burden on Williams. Although a trust fund had been set up in his name, he clashed with the trustees over access to it, especially after he left the University of British Columbia.

He decided to run in an indoor series of races in the eastern United States that traditionally offered under-the-counter appearance money. In what he called the "Tour of Guts," he raced events of different distances on unfamiliar tracks against fresh opponents. He won 14 of the 17 races he entered, set a new world record for the 60 metres, and tied three others.[66] It was, he felt, a greater accomplishment than his double in the Netherlands.

In reality, though, few were aware of his Tour of Guts, whereas almost every living Canadian knew what he had done in 1928.

Williams's last great race was the finals of the 100-yard dash in the first British Empire Games, held in Hamilton, Ontario, in August 1930. The day was cold and after the runners had removed their warm sweatsuits, they were kept waiting for 10 minutes. After the gun went, Williams burst into the lead at a record-breaking pace, only to pull a muscle in his left thigh at the two-thirds mark. He ran through the pain, set a winning time of 9.9 seconds, and collapsed on the track. His leg was never the same.[67] Although he ran for another year and tried out for the 1932 Olympics in Los Angeles, the peerless one did not qualify.[68] It was the last track meet he ever attended, as athlete or spectator.

Catherwood, a small-town girl, had been burdened by her beauty and surprised by her success. Hers was an unexpected and jolting entry into sports when, at a 1926 high-school meet, she jumped five feet. During the Olympics, Ethel won as much praise for her attractiveness as her athleticism. She was, after all, the most photographed athlete at the Games. Like Williams, Catherwood's significant natural talent allowed her to compete without appearing to go through the training needed by others. Also, like Williams, she enjoyed team sports but lacked a great passion for the sport that she would soon dominate.

After the Olympics, she briefly returned to Saskatoon to celebrate her Olympic victory before going back to Toronto. Catherwood resented her loss of privacy and the invasiveness of adoring fans. She competed sporadically for a few years, missing the 1929 Canadian championships because of injuries but winning both the high jump and javelin championships the following year. The end came in 1931 when at the nationals held in Wetaskiwin, Alberta, she finished in third place, unable to clear 4'9". It was the first time she had been beaten.

Catherwood's post-Olympic life was upended when she became the subject of the exposé press. In November 1929, she secretly married James McLaren, a Toronto bank clerk, amid rumours that she was pregnant.[69] Shortly after her marriage, she met and fell in love with Byron Mitchell. In December 1931, a Toronto paper broke the story that she had moved to

The statuesque "Saskatoon Lily," Ethel Catherwood.

Reno, Nevada, to obtain a quick divorce. Dozens of Canadian and American papers seized the story.[70] In that same month, the press reported that she had been born in Hannah, North Dakota, and had moved to Saskatchewan only in 1910. Bitter at the way the Toronto press had treated her, she never returned to Canada. Catherwood considered representing the United States in the 1932 Olympics in Los Angeles but decided against it. In later years, she got rid of all her medals and trophies, refused offers to attend team reunions or hall-of-fame ceremonies, and lived the life of a recluse in California.[71]

As for Williams, in 1953 there had been talk of naming a new stadium for the British Empire Games after him. He told organizers that he was uncertain if he could attend the sod-turning event and suggested that he would ask his mother. The naming idea was quickly dropped, and the new building was called Empire Stadium. He was equally uninterested in helping to publicize a new track meet to be called the Percy Williams Invitational. That name was changed. In 1976, Williams, like other living Canadian gold medallists, was invited to Montreal for a special ceremony to celebrate the Olympics. He was the only one who did not attend.[72]

After his athletic career, Percy worked as an insurance salesman, played golf, learned to fly, and lived with his mother until she died in 1980. In his later years, he became bitter and isolated. He began to drink heavily and was expelled from the Capilano Golf Club for stealing liquor from other members. In November 1982, Percy Williams, in a bitterly ironic act, killed himself with a shotgun he had received as a gift in that glorious summer of 1928.

Catherwood and Williams presented difficult narratives for the Canadian public to digest. Fans, understandably, find it hard to love athletes who don't love their sport or, at the very least, demonstrate little reverence for their own important place in it. In 1980, Catherwood referred to the Olympics as an unfortunate period in her life. The Saskatoon Lily believed that she had never been an athlete: "I was a natural. It was no big thing. I went, I did it, and quite frankly I'm sick and tired of the whole thing." Williams's retrospection on sudden fame struck a sympathetic chord: "I didn't like running. … Oh, I was so glad to get out of it all."[73]

It is hardly surprising, then, that Williams and Catherwood developed a friendship. It was a kinship based on an understanding of what the burden of fame really meant. They shared the melancholy of having a life defined by one summer in Amsterdam. Back then, during the very last events of the 1928 Games, these two friends sat together. Perhaps they found comfort in one another, both of them unbelonging, quietly anticipating the difficult path that lay ahead.

Percy Williams on the shoulders of Phil Edwards and Brant Little after his victory in the 100-metre sprint.

FORGOTTEN:
A BENEDICTION

BY THE EARLY 20TH CENTURY, THE PLAYING AND WATCHING OF sports had exploded in popularity across North America. Newspaper owners understood that they could boost sales of their papers and increase their revenue from advertising by carrying extensive coverage of sports. The result was that by the start of the 20th century, readers had access to a wide coverage of sporting news. And it wasn't just the large papers that covered sporting events. A subscriber to a small market paper such as the *Medicine Hat News*, for example, could find an entire page dedicated to the coverage of sports. Besides items on local contests, the paper had regular reports on professional boxing, cricket from England, soccer from Scotland, and baseball from New York.[1] The papers fed the growing interest in sports celebrities. It made them famous.

The degree of fame accorded an athlete reflects the importance and value placed on sports by a given audience. Certain sports — especially international contests such as sprints in the Olympics — carry more prestige because they draw a huge pool of competitors and are followed by a worldwide audience. In Canada's early years, there was a very real link between sport and "nation building," and that link informed the general public's interest in sports. In Canada, victory in some sports was more important than in others. This was so, of course, in hockey. As such, fame favoured those partaking in the nation's already popular games. The top three male athletes of the 20th century, in a survey conducted by the Canadian Press in 1999, were hockey players.

And fame could come quickly. It came fast for Percy Williams — a largely unknown athlete — after only two races one summer in Amsterdam. With the "double" in Olympic sprints, Williams was, at least for a time, the world's fastest man. Fame came quickly for Ethel Catherwood as well. Her athletic prowess was impressive, but hers was a fame troubled by beauty. It is difficult to assess whether she was best remembered for being the only Canadian female to have won a gold medal in an Olympic field event, or because she was the most photographed athlete at the 1928 Olympics.

Indeed, fame can be gendered. The incredible accomplishments of basketball's Edmonton Grads (a team that continues to hold the best winning percentage in the history of North American women's sports) or hockey's Preston Rivulettes (who, in approximately 350 games, lost only twice and drew only three times) have been utterly undervalued. The "Old Boys' Club," also known as the Hockey Hall of Fame, inducted its first women — Cammi Granato and Angela James — only in 2010! Of the 293 players who have been inducted into that Hall, only 9 have been women. In contrast, 16 on-ice officials have been inducted. The Rivulettes's incomparable sniper, Hilda Ranscombe, who was twice a finalist for the Lou Marsh Trophy (now the Northern Star Award) and who *has* been inducted into the CSHF, remains outside of hockey's hallowed hall.

Fame can also be fleeting. Louise Armaindo had a Hollywood-eligible personal life and athletic triumphs (including those against men) but enjoyed only a brief and sometimes painful spell of fame. Her star had long faded by the time she was forced to jump out of a window during a hotel fire. She was buried without a gravestone. It was much the same for George Dixon, who was the first North American boxer to go to Britain and win an international title. Having scaled the heights of his sport — as much as a Black man could at that time — Dixon had fought a little too long and drank a lot too much to secure any lasting fame beyond his own time.

Fame has its own fickle demands. Up until the early 20th century, few fans could get a personal view of sporting celebrities. With the advent of radio, news, film, and television, the apparent personality, behaviour, and appearance of an athlete became as important, and sometimes even more important, as athletic achievement when it came to creating and preserving fame. Bobbie Rosenfeld was completely comfortable in the limelight. Percy

Williams and Ethel Catherwood were not. At face value, Walter Knox's accomplishments were staggering and his contribution to the careers of many young athletes was laudable, but he was unable to wrest lasting fame away from his shady past. He gambled his own legacy, and it did not pay.

Fame can be racist. John "Army" Howard, George Godfrey, Alex Decoteau, and so many others were never really given their due during their lives. Coverage of their successes was often laden with either coded or explicit racism. Still, athletes who belonged to groups once marginalized and whose accomplishments had been undervalued or ignored during their careers because of prejudice are now getting some of the recognition they deserve. Sam Langford's exceptional career, for example, has been properly reassessed in recent times and has been rescued by boxing's intelligentsia.[2] His life story was the subject of a recent short docudrama titled *Bonecrusher*.[3] More broadly, in 2015, the CSHF introduced a new category of inductees: Sports Legends. The category is specifically for those athletes whose careers took place before 1955 and has allowed the Hall to make needed corrections, resulting in an uptick of diversity among inductees.[4]

Finally, lasting fame can be arbitrary. Bobbie Rosenfeld, Tom Longboat, and Lionel Conacher all have their names tied with popular sports awards. Invariably, scores of people will Google these names when the nominees and eventual winners are announced each year. It is the same for baseball's Tip O'Neill. No doubt, fans of the young star of the Toronto Blue Jays, Vladimir Guerrero Jr., became familiar with, if not genuinely knowledgeable of, the "Woodstock Wonder's" name when the former won the award in 2021.

But what of those who don't have a named award in their honour? To be sure, there are a great many more of these athletes. One thinks of Edward Ogden, whose glorious day at Lord's in 1887 should have comfortably placed him at the centre of Canadian cricket lore. And yet, he is scarcely mentioned in any works on Canadian cricket since J.E. Hall and R.O. McCulloch's *Sixty Years of Canadian Cricket* (1895). Alas, there is no Teddy Ogden Trophy. It is hoped, then, that this rescue mission may inspire others to search for all of Canada's forgotten "Teddy Ogdens" in the histories of all the popular and not-so-popular sports, who toiled away with success and were for a time — in their time — famous.

Select Bibliography

BOOKS

Aycock, Colleen and Mark Scott, eds., *The First Black Boxing Champions.* Jefferson, NC: McFarland & Co., 2011.

Bax, Clifford, *W.G. Grace.* London: Phoenix House, 1952.

Beauvais, Johnny, *Kahnawake: A Mohawk Look at Canada and Adventures of Big John Canadian, 1840–1919.* Montreal: Techno Couleur, 1985.

Beers, William George, *Lacrosse: The National Game of Canada.* Montreal: Dawson Brothers, 1869.

Birley, Derek, *Land of Sport and Glory: Sport and British Society, 1887–1910.* Manchester: Manchester University Press, 1995.

Block, David, *Baseball Before We Knew It: A Search for the Roots of the Game.* Lincoln, NB: University of Nebraska Press, 2005.

Bouchier, Nancy, *For the Love of the Game: Amateur Sport in Small-Town Ontario, 1838–1895.* Montreal and Kingston: McGill-Queen's University Press, 2003.

Cosentino, Frank, *Afros, Aboriginals and Amateur Sports in Pre World War One Canada.* Canada's Ethnic Groups Series, Booklet No. 16. Ottawa: Canadian Historical Association, 1998.

Culin, Stewart, *Games of the North American Indians.* Lincoln, NB: University of Nebraska Press, 1992.

Denison, Merrill, *Klondike Mike: An American Odyssey.* New York: William Morrison, 1943.

Downey, Allan, *The Creator's Game: Lacrosse, Identity, and Indigenous Nationhood.* Vancouver: University of British Columbia, 2018.

Early, Gerald, ed., *The Cambridge Companion to Boxing.* New York: Cambridge University Press, 2019.

Farr, Finis, *Black Champion: The Life and Times of Jack Johnson.* New York: Charles Scribner's Sons, 1964.

Fisher, Donald M., *Lacrosse: A History of the Game.* Baltimore: Johns Hopkins University Press, 2002.

Gilles, Roger, *Women on the Move: The Forgotten Era of Women's Bicycle Racing.* Lincoln, NB: University of Nebraska Press, 2018.

Gorn, Elliott J., *The Manly Art: Bare-Knuckle Prize Fighting in America.* Ithaca, NY: Cornell University Press, 2010.

Guroff, Margaret, *The Mechanical Horse: How the Bicycle Reshaped American Life.* Austin, TX: University of Texas Press, 2016.

Guttmann, Allan, *Games and Empires.* New York: Columbia University Press, 1994.

Hall, M. Ann, *The Girl and the Game: A History of Women's Sport in Canada.* Toronto: University of Toronto Press, 2016.

———, *Muscle on Wheels: Louise Armaindo and the High-Wheel Racers of Nineteenth-Century America.* Montreal: McGill-Queen's University Press, 2018.

Hardy, Stephen, *How Boston Played: Sports, Recreation, and Community, 1865–1915.* Boston: Northeastern University Press, 1982.

Hawley, Samuel, *I Just Ran: Percy Williams, World's Fastest Human.* Vancouver: Ronsdale Press, 2011.

Herlihy, Edward V, *The Lost Cyclist: The Epic Tale of an American Adventurer and His Mysterious Disappearance.* Boston: Houghton Mifflin Harcourt, 2010.

Hotchkiss, Ron, *The Matchless Six: The Story of Canada's First Women's Olympic Team.* Toronto: Tundra Press, 2006.

———, *Queen of the Cinder Track: The Life and Times of Rosa Margueretta Grosse.* Altona, MB: Friesen Press, 2021.

Howell, Colin, *Blood, Sweat and Cheers.* Toronto: University of Toronto Press, 2001.

Humber, William, *Diamonds of the North: A Concise History of Baseball in Canada.* Toronto: Oxford University Press, 1995.

———, *Freewheeling: The Story of Bicycling in Canada.* Erin, ON: Boston Mills Press, 1986.

———, *A Sporting Chance: Achievements of African-Canadian Athletes.* Toronto: Natural Heritage Books, 2004.

Isenberg, Michael, *John L. Sullivan and His America.* Champaign-Urbana, IL: University of Illinois Press, 1994.

Johnson, Leo A., *The History of Guelph 1827–1927*. Guelph, ON: Guelph Historical Society, 1977.

Kidd, Bruce, *The Struggle for Canadian Sport*. Toronto: University of Toronto Press, 1996.

Kinsman, Brian, *Around the World Awheel: The Adventures of Karl M. Creelman*. Hantsport, NS: Lancelot Press, 1993.

Kirsch, George B., *Baseball in Blue and Grey: The National Pastime During the Civil War*. Princeton, NJ: Princeton University Press, 2007.

Laffoley, Steven, *Shadowboxing: The Rise and Fall of George Dixon*. Lawrencetown Beach, NS: Pottersfield Press, 2012.

Llewellyn, Matthew, *Rule Britannia, Nationalism, Identity and the Modern Olympic Games*. New York: Routledge, 2011.

Lumsden, Louisa Innes, *Yellow Leaves: Memories of a Long Life*. London: William Blackwood and Sons, 1933.

Mangan, J.A., ed., *Pleasure, Profit, Proselytism: British Culture and Sport at Home and Abroad 1700–1914*. London: Frank Cass, 1988.

Mangan, J.A., Fan Hong, and Boria Majumdar, eds., *Freeing the Human Body: Inspirational Icons*. London: Frank Cass, 2001.

Martin, Brian, *The Tecumsehs of the International Association: Canada's First Major League Baseball Champions*. Jefferson, NC: McFarland, 2015.

Matthews, George R., *America's First Olympics: The St. Louis Games of 1904*. St. Louis: University of Missouri Press, 2005.

McCaffery, Dan, *Tommy Burns: Canada's Unknown World Heavyweight Champion*. Toronto: James Lorimer, 2000.

Meredith, Anthony, *W.G. Grace: In the Steps of a Legend*. Stroud, Gloucestershire: Amberley Publishing, 2015.

Metcalfe, Alan, *Canada Learns to Play: The Emergence of Organized Sports, 1807–1914*. Don Mills, ON: Oxford University Press, 1987.

Middleton, Richard, *Pontiac's War: Its Causes, Course and Consequences*. New York: Routledge, 2007.

Milloy, John S., *A National Crime: The Canadian Government and the Residential School System, 1879–1986*. Winnipeg: University of Manitoba Press, 1999.

Moore, Louis, *I Fight for a Living: Boxing and the Battle for Black Manhood, 1880–1915*. Champaign-Urbana, IL: University of Illinois Press, 2017.

Morrow, Don and Kevin B. Wamsley, *Sport in Canada: A History*, 4th ed. Don Mills, ON: Oxford University Press, 2017.

Moyle, Clay, *Sam Langford: Boxing's Greatest Uncrowned Champion*. Seattle: Bennett & Hastings, 2012.

Nicholson, Kelly Richard, *Hitters, Dancers and Ring Magicians: Seven Boxers of the Golden Age and Their Challengers*. Jefferson, NC: McFarland, 2010.

Norcliffe, Glen, *The Ride to Modernity: The Bicycle in Canada, 1869–1900*. Toronto: University of Toronto Press, 2001.

Pfeifer, Michael J., *Rough Justice: Lynching and American Society, 1874–1947*. Champaign-Urbana, IL: University of Illinois Press, 2006.

Poulter, Gillian, *Becoming Native in a Foreign Land: Sports, Visual Culture, and Identity in a Foreign Land*. Vancouver: University of British Columbia Press, 2009.

Pratt, Mary Louise, *Imperial Eyes: Travel Writing and Transculturation*. London: Routledge, 1992.

Rader, Benjamin, *Baseball: A History of America's Game*, 4th ed. Champaign-Urbana, IL: University of Illinois Press, 2018.

Rae, Simon, *W.G. Grace: A Life*. London: Faber and Faber, 1999.

Radforth, Ian Walter, *Royal Spectacle: The 1860 Visit of the Prince of Wales to Canada and the United States*. Toronto: University of Toronto Press, 2004.

Sandiford, Keith, *Cricket and the Victorians*. Aldershot, UK: Scholar Press, 1994.

Sentance, P. David, *Cricket in America, 1710–2000*. Jefferson, NC: McFarland & Company, 2006.

Thiessen, Dennis, *Tip O'Neill and the St. Louis Browns of 1887*, Jefferson, NC: McFarland & Company, 2019.

Town, David F., *Hot Foot: Walter Knox's Remarkable Life as a Professional in an Amateur World*. Altona, MB: Friesen Press, 2014.

Vennum, Thomas, *Lacrosse Legends of the First Americans*. Baltimore: Johns Hopkins University Press, 2007.

Voorhies, Barbara, ed., *Prehistoric Games of North American Indians: Subarctic to Mesoamerica*. Salt Lake City: University of Utah Press, 2017.

Winders, Jason, *George Dixon: The Short Life of Boxing's First Black World Champion, 1870–1908*. Fayetteville: University of Arkansas Press, 2021.

PUBLISHED PRIMARY SOURCES

Beers, William George, *Lacrosse: The National Game of Canada*. Montreal: Dawson Brothers, 1869.

Burns, Tommy, *Scientific Boxing and Self Defence*. London: Health and Science, 1908.

Deacon, Bruce W., *Physical Education Curriculum Review Report*. Vancouver: Ministry of Education Curriculum Branch, 2001.

Fitzgerald, R.A., *Wickets in the West, or The Twelve in America*. London: Tinsley Brothers, 1873.

Hall, J.E. and R.O. McCulloch, *Sixty Years of Canadian Cricket*. Toronto: Bryant Printing and Publishing, 1895.

Jacomb, William J., *Boxing for Beginners, With Chapter Showing Its Relationship to Bayonet Fighting*. Philadelphia: Lea & Febiger, 1918.

Lillywhite, Fred, *The English Cricketers' Trip to Canada and the United States*. London: Kent & Co., 1860.

Lindsey, Goldwin and Dyce W. Saunders (a.k.a. Two of the Vagrants), *Cricket Across the Sea, or, The Wanderings and Matches of the Gentlemen of Canada, 1887*. Toronto: James Murray, 1887.

Marylebone Cricket Club, *The Laws of Cricket 2017 Code*, 2nd ed. London: Marylebone Cricket Club, 2019.

McAllister, Robert, *The Kind of Guy I Am*. New York: McGraw Hill, 1957.

Pardon, Sydney H., ed., "Obituaries," *John Wisden's Cricketers' Almanack for 1914*. London: John Wisden and Co., 1914; espncricinfo.com.

Twain, Mark, "Taming the Bicycle," in Mark Twain, *Collected Tales, Sketches, Speeches, and Essays, 1852–1890*. New York: Library of America, 1992.

Notes

FAMOUS: AN INTRODUCTION

1 Bruce Kidd, "The Making of a Hockey Artifact: A Review of the Hockey Hall of Fame," *Journal of Sport History* 23, no. 3 (Fall 1996): 332.

2 "Indigenous Woman Named to Canada's Sports Hall of Fame," *Indian Life* 40, no. 3 (Nov–Dec 2019).

CHAPTER I — THE CREATOR'S GAME AND CANADIAN IDENTITY: LACROSSE, 1800S

1 See, *inter alia*, Daniel Francis, *The Imaginary Indian: The Image of the Indian in Canadian Culture* (Vancouver: Arsenal Pulp Press, 2012); John S. Milloy, *A National Crime: The Canadian Government and the Residential School System, 1879 to 1986* (Winnipeg: University of Manitoba Press, 1999); John S. Milloy, "Indian Act Colonialism: A Century of Dishonour, 1869–1969" (National Centre for First Nations Governance, 2008).

2 As early as September 1834, the *Montreal Gazette* carried accounts of a Kahnawake team putting on a demonstration of the sport before a large audience at the St. Pierre racecourse in Montreal. See *Montreal Gazette*, September 25, 1834.

3 *Montreal Gazette*, August 29, 1844; Gillian Poulter, *Becoming Native in a Foreign Land: Sports, Visual Culture, and Identity in a Foreign Land* (Vancouver: University of British Columbia Press, 2009), 117.

4 H.H. Roxborough, "Can Lacrosse Come Back?" *Maclean's Magazine* (August 15, 1929).

5 Allan Downey, *The Creator's Game: Lacrosse, Identity, and Indigenous Nationhood* (Vancouver: University of British Columbia, 2018), 145.

6 Mary Louise Pratt, *Imperial Eyes: Travel Writing and Transculturation* (London: Routledge, 1992), 4.

7 The French colonists had used the term *la crosse* (game of the crozier) to refer to Indigenous people's stick-and-ball games in general.

8 Thomas Vennum, *Lacrosse Legends of the First Americans* (Baltimore: Johns Hopkins University Press, 2007), 25.

9 Ronald F. Williamson and Martin S. Cooper, "He Must Die Unless the Whole Country Shall Play Crosse: The Role of Gaming in Great Lakes Indigenous Societies," in Barbara Voorhies (ed.), *Prehistoric Games of North American Indians: Subarctic to Mesoamerica* (Salt Lake City: University of Utah Press, 2017), 49.

10 North American Indian Traveling College, *Tewaarathon (LaCrosse), Akwesasne's Story of Our National Game* (Akwesasne: NAITC, 1978), 35.

11 Cited in Michael A. Robidoux, "Imagining a Canadian Identity Through Sport: A Historical Interpretation of Lacrosse and Hockey," *Journal of American Folklore* 115, no. 456, (Spring 2002).

12 Jonathan Carver and Edward G. Bourne, "The Travels of Jonathan Carver," *American Historical Review* 11, no. 2 (January 1906): 287–302; Stewart Culin, *Games of the North American Indians* (Lincoln, NB: University of Nebraska Press, 1992), 566.

13 Richard Middleton, *Pontiac's War: Its Causes, Course and Consequences* (New York: Routledge, 2007), 91–2.

14 Robidoux, "Imagining a Canadian Identity Through Sports," 213–14.

15 Fabrice Delsahut, "From Baggataway to Lacrosse: An Example of the Sportization of Native American Games," *International Journal of the History of Sport* 32, no. 7 (2015): 923.

16 Johnny Beauvais, *Kahnawake: A Mohawk Look at Canada and Adventures of Big John Canadian, 1840–1919* (Montreal: Techno Couleur, 1985), 4.

17 In 1833, Montreal sportsmen could watch a game between Kahnawake and Kanesatake teams played as part of the ceremony to initiate five new chiefs; see Poulter, *Becoming Native in a Foreign Land*, 138.

18 A term coined by the author R.G. Haliburton in Montreal in 1869. See Robert Grant Haliburton, *The Men of the North and Their Place in History: A Lecture Delivered Before the Montreal Literary Club, March 31st, 1869* (Ottawa: 1869), passim.

19 The notion still has currency in the 21st century. Witness the National Basketball Association's Toronto Raptors and their PR campaign "We the North." Although far more inclusive, it still plays on the agency of the land

and the pioneering spirit that the anglophones of Montreal were using in the 19th century.

20 Gillian Poulter, "'Eminently Canadian': Indigenous Sports and Canadian Identity in Victorian Montreal," in Davis Newhouse, Cora Voyageur, and Dan Beavon (eds.), *Hidden in Plain Sight: Contributions of Aboriginal People to Canadian Identity and Culture* (Toronto: University of Toronto Press, 2005), 353.

21 Ian Walter Radforth, *Royal Spectacle: The 1860 Visit of the Prince of Wales to Canada and the United States* (Toronto: University of Toronto Press, 2004), 219.

22 Johnny Beauvais suggests that the inclusion of such "Indian dances" was based on the rule to give "the audience what it wants whether it is fact or fancy." Beauvais, *Kahnawake*, 37–8.

23 Radforth, *Royal Spectacle*, 220.

24 *Montreal Gazette*, November 14, 1867.

25 "The Game of Lacrosse: A Sport for Which Whites Are Indebted to Indians," *Chicago Daily Tribune*, February 20, 1887.

26 Dan McCaffery, *Tommy Burns: Canada's Unknown World Heavyweight Champion* (Seattle: James Lorimer, 2000), 111.

27 "Lacrosse Match: Toronto vs the Six Nation Indians," *Globe*, September 26, 1867, cited in Downey, *Creator's Game*, 50.

28 Grant Jarvie and Joseph Maguire, *Sport and Leisure in Social Thought* (London: Routledge, 1994).

29 Robidoux, "Imagining a Canadian Identity Through Sports," 212.

30 William George Beers, *Lacrosse: The National Game of Canada* (Montreal: Dawson Brothers, 1869), 76.

31 *Montreal Daily Star*, August 25, 1879.

32 The Indigenous team in the first tour was sponsored by the Montreal Lacrosse Club and organized by Captain William B. Johnson of the Canadian Volunteers. In another instance, Big John Taiaiake Rice put together a team of 18 Indigenous players from Kahnawake who were paid to accompany and play against amateur players from the MLC. Although the 6'7" Taiaiake was not an active player at the time, being 56 years old, "he projected a charisma" that helped promote the tour. He also countered existing British stereotypes of Indigenous people. See "Canadian Summary," *The British Columbian*, October 5, 1867; Downey, *The Creator's Game*, 56; Beauvais, *Kahnawake*, 101.

33 Colin D. Howell and Daryl Leeworthy, "Playing on the Border: Sports, Borderlands and the North Atlantic," *Sport in Society* 20, no. 3 (2017): 1358.

34 "La Crosse at Kennington Oval," *London Daily News*, June 6, 1876.

35 "Exciting Games of Lacrosse by the Montreal Club and the Indians," *New York Herald*, August 17, 1876.

36 "Canada," *Colonies and India*, September 7, 1883: 14.

37 Rule IX section 6, Beers, *Lacrosse*, 254.

38 In response, the Indigenous teams formed an annual competition called the "Indian Championship of the World." Won first by a Kahnawake team (1880–84), the title was then held for 20 years by Akwesasne teams. A.W. Weyand and M.R. Roberts, *The Lacrosse Story* (Baltimore: H. and A. Herman, 1965), 39–40.

39 Donald Fisher, *Lacrosse: A History of the Game* (Baltimore: Johns Hopkins University Press. 2002), 37.

40 In a few areas, women played a version of stickball called double ball. In this game, two balls were fastened together by string or thong and players used sticks with a slight curve on the end to catch and throw the double ball.

41 For further discussion on Canada's "Crisis in Masculinity" as it pertains to hockey, see Jason Wilson, "Skating to Armageddon: Of Canada, Hockey and the First World War," *International Journal of the History of Sport* 22, no. 3 (Oxford: Routledge, May 2005): 315–43.

42 Louisa Innes Lumsden, *Yellow Leaves: Memories of a Long Life* (London: William Blackwood and Sons, 1933), 81.

43 Some sport historians, such as Melissa C. Wiser, now argue that although men's and women's lacrosse share a name, they evolved within very different race, class, and gender expectations into different sports. See Melissa C. Wiser, "Lacrosse History, a History of One Sports or Two? A Comparative Analysis of Men's Lacrosse and Women's Lacrosse in the United States," *International Journal of the History of Sport* 31, no. 13 (2014): 1656–76.

44 George R. Matthews, *America's First Olympics: The St. Louis Games of 1904* (St. Louis: University of Missouri, 2005), 124.

45 John S. Milloy, *A National Crime: The Canadian Government and the Residential School System, 1879–1986* (Winnipeg: University of Manitoba Press, 1999), 52.

46 The Truth and Reconciliation Commission confirmed that there were at least 4,100 student deaths resulting from abuse, negligence, lack of medical care, and suicide in residential "schools." The commission estimated that the number in reality is closer to 6,000 children.

47 Downey, *The Creator's Game*, 89.

48 John Reid, "Space, Environment, and Appropriation: Sport and Settler Colonialism in Mi'kma'ki," *Journal of Sport History* 46, no. 2 (Summer 2019): 248.

49 Ted Reeve, "Box Lacrosse," *Maclean's Magazine*, August 15, 1931.

50 The run was part of a larger attempt to have the two gold medals won by Thorpe at the 1912 Stockholm Games — which were stripped from him when it was revealed that he had earned $5 a game in semi-pro baseball in 1909 — returned to his family. New medals were presented to Thorpe's family in 1983 after it was established that the committee had violated its own rules about challenging any of the results.

51 The Haudenosaunee Confederacy had issued its own passports as early as 1923.

CHAPTER II — TIP AND TEDDY: BASEBALL V. CRICKET, 1887

1 George Goldwin Smith Lindsey and Dyce W. Saunders (a.k.a. Two of the Vagrants), *Cricket Across the Sea, or, The Wanderings and Matches of the Gentlemen of Canada, 1887* (Toronto: James Murray & Co., 1887), 129.

2 "Base-Ball and Athletics," *St. Louis Globe-Democrat*, August 3, 1887: 8.

3 R.A. Fitzgerald, *Wickets in the West, or, The Twelve in America* (London: Tinsley Brothers, 1873), 6.

4 *Patriot*, July 15, 1836.

5 J.E. Hall and R.O. McCulloch, *Sixty Years of Canadian Cricket* (Toronto: Bryant Printing and Publishing, 1895), 1.

6 Leo A. Johnson, *The History of Guelph 1827–1927* (Guelph, ON: Guelph Historical Society, 1977), 321.

7 *Guelph Daily Mercury*, July 17, 1876; May 14, 1877; May 25, June 2, 1881.

8 R.A. Fitzgerald, "Letter to T.C. Patteson, Esq." (September 16, 1872). As found in Hall and McCulloch, *Sixty Years of Canadian Cricket*, 331–32.

9 Fitzgerald, *Wickets in the West*, 54.

10 Hall and McCulloch, *Sixty Years of Canadian Cricket*, 264–65.

11 Unlike the more famous case of the 1838 game at Beachville, there was no description of the rules under which it was played. *Military Encampment: Souvenir Book and Program* (Hamilton, ON: Ladies' Committee of the Wentworth Historical Society, 1895), 45, cited in Ben Robinson, "Fields of Engagement: Baseball in Rural Ontario, 1879–1925," *Ontario History* 102, no. 1 (Spring 2010): 40–55.

12 "Ball Play," *New York Clipper*, September 27, 1856.

13 The names given to many of the first baseball clubs — American, Columbia,

Eagle, Young America, Washington, Union, Liberty, and National — reflect an early attempt to proclaim the games as American. Benjamin Rader, *Baseball: A History of America's Game*, 4th ed. (Champaign-Urbana, IL: University of Illinois Press, 2018), 17.

14 David Block, *Baseball Before We Knew It: A Search for the Roots of the Game* (Lincoln, NB: University of Nebraska Press, 2005), 62–63.

15 Because Ford, writing from Denver, referred to baseball as "our national game," he had come to see himself as an American.

16 Lacrosse was the one exception, and it provided the necessary conditions for some to call it the national game.

17 Nancy Bouchier, *For the Love of the Game: Amateur Sport in Small-Town Ontario, 1838–1895* (Montreal and Kingston: McGill-Queen's University Press, 2003), 114.

18 *Guelph Daily Mercury*, June 18, 1877.

19 William Humber, *Diamonds of the North: A Concise History of Baseball in Canada* (Toronto: Oxford University Press, 1995), 31.

20 "Baseball Was Started in Guelph in 1861," *Guelph Mercury*, unknown date, 1916.

21 "Base-ball in Canada," *Harper's Magazine*, September 12, 1874: 761–62.

22 Brian Martin, *The Tecumsehs of the International Association: Canada's First Major League Baseball Champions* (Jefferson, NC: McFarland, 2015), 944.

23 At least four hotels in Woodstock and two in Ingersoll "promoted baseball avidly." See Bouchier, *For the Love of the Game*, 103.

24 *New York Clipper*, June 22, 1861.

25 Bouchier, *For the Love of the Game*, 104.

26 "Base Ball Notes. The Woodstock Actives Defeat the Leafs by a Score of 1 to 0," *Guelph Mercury*, August 23, 1878; Dennis Thiessen, *Tip O'Neill and the St. Louis Browns of 1887*, foreword by Mark O'Neill (Jefferson, NC: McFarland & Company, 2019), 27.

27 "Notes," *St. Louis Post-Dispatch*, August 15, 1885: 12.

28 "One of the World-Beaters: 'Tip' O'Neill of the St. Louis Browns Arrives Home," *Woodstock Sentinel-Review*, November 11, 1886.

29 "Diamond Doings," *St. Louis Post-Dispatch*, August 2, 1887: 8.

30 "Base-Ball and Athletics," *St. Louis Globe-Democrat*, August 3, 1887: 8.

31 Thiessen, *Tip O'Neill and the St. Louis Browns of 1887*, 105.

32 Mike Axisa, "Brewers' Christian Yelich becomes fifth player in MLB history with two cycles in one season," cbssports.com, September 17, 2018; Thiessen, *Tip O'Neill and the St. Louis Browns of 1887*, 1–3.

33 "Single Season Leaders for Batting Average," baseball-almanac.com, baseball-almanac.com/hitting/hibavg2.shtml (as of January 1, 2023).

34 C.E. Horner, "English Gentlemen in Canada in 1885," as found in Hall and McCulloch, *Sixty Years of Canadian Cricket*, 426–29.

35 "Britain vs. America," *Daily Inter Ocean*, June 18, 1887, morning edition: 3.

36 An "all-rounder" refers to a cricketer who is adept at both bowling and batting. For more on Ogden's time in Chicago, see Jerome Flannery (ed.), *The American Cricket Annual for 1890* (New York: Sports Publishing), 17; P. David Sentance, *Cricket in America, 1710–2000* (Jefferson, NC: London: McFarland & Company, 2006), 113.

37 "Dr. Edward Russell Ogden," *Spalding's Official Cricket Guide for 1914* (New York: American Sports, 1914), 203.

38 "The Gentlemen of Canada," *Cricket: A Weekly Record of the Game* (April 14, 1887): 54.

39 Lindsey and Saunders, *Cricket Across the Sea*, 12–13.

40 The 1887 Canadian team included, among others, George Goldwin Smith Lindsey (tour organizer, secretary of the TCC, distinguished Toronto lawyer, UCC, University of Toronto and publisher of *Canadian Cricket Field*); Wallace W. Jones (UCC Old Boy, Trinity College, and TCC); Dyce W. Saunders (Trinity College, TCC); George W. Jones (Merchiston Castle School, Edinburgh, St. John, New Brunswick); and, of course, Dr. E.R. Ogden of Chicago. George Goldwin Smith Lindsey, *Tour of Mr. Lindsey's Eleven of the Gentlemen of Canada in England*, Jubilee Year, official itinerary (Toronto: Toronto Public Library Digital Archive, 1887); "The Gentlemen of Canada," *Cricket: A Weekly Record of the Game*, April 14, 1887: 54–55.

41 "The Anchor Steamer *Furnessia*," *Cricket: A Weekly Record of the Game* (July 14, 1887): 265.

42 "The Canadians' Tour," *Globe*, August 23, 1887: 3.

43 Lindsey and Saunders, *Cricket Across the Sea*, 48.

44 "The Canadian Cricketers: Summary of the Tour," *Cricket: A Weekly Record of the Game* (September 8, 1887): 398.

45 Lindsey and Saunders, *Cricket Across the Sea*, 120.

46 Ibid., 121.

47 Dyce W. Saunders, as quoted in Hall and McCulloch, *Sixty Years of Canadian Cricket*, 447–49.

48 "M.C.C. v. Gentlemen of Canada," *Cricket: A Weekly Record of the Game* (August 4, 1887): 306.

49 "The Canadian Cricketers: Summary of the Tour," *Cricket: A Weekly Record of the Game* (September 8, 1887): 398.
50 W.G. Grace, as quoted in Simon Rae, *W. G. Grace: A Life* (London: Faber and Faber, 1999), 110.
51 Lindsey and Saunders, *Cricket Across the Sea*, 161–62.
52 John Kalbfleisch, "Cricket match was no picnic: Players stopped balls bowled by British cricket legend W.G. Grace — the Leviathan — with their heads and stomachs," *Montreal Gazette* (August 19, 2007).
53 Lindsey and Saunders, *Cricket Across the Sea*, 166–67.
54 "The Canadian Cricketers: Summary of the Tour," *Cricket: A Weekly Record of the Game* (September 8, 1887): 398.
55 "They Need Not Be Ashamed of their Record," *New York Times*; *Globe*, September 3, 1887: 7.
56 "Mr. Dyce Willcocks Saunders," *Cricket: A Weekly Record of the Game* (August 25, 1887): cover page.
57 Lindsey and Saunders, *Cricket Across the Sea*, 216–7.
58 "The Canadian Cricketers: Summary of the Tour," *Cricket: A Weekly Record of the Game* (September 8, 1887): 398.
59 "Bisons Badly Trounced" and "Good Games of Cricket," *Chicago Tribune*, August 12, 1890: 6.
60 In the five-year period from 1885 to 1889, as Thiessen confirmed, O'Neill "had the best batting average with a cumulative five-year percentage of .370, ahead of Pete Browning (.360) and Dave Orr (.341), two of the leading batsmen in the American Association, and Dan Brouthers (.367), Cap Anson (.359), and Roger Connor (.344), three of the leading batsmen in the National League. O'Neill was in the top three in the majors in hits, runs batted in, slugging percentage, and on-base plus slugging percentage, and fourth best in total bases." Thiessen, *Tip O'Neill and the St. Louis Browns of 1887*, 159–60.
61 "Brotherhood," *Daily Inter Ocean*, August 23, 1890, morning edition: 3.
62 Sydney H. Pardon (ed.), "Obituaries," *John Wisden's Cricketers' Almanack for 1914* (London: John Wisden and Co., 1914; espncricinfo.com).
63 "The Gentlemen of Canada," *Cricket: A Weekly Record of the Game* (April 14, 1887): 54.
64 "Dr. Edward Russell Ogden," *Spalding's Official Cricket Guide for 1914*, 203.
65 The Ashes remains one of the world's oldest sporting contests, played between England and Australia at least once every two years. David Cooper, "Canadians Declare 'It Isn't Cricket,'" *Journal of Sport History* 26, no. 1 (Spring 1999), 75. For a variety of theories on why cricket failed in

Canada, see Alan Metcalfe, *Canada Learns to Play* (Toronto: McClelland and Stewart, 1987), 20, 80–4; Allan Guttmann, *Games and Empires* (New York: Columbia University Press, 1994), 23, 112; Derek Birley, *Land of Sport and Glory: Sport and British Society, 1887–1910* (Manchester: Manchester University Press, 1995), 67, 158; Keith Sandiford, *Cricket and the Victorians* (Aldershot, England: Scholar Press, 1994), 148.

CHAPTER III – SCORCHERS AND WANDERERS: CANADA'S CYCLING CRAZE, 1883–1901

1 Jeffery S. Murray, "Riding the Cycling Craze," *Legion: Canada's Military History Magazine* (September 2006): 1.

2 Mark Twain, "Taming the Bicycle," in Mark Twain, *Collected Tales, Sketches, Speeches, and Essays, 1852–1890* (New York: Library of America, 1992), 899.

3 *Canadian Wheelman,* October 1887: 148.

4 Glen Norcliffe, "National Identity, Club Citizenship, and the Formation of the Canadian Wheelman's Association, 1883–87," *Journal of Canadian Studies* 51, no. 2 (Spring 2017): 462.

5 Despite the British background of many members, these clubs tended to follow the rules and hierarchy set down by Charles E. Pratt, a Civil War veteran. See Charles E. Pratt, *The American Bicycler* (Boston: Rockwell and Churchill, 1880).

6 The League of American Wheelmen, perhaps the most influential cycling club, had a number of Canadian members. Murray, "Riding the Cycling Craze," 3.

7 "Sporting World," *Winnipeg Daily Tribune,* June 17, 1896.

8 Rebecca Beausaert has studied small, turn-of-the-century cycling clubs in Tillsonburg and Ingersoll that admitted women members. The clubs lost their virulent masculinity, but the women were not truly accepted as full members. Rebecca Beausaert, "'Young Rovers' and 'Dazzling Lady Meteors': Gender and Bicycle Club Culture in Turn-of-the-Century Small-Town Ontario," *Scientia Canadensis* 36, no. 1 (2013): 46–50.

9 Lachapelle was born in Montreal in 1859 and moved to the United States with her husband around 1877.

10 M. Ann Hall, *Muscles on Wheels: Louise Armaindo and the High-Wheel Racers of Nineteenth-Century America* (Montreal: McGill-Queen's University Press, 2018), 15, 49.

11 Norcliffe, *The Ride to Modernity: The Bicycle in Canada, 1869-1900* (Toronto: University of Toronto Press, 2001), 18.

12 Steve Brearton, "Peterborough's Rich Bicycle History," *The Bicycle Museum,* November 2018.

13 One of the Tillsonburg Meteor rides in 1895 described by Beausaert was composed of 20 men and 11 women. That was about the same gender breakdown that the *Toronto Evening Star* found in its census of riders leaving the city on a Sunday in 1896. Beausaert, "'Young Rovers' and 'Dazzling Lady Meteors,'" 54; Murray, "Riding the Cycling Craze," 4.

14 For examples of two views on this issue, see Heather Watts, "Silent Steeds: Cycling in Nova Scotia to 1900" (Halifax: Nova Scotia Museum, 1985); and Anita Rush, "The Bicycle Boom of the Gay Nineties: A Reassessment," *Material History Review* 18 (1983): 1–12.

15 Colin Howell, *Blood, Sweat, and Cheers: Sport and the Making of Modern Canada* (Toronto: University of Toronto Press, 2001), 114–15.

16 M. Ann Hall, *The Girl and the Game: A History of Women's Sport in Canada* (Toronto: University of Toronto Press, 2002), 15.

17 Fittingly, Mary Marshal, one of the first Canadian professional pedestrians and then high-wheel racer, had supported herself and her son by working as a door-to-door bookseller. M. Ann Hall, *Muscle on Wheels*, 20–21.

18 The two cyclists clearly had a complex relationship. They were, at different times, both competitors and colleagues. When they started travelling together, they let people believe they were married. Although they may have been lovers, they were never married.

19 Roger Gilles, *Women on the Move: The Forgotten Era of Women's Bicycle Racing* (Lincoln, NB: University of Nebraska Press, 2018), 32–33.

20 Hall, *Muscle on Wheels*, 90–92.

21 "The Wonderful Riders of the Flying Wheels Who Have Beaten Man and Beast," *National Police Gazette*, May 10, 1884: 6.

22 "A Strange Contest," *Winnipeg Daily Sun*, August 19, 1884.

23 "Here and There," *Bicycling World*, November 4, 1887: 6, cited in Hall, *Muscle on Wheels,* 113. Ironically, when Armaindo did marry in 1888, it turned out to be an exploitative marriage to a much younger man that only hurt her career.

24 "Bicycle Tournament," *Saint Joseph Daily Express*, February 15, 1889.

25 In a January 1896 six-day race in Madison Square Garden, the winners of the race, Frankie Nelson and her partner, May Allen, both used the patent medicine bovinine. It was a mixture of beef blood, glycerin, and sodium chloride. It was not a covert act. Both racers were monitored by a physician and the results published in *Modern Medical Science*. Nelson testified that she was not properly

fit at the start of the race, but once she began taking bovinine under the guidance of a physician, "I soon regained my strength and vigor, and suffered no inconvenience from the violent exertions that I was obliged to put forth." See, "From the Female Champion," *Modern Medical Science* 8, no. 9 (March 1896): 134, 596–98, cited in Hall, *Muscle on Wheels,* 152.

26 The *Winnipeg Tribune* carried daily reports of the competition from June 9 to 17, 1896.

27 Hall, *Muscle on Wheels*, 158–9.

28 "Sporting World," *Winnipeg Tribune*, June 17, 1896.

29 The *Journal* described her as standing "less than four and one-half feet." William Humber, *Freewheeling: The Story of Bicycling in Canada* (Erin, ON: Boston Mills Press, 1986), 124; *Ottawa Journal*, November 22, 1900.

30 *49 Boston Post*, August 28, 1902: 2; Hall, *Muscle on Wheels, 168.*

31 Humber, *Freewheeling*, 15–17.

32 The Montreal Bicycle Club joined the LAW in 1880 but subsequently left to join the CWA in 1883. See Norcliffe, "National Identity, Club Citizenship," 465.

33 Steve Brearton, "A History of CCM in Weston, Ontario," Dandyhorse, posted October 13, 2018, dandyhorsemagazine.com.

34 Glen Norcliffe, *The Ride to Modernity*, 113.

35 Carman Miller, "Framing Canada's Great War: a case for including the Boer War," *Journal of Transatlantic Study* (April 2008): 4.

36 Eva Chen, "'The Hate that Changed': Cycling Romance and the Aestheticization of Women Cyclists," *Victorian Periodicals Review* 52, no. 3 (Fall 2019): 491.

37 Margaret Guroff, *The Mechanical Horse: How the Bicycle Reshaped American Life* (Austin: University of Texas Press, 2016), 114.

38 Carlton Reid, *Roads Were not Built for Cars: How Cyclists Were the First to Push for Good Roads and Became the Pioneers of Motoring* (Washington, D.C.: Island Press, 2017), 190.

39 Jaroslav Petryshyn, "Russell, Thomas Alexander," *Dictionary of Canadian* Biography, 16.

40 Norcliffe, *The Ride to Modernity*, 121–23.

41 The Toronto Athenaeum Club built its own storage facility to accommodate the 1,000 bicycles of the club members.

42 Murray, *Riding the Cycling Craze*, 3.

43 William Humber, "Bicycling," *The Canadian Encyclopedia* (2015).

44 Canadian *Wheelman,* October 1887: 146.

45 Beausaert, "'Young Rovers' and 'Dazzling Lady Meteors,'" 43–44.
46 Norcliffe, *The Ride to Modernity*, 175; Murray, "Riding the Cycling Craze," 41.
47 John C. Lehr and H. John Selwood, "Two-Wheeled Workhorse: The Bicycle as Personal and Commercial Transport in Winnipeg," *Urban History Review* 28, no. 1 (October 1999): 6.
48 Norcliffe argues that Canadian cyclists had less influence than their American counterparts, who had joined the Good Roads Movement in 1889. Although cyclists were most active for only a limited period of time, their position in society gave them significant political influence. Norcliffe, *The Ride to Modernity*, 150–51.
49 That feeling motivated Creelman's biographer, Brian Kinsman, *Around the World Awheel: The Adventures of Karl M. Creelman* (Hantsport, NS: Lancelot Press, 1993), and also photojournalist and blogger, Louise Trotter, who is — at the time of writing — retracing Creelman's travels in the *Karl Chronicles*. For more see louisetrotter.photo/about-karl.
50 The first cyclist to circle the world, Thomas Stevens, had published his account of his journey in *Around the World on a Bicycle* in 1887.
51 "Creelman Reaches Vancouver," *Seattle Post-Intelligencer*, November 10, 1899.
52 On the outskirts of Truro, he gave the money he had in his pocket — $0.03 — to three paper boys. Kinsman, *Around the World Awheel*, 20.
53 While in Montreal, in one case, he visited the *Montreal Star* office, and shortly thereafter the paper began to carry his accounts of his travels. Papers in Truro, Vancouver, Kingston, and Sydney all carried frequent accounts of his travels.
54 "A Long Cycle Tour," *Brandon Western Sun*, August 31, 1899.
55 The company had retail outlets in both Sydney, Australia, and Cape Town, South Africa, where Creelman expected to tour.
56 Kinsman, *Around the World Awheel*, 37, 108.
57 "Globe Trotter Visits Brandon Once Again," *Brandon Daily Sun*, October 13, 1917.
58 "Creelman Reaches Vancouver," *Seattle Post-Intelligencer*, November 10, 1899; *Armidale Chronicle*, May 5, 1900.
59 See Jim Fitzpatrick, "A Glimpse of Australia's Cycling History," in Jennifer Bonham and Marilyn Johnson (eds.), *Cycling Futures* (Adelaide: University of Adelaide Press, 2015), 25–6; "Round the World," *Gympie Times*, April 26, 1900.
60 Much of his writing was done before he contracted malaria. "Around the World Awheel," *Agassiz Record* (BC), January 11, 1901.
61 Creelman, as quoted in Kinsman, *Around the World Awheel*, 94.

62 Duncan R. Jamieson, *The Self-Propelled Voyager: How the Cycle Revolutionized Travel* (Washington, D.C.: Rowman & Littlefield Publishers, 2015), 86.
63 "Wanderings of a Locomotive Fireman," *Brotherhood of Locomotive Firemen and Enginemen's Magazine*, (February 1908): 187.
64 And even here, Verne had given himself 80 days. Creelman offered no such limitations.

CHAPTER IV – "THE GREATEST ALL-ROUND ATHLETIC MACHINE OF MODERN TIMES": WALTER KNOX

1 Don Morrow, "A Case-Study in Amateur Conflict: The Athletic War in Canada, 1906–08," *British Journal of Sports History* (September 1986): 174.
2 H.H. Roxborough, "Where Are Canada's Field Athletes?" *Maclean's Magazine*, April 15, 1926.
3 Walter Knox, "Hot Foot: Fifty Years in Sport," 149. An uncompleted autobiographical manuscript compiled in 1951, along with a scrapbook of newspaper clippings, and both held by the Orillia Museum of Art and History, Orillia, Ontario.
4 Ibid., 150–51.
5 David F. Town, *Hot Foot: Walter Knox' Remarkable Life as a Professional in an Amateur World* (Friesen Press, 2014), 146–49.
6 "Mr. Knox Makes Record," *Bozeman Chronicle*, Knox Scrapbook, October 1907.
7 In his uncompleted autobiography, Knox denied any ill feelings toward Bricker. "Mr. Knox Makes Record," *Bozeman Chronicle,* Knox Scrapbook, 1907.
8 "W.R. Knox Apply for Readmission," Knox Scrapbook, 1907.
9 "C.A.A.U. Meets," *Winnipeg Tribune*, June 18, 1907.
10 Knox, "Hot Foot: Fifty Years in Sport," 4.
11 Ibid., 3.
12 Ibid., 23–24.
13 Gray held the international record for shot putting, a distance of 43'11", from 1887 to 1902, and was the Canadian amateur champion for 17 years and the American champion for 10 before retiring undefeated in 1902. Gill, who had a long and successful coaching career at the University of Illinois, was also an international champion.
14 In early 1898, Long had approached Knox, whom he thought was "just about the smartest shingle man in town," to run a new machine being installed in

Verner. The incentives were an increase in pay and the promise that it was a sporting town. Knox, "Hot Foot: Fifty Years in Sport," 27–28.

15 Knox, "Hot Foot: Fifty Years in Sport," 30–31.

16 Ibid., 5–7.

17 "Canadian Championships," *Winnipeg Free Press,* September 24, 1900.

18 Knox, "Hot Foot: Fifty Years in Sport," 41.

19 Ibid., 42.

20 "Activity in College Athletics," *New York Times,* May 24, 1903.

21 The existing record was held by a University of Chicago vaulter, and one of the judges, a Chicago alumnus, wanted a remeasurement.

22 Howell, *Blood, Sweat and Cheers,* 60.

23 Ibid.

24 *Guelph Weekly Mercury,* July 21, 1881.

25 Bouchier, *For the Love of the Game,* 11.

26 Knox, "Hot Foot: Fifty Years in Sport," 115.

27 Ibid., 111.

28 Town, *Hot Foot: Walter Knox' Remarkable Life,* 103–5.

29 "Big Race Today," *Slocan Drill,* October 21, 1904.

30 "Sprinters Run for Big Purse," "Renwick is Walter Knox," *Spokane Press,* August 8, 1905.

31 "Wilson Too Fast for Ferguson," *Nanaimo Free Press,* June 1, 1906.

32 Town, *Hot Foot: Walter Knox' Remarkable Life,* 146–49.

33 "New Athletic Records Shot Put and Pole Vault," *Orillia Times,* August 9, 1906.

34 In winning, Knox tied Poage's state record. Town, *Hot Foot,* 71.

35 "Many Entries in Amateur Events," *Los Angeles Herald,* July 11, 1909.

36 "Walter Knox is Identified As a 'Ringer,'" Knox Scrapbook, 1909; "Frisco Athletics on Carpet," *Victoria Daily Colonist,* September 14, 1909.

37 Knox, "Hot Foot," 159–60.

38 Ibid., 177.

39 Douglas Baldwin and David F. Duke, "'A Grey Wee Town': An Environmental History of Early Silver Mining in Cobalt, Ontario," *Urban History Review* 34, no. 1 (Fall 2005): 71.

40 Knox, "Hot Foot: Fifty Years in Sport," 187.

41 Lou Marsh, "Short Time Gives Olympic Coach but Little Chance," *Toronto Star,* May 1912. The Lou Marsh Trophy was renamed the Northern Star Award in November 2022.

42 Tom Flanagan, "Canada's Olympic Team Looks Weak and Has Little Chance to Score," *Winnipeg Free Press,* June 22, 112.

43 *Winnipeg Free Press*, June 27, 1912. His grandson was Harry Jerome, bronze medallist in the 1964 Games.

44 "Wonderful Record of Canadian Champion," Knox Scrapbook, October 1912.

45 "A Great All-Round Athlete," *Edinburgh Winning News*, Knox Scrapbook, August 6, 1913.

46 The fund-raising results, about £10,000, fell well short of the target. Matthew Llewellyn, *Rule Britannia, Nationalism, Identity and the Modern Olympic Games* (Oxford: Routledge, 2011), 107, 109, 112, 114.

47 Peter Lovesey, "Conan Doyle and the Olympics," *Journal of Olympic History* 10 (Dec. 2001/ Jan. 2002): 8.

48 "Mr. Walter R. Knox," *Sport and Play*, May 9, 1914.

49 "In Colorful Career Won 411 Firsts," *Orillia News Letter*, April 27, 1931.

50 "Walter R. Knox Has Retired from Athletic Activity," *Orillia Daily Times*, April 28, 1915.

51 "Knox Is Busy Organizing Schools for Athletics," Knox Scrapbook, September 1923.

52 "Walter Knox in Soo Today; Canada's Greatest Athlete," *Sault Weekly Star*, August 28, 1913.

53 Town, *Hot Foot: Walter Knox' Remarkable Life*, 391.

54 Bruce Kidd, "Making the Pros Pay, for Amateur Sports: the Ontario Athletic Commission, 1920–1947," *Sport in Society: Cultures, Commerce, Media, Politics* 16, no. 4 (2013): 539.

55 Ron Hotchkiss, *Queen of the Cinder Track: The Life and Times of Rosa Margueretta Grosse* (Altona, MB: Friesen Press, 2021), 16–17, 170.

56 Fred "Teddy" Oke was a former hockey player, a war veteran, and self-made millionaire who, until the stock market crash in 1929, was willing to spend money to make Parkdale the premier women's club. Hall, *The Girl and the Game*, 45; David MacDonald, "The Golden Age of Women and Sport in Canada," *Canadian Woman Studies* 15, no. 4 (1995): 14.

57 "'Guess They Forgot Me': Knox Was Disappointed Man," *Toronto Star*, March 5, 1951.

CHAPTER V – BARE-KNUCKLE BRAWLERS AND MEN OF MEANS: BOXING, 1881–1908

1 See Louis Moore, "Race and Boxing in the Nineteenth Century," in Gerald Early (ed.), *The Cambridge Companion to Boxing* (New York: Cambridge University Press, 2019), 59.

2 Sullivan won the title under the bare-knuckle London Prize Ring rules and would defend it according to the modern-era Marquess of Queensbury Rules.

3 Moore, "Race and Boxing in the Nineteenth Century," 60.

4 Jack Broughton taught boxing at his London Academy in the mid-1700s. See Elliot J. Gorn, "The Bare-Knuckle Era," in Early (ed.), *The Cambridge Companion to Boxing*, 35.

5 Lesley Choyce, "Fighting Fever in the Maritimes," *Maclean's Magazine*, February 8, 1982.

6 Mitchell Lawrence, "Ernest Hemingway: In the Ring and Out," *Hemingway Review*, September 22, 2011; Morley Callaghan, *That Summer in Paris* (Toronto: Macmillan Canada, 1963), 250.

7 Dan McCaffery, *Tommy Burns*, 186.

8 Louis Moore, *I Fight for a Living: Boxing and the Battle for Black Manhood, 1880–1915* (Champaign-Urbana, IL: University of Illinois Press, 2017), 1.

9 "Professor Godfrey," *San Francisco Chronicle*, July 30, 1888.

10 Stephen Hardy, *How Boston Played: Sports, Recreation, and Community, 1865–1915* (Boston: Northeastern University Press, 1982), 176.

11 Tony Triem, "George Godfrey: First Coloured Heavyweight Champion," in Colleen Aycock and Mark Scott (eds.), *The First Black Boxing Champions* (Jefferson, NC: McFarland & Co., 2011), 23–24.

12 "G. Godfrey First Race Fighter," *Chicago Defender*, July 3, 1920, cited in Jason Winders, *George Dixon: The Short Life of Boxing's First Black World Champion, 1870–1908* (Fayetteville: University of Arkansas Press, 2021), 37–38.

13 Triem, "George Godfrey," 24.

14 Ibid., 27.

15 Cardiff was born in Renfrew County, Ontario, and had moved to the United States in 1881 when he was about 18. A tough and durable heavyweight, Cardiff fought a six-round draw with John L. Sullivan in 1887. During his career, 1884 to 1892, he was heavyweight champion of Illinois and heavyweight champion of the Northwest. In 1907, he owned a prosperous house-moving business in Portland, Oregon.

16 Moore, *I Fight for a Living*, 95–96.

17 Ibid., 3.

18 Winders, *George Dixon*, 40.

19 He reportedly wore weighted shoes in his first weigh-ins in order to make the mandatory 100 pounds for any fighter. See Cyber Boxing Zone, cyberboxingzone.com/boxing/dixon-g.htm.

20 Winders, *George Dixon*, 33.

21 "A Game Fighter Is He," *Washington Post*, March 11, 1894, cited in Winders, *George Dixon*, 73.
22 "Wife of Fighter Dixon," *Boston Daily Globe*, July 30, 1891.
23 "Slugger Dixon," *Winnipeg Daily Tribune*, February 5, 1890.
24 "Lively Bouts," *Brooklyn Daily Eagle*, April 3, 1889, cited in Winders, *George Dixon*, 50.
25 Mike Glenn, "George Dixon: World Bantamweight and Featherweight Champion," in Aycock and Scott (eds.), *The First Black Boxing Champions*, 50–51.
26 "Referee's Remarks," *National Police Gazette*, July 19, 1890.
27 Glenn, "George Dixon," 52.
28 *New Orleans Weekly Times Democrat*, September 7, 1892, cited in Elliot J. Gorn, *The Manly Art: Bare-Knuckle Prize Fighting in America* (Ithaca, NY: Cornell University Press, 2010), 204, 243.
29 There were an estimated 4,500 victims of lynching in the United States from 1883 to 1941, of whom 2,300 were African American. For more information on the subject, see Michael J. Pfeifer, *Rough Justice: Lynching and American Society, 1874–1947* (Champaign-Urbana, IL: University of Illinois Press, 2006).
30 Gorn, *The Manly Art*, 204, 243.
31 John L. Sullivan started the tradition of a boxing champion appearing on stage taking part in vaudeville acts or exhibition bouts. McCaffery, *Tommy Burns*, 73, 123.
32 Advance notice of a $50 prize to anyone who could last four rounds against the champion was often given. Winders, *George Dixon*, 199–200.
33 See Cyber Boxing Zone, cyberboxingzone.com/boxing/dixon-g.htm.
34 "Jolts from 'John L.,'" *Boston Daily Globe*, January 26, 1908.
35 Winders, *George Dixon*, 217.
36 He and a friend had spent the pre-boarding time drinking, and when an elderly and racist white man objected to having a Black man sit beside him, the boxer supposedly became angry and threatening. Winders, *George Dixon*, 201–2.
37 "George Dixon Still Winning," *National Police Gazette*, April 23, 1904.
38 Clay Moyle, "Sam Langford: Heavyweight Champion of Australia, Canada, England and Mexico," in Aycock and Scott (eds.), *The First Black Boxing Champions*, 159.
39 "He Fairly Outclassed the Champion," *Boston Daily Globe*, December 9, 1903.
40 Ketchel was training at a friend's ranch in Missouri when, in a robbery gone bad, a hired hand, Walter Dipley, shot the boxer as he ate breakfast.

41 He also refused to fight other Black boxers. See John Demont, "Requiem for a Heavyweight," *Maclean's Magazine,* May 28, 2001.
42 Hardy, *How Boston Played*, 176.
43 "Sam Langford Entitled to Jack Johnson's Crown," *Winnipeg Free Press*, August 17, 1912.
44 McVey, whom Langford fought 15 times, weighed about 220 pounds for most of his fights while Wills, whom the Canadian faced 18 times, weighed up to 230 pounds.
45 "International Fighting," *The Winnipeg Tribune*, 23 April, 1907.
46 Sam McVey was also fighting on the card and defeated his British opponent. "Americans Beat British," *Agassiz Record*, June 4, 1907.
47 "Sammy Langford Explains Why He Quit to Fred Fulton in Boston," *Halifax Herald*, September 18, 1924, cited in Moyle, "Sam Langford," 164.
48 "Sam Langford Wins Spanish Title," *New York Times*, April 9, 1923.
49 "Al Laney's Prose," *New York Times,* December 3, 1978, Section S, 3.
50 Trent Frayne, "The Greatest Fighter Who Ever Lived," *Maclean's Magazine*, February 15, 1955.
51 Kieran Mulvaney, "The Greatest Fighter Almost Nobody Knows," Espn.com (February 7, 2007), espn.com/espn/blackhistory2007/news/story?id=2755803.
52 The other titles were the world light-heavyweight, the British Empire heavyweight, and both the U.S. Pacific Coast and Michigan middleweight titles. See McCaffery, *Tommy Burns*, 3–4.
53 Ibid., 35.
54 See Cyber Boxing Zone, cyberboxingzone.com/boxing/burns.htm; "Brusso Knocked Out McCune," *Globe*, December 29, 1902; Cincinnati *Commercial Tribune*, December 27, 1902.
55 Al Rosaasen interview as cited in McCaffery, *Tommy Burns*, 64.
56 Tommy Burns, *Scientific Boxing and Self Defence* (London: Health and Science, 1908).
57 "Arrest Prize Fighter," *Bloomington Weekly Pantagraph*, January 29, 1904.
58 Legend had it that Klondike Mike even carried a piano through the Pass. See Merrill Denison, *Klondike Mike: An American Odyssey* (New York: William Morrison, 1943), 182–87.
59 Ibid., 298–99.
60 Red Wilson interview, cited in McCaffery, *Tommy Burns*, 126.
61 "Brusso's Good Showing," *London Free Press*, March 8, 1905.
62 Finis Farr, *Black Champion: The Life and Times of Jack Johnson* (New York: Charles Scribner's Sons, 1964), 40–41.

63 Stephen Jones Gamester, "When Little Tommy Burns Outslugged the Biggest Brutes in Boxing," *Maclean's Magazine*, February 6, 1965, 32.
64 Ibid.
65 *National Police Gazette*, September 25, 1906.
66 *Racine Daily Journal*, February 23, 1906; *Salt Lake City Herald*, April 1, 1906.
67 The two fights were announced in the papers as title bouts. "Tommy Burns Goes Some," *Agassiz Record*, March 30, 1906.
68 McCaffery, *Tommy Burns*, 141.
69 The issue was never *if* Burns would fight Johnson, but only *when*, and under what terms. The issue for Johnson was that he was taking too long to come back to America.
70 "Boxing Championship," *London Evening News*, May 25, 1908.
71 *Globe*, May 1, 1908, cited in McCaffery, *Tommy Burns*, 174.
72 Kerry Banks, "Lonely Warrior," *Canada's History* (February–March 2021): 42.
73 Sam Langford Plans Fight in London with Tommy Burns," *Dubuque Telegraph Herald*, July 26, 1909.
74 McCaffery, *Tommy Burns*, 184.
75 When Johnson was finally forced by the International Boxing Union in 1913 to fight a Black boxer, he selected a second-tier fighter, "Battling Jim" Johnson. Neither boxer put up much of a fight and it ended in a draw.
76 Jason Wilson, "Langford v. Johnson II," *The Peacemaker's Chauffeur* (Wheel Records, 2008).

CHAPTER VI – PEERLESS PERCY AND THE MATCHLESS SIX: AMSTERDAM, 1928

1 Ron Hotchkiss, *The Matchless Six: The Story of Canada's First Women's Olympic Team* (Toronto: Tundra Press, 2006), 126.
2 In the early 20th century, Britain and North America retained the imperial measurements in track and field, but the Olympics, except for a few events in 1904 and 1908, used the metric system.
3 Ray Gardner, "How Percy Williams Swept the Olympic Sprints," *Maclean's Magazine* November 24, 1956: 32; Geoff D'Auria, "Vancouver's Forgotten Track Star," *The Tyee*, August 4, 2012.
4 Roxborough, "Where Are Canada's Field Athletes?"
5 Earl Thomson won gold in the 110-metre hurdles but declined to compete in any other event.

6 Caryne Brown, "Taking the Track," *American History* 31, no. 2 (May/June 1996): 43.
7 Hall, *The Girl and the Game*, 74.
8 Susan L. Forbes, "Gendering Corporate Welfare Practices: Female Sports and Recreation in Eaton's During the Depression," *Rethinking History* 5, no. 1 (2001): 61.
9 One of the most active groups was a women's basketball team from the Edmonton store, the Fur Trappers, who played in a ladies' mercantile basketball league, and by 1924 was the best "100 percent mercantile" team in the province. Hall, *The Girl and the Game*, 74.
10 Hotchkiss, *The Matchless Six*, 44.
11 Bruce W. Deacon, *Physical Education Curriculum Review Report* (Vancouver: Ministry of Education Curriculum Branch, 2001), 8.
12 Kidd, "Making the Pros Pay": 54
13 Hall, *The Girl and the Game*, 46.
14 Hotchkiss puts the comment in quotation marks, but here, as elsewhere, he provides no citation. Hotchkiss, *Queen of the Cinder Track*, 9, 10.
15 Oke's influence diminished with the onset of the Great Depression. David McDonald, "The Golden Age of Women and Sport in Canada," 14; Hall, *The Girl and the Game*, 45, 75; "F.G. 'Teddy' Oke: Sports Lover and Mining Man Dead," *Ottawa Citizen*, April 30, 1937: 4.
16 The society offered life and disability insurance to its members at cost.
17 The field day had been first added in 1909 as a way of maintaining interest in the Ex and showcasing Olympic notables. It was a success from the start and had become one of the premier track events on the continent.
18 Hotchkiss, *Queen of the Cinder Track*, 54.
19 Hotchkiss, *Queen of the Cinder Track*, 60.
20 The first woman to compete, however, was Hélène de Pourtalès of Switzerland in the one- to two-ton sailing event on May 22, 1900.
21 Hall, *The Girl and the Game*, 47.
22 Brown, "Taking the Track," 42.
23 The seventh woman was Dorothy Prior, who swam the 200-metre breaststroke.
24 The countries were Great Britain, Canada, and Czechoslovakia.
25 M. Ann Hall, "Alexandrine Gibb: In 'No Man's Land of Sport,'" as found in J.A. Mangan, Fan Hong, and Boria Majumdar (eds.), *Freeing the Human Body: Inspirational Icons* (London: Frank Cass, 2001), 151, 153; "Confirms Appointment of Miss 'Alex' Gibb," *Globe and Mail*, July 9, 1925.

26 Interestingly, on the same day that Gibb's team was competing, Rosa Grosse set a new world record for the 220-yard dash at a meet in Brantford, Ontario.

27 Hotchkiss, *Queen of the Cinder Track*, 272.

28 By 1926, she had also developed the reputation of being a sprinter who tried to "jump the gun" to better her chance of winning. See Hotchkiss, *Queen of the Cinder Track*, 218.

29 At this time, there was no internationally recognized way of officially recording and recognizing event results.

30 Joseph Levy, Danny Rosenberg, and Avi Hyman, "Fanny 'Bobbie' Rosenfeld: Canada's Woman Athlete of the Half Century," *Journal of Sport History* 26, no. 2 (Summer 1999): 392. See also Christina Burr and Carol A. Reader, "Fanny 'Bobbie' Rosenfeld: A 'Modern Woman' of Sport and Journalism in Twentieth-Century Canada," *Sport History Review* 44 (2013): 121.

31 Officials initially thought Thompson's time was a new world record, but in Germany, Lina Radke had just run 800 metres in under 2 minutes and 24 seconds. Hotchkiss, *Queen of the Cinder Track*, 283.

32 David Dupuis, "Penetanguishene's First Olympic Star," Penetanguishene Sports Hall of Fame, pshof.ca/uploads/6/8/9/5/6895306/jean_thompson.pdf.

33 Samuel Hawley, *I Just Ran: Percy Williams, World's Fastest Human* (Vancouver: Ronsdale Press, 2011), 18–19.

34 Hawley, *I Just Ran*, 19.

35 Kerry Banks, "Forgotten Champion," *Canada's History*, 99, 4 (August/September 2011): 39.

36 Of course, by emphasizing Williams's travesty of form or his running like "a poorly trained trotting horse," Granger emphasized his own contributions to Williams's success. Bob Granger, "The Human Flash: The Story of Percy Williams, Breaker of Speed Records," *American Magazine* (November 1930): 63.

37 Gardner, "How Percy Williams Swept the Olympic Sprints," 34.

38 Hawley, *I Just Ran*, 62.

39 D'Auria, "Vancouver's Forgotten Track Star."

40 The races were in metres to help prepare the runners for the Olympics.

41 Hawley, *I Just Ran*, 86.

42 There was no athletes' village then, and the limited accommodation had to be arranged by individual countries, while Olympic events ran from July 28 to August 12.

43 After the Amsterdam Olympics, Edwards entered the McGill University medical school and became a specialist in tropical medicine. Although he ran for Guiana in the British Empire Games, he ran for Canada in the 1932 and

1936 Olympics, where he won another four bronze medals. Hawley, *I Just Ran*, 92–3; William Humber, *A Sporting Chance: Achievements of African-Canadian Athletes* (Toronto: Natural Heritage Books, 2004).

44 After rumours circulated that Americans were allowed to use the stadium, Mulqueen and Robinson lodged a protest. "Canadians Win Same Olympic Rights As U.S.," *Toronto Star*, July 27, 1928.

45 One of the Canadians not advancing, Buck Hester, had a banner blow across the track, causing him to ease up. Pat Mulqueen of the Canadian Olympic Committee and Bobby Robinson protested the results and demanded a re-run, to no avail. Hawley, *I Just Ran*, 115.

46 Hawley, *I Just Ran*, 146.

47 By contrast, little criticism was directed at Frank Wykoff when the American burst into tears after finishing fourth in the 100-metre race. Robert McAllister, *The Kind of Guy I Am* (New York: McGraw Hill, 1957), 271.

48 John Eaton, "The Life and Professional Contributions of Arthur Stanley Lamb, M.D., to Physical Education in Canada" (Ph.D. diss., Ohio State University, 1964), 149.

49 Archie Hahn in 1904 and Ralph Craig in 1912 won the double, but they faced fewer competitors and ran fewer heats.

50 Gardner, "How Percy Williams Swept the Olympic Sprints," 43.

51 Ibid.

52 Colleen English, "'Not a Very Edifying Spectacle': The Controversial Women's 800-Metre Race in the 1928 Olympics," *Sports in American History* (October 2015), ussporthistory.com/2015/10/08/not-a-very-edifying-spectacle-the-controversial-womens-800-meter-race-in-the-1928-olympics/.

53 Knute Rockne, "Yankees Have Another Dull Day in Olympics," *Pittsburgh Press*, August 3, 1928, Sports Section: 21.

54 William Shirer, "Americans Beaten in 4 Olympic Tests," *New York Times*, August 3, 1928, Sports Section: 32.

55 Lou F. Marsh, "Jean Thompson Loses but Beats World Mark with Fanny Rosenfeld," *Toronto Star*, August 3, 1928, News Section: 1.

56 When the bar was remeasured, the actual height recorded was 5'2".

57 Marples was the secretary-treasurer of the Canadian Olympic Committee. He had served as an on-field official for some of the events in 1928.

58 The women's 800 metres would not return to the Olympic program until 1960. English, "Not a Very Edifying Spectacle."

59 *Montreal Herald*, August 8, 1928, cited in Eaton, "The Life and Professional Contributions of Arthur Stanley Lamb," 150.

60 Hall, "Alexandrine Gibb," 161.

61 Alexandrine Gibb, "Canada at the Olympics," *Maclean's Magazine*, October 1, 1928: 49.

62 Voters also selected the team of the 20th century. It was the 1972 Team Canada.

63 Rosenfeld had already been named Canada's female athlete of the half century, narrowly beating out Barbara Ann Scott. That Rosenfeld would win the award in an era of widespread anti-Semitism said much about her personality and abilities.

64 Levy, Rosenberg, and Hyman, "Fanny 'Bobbie' Rosenfeld," 393, 394.

65 Hotchkiss, *The Matchless Six*, 127.

66 Kerry Banks, "Forgotten Champion," 41; "Percy Williams and Ethel Catherwood Equal Records," *Winnipeg Free Press*, April 18, 1929.

67 Gardner, "How Percy Williams Swept the Olympic Sprints."

68 "Percy Williams, 1928 Olympic Winner, Poor Fourth," *Ames Daily Tribune*, June 20, 1931; "New Champion Crowned in Olympic Century Dash," *Winnipeg Free Press*, August 2, 1932.

69 McLaren claimed the marriage was kept secret because the bank did not allow a man making less than $2,000 to marry. "Miss Catherwood Married in 1929," *Winnipeg Free Press*, December 11, 1931.

70 Virtually all the papers referred to Ethel as a world champion and the prettiest, or most beautiful, girl at the Olympics, while McLaren was described in some stories as a bank teller or a wealth banker in others. Mitchell was depicted as part of the San Francisco elite. "Former Bear Oarsman Wins Pretty Champion," *Berkeley Daily Gazette*, December 14, 1931.

71 Kevin Mitchell, "The Strange Life of Ethel Catherwood, the Only Canadian Woman to Win an Individual Olympic Gold in Athletics," *National Post*, July 20, 2021.

72 Kerry Banks, "Forgotten Champion," 44.

73 Gardner, "How Percy Williams Swept the Olympic Sprints."

FORGOTTEN: A BENEDICTION

1 See, for example, "The Doings in Sportsdom," *Medicine Hat News*, May 22, 1913.

2 Kieran Mulvaney, "The Greatest Fighter Almost Nobody Knows."

3 Jim Morrison IV (dir.), *Bonecrusher* (Toronto: Republic Seven, 2020), short film.

4 Among the 32 inductees to date in the Sports Legends category, 11 are female, 4 are Indigenous athletes, and 3 are Black Canadians.

Image Credits

Canadian Baseball Hall of Fame and Museum: 56, 60
Colchester Historeum — Museum and Archives: 99
Hockey Hall of Fame/Library and Archives Canada, PA-050248: 201
Library and Archives Canada, PA-016114: 81
Library and Archives Canada, PA-150983: 203
Library and Archives Canada, PA-150997: 193
Library and Archives Canada, PA-151007: 195
Library and Archives Canada, PA-151016: 196
M. Ann Hall: 88
McCord Stewart Museum: 3, 8, 15, 24, 27, 29, 44, 48, 76
Nova Scotia Archives: 143, 147, 155
Orillia Museum of Art and History: 106, 123, 133
Sixty Years of Canadian Cricket: 64, 70
Stratford-Perth Archives: 79

Index

About the Authors

Jason Wilson is a bestselling Canadian historian, a two-time Juno Award nominee, and winner of the Ontario Historical Society's Joseph Brant Award. An adjunct professor of history at the University of Guelph, Dr. Wilson has seven books to his name and lives in Stouffville, Ontario.

Richard M. Reid is a professor emeritus at the University of Guelph. He is the author of several books including the C.P. Stacey Award–winning *African Canadians in Union Blue*. He lives in Guelph, Ontario.